*International Law
and Contemporary Commonwealth Issues*

International Law
and Contemporary
Commonwealth Issues

Robert R. Wilson

Number 38 in a series published for the
Duke University Commonwealth–Studies Center
Duke University Press, Durham, N.C.
1971

© 1971, Duke University Press
Library of Congress Catalogue Card number 79-142294
I.S.B.N. 0-8223-0246-2

Printed in the United States of America
by Kingsport Press, Inc., Kingsport, Tennessee

Preface

In his foreword to the first number of *Law and Contemporary Problems* (the number for December, 1933) the editor, Professor David Cavers, then of the Duke Law School faculty, wrote that "our social order has entered into a period of accelerating change. Law is at once a barrier to political change and a mechanism through which it may be effected. Its relations to the problems of today cannot be ignored by lawyers or laymen." The generalization would seem to hold in 1970 even more clearly, if possible, than it did in 1933 and to be applicable to public as well as private law, with no exception for public international law.

Conceptions of international legal rights and duties invite examination in relation to current as well as past developments. In the present volume there has been effort to discern and evaluate invocations and utilization of public international law in relation to certain contemporary issues in the Commonwealth. To carry out this purpose, even for a very limited number of issues, in a single monograph has involved the assumption that it could be done with relatively brief attention to the historical background. The five issues chosen are ones that have given rise to policy and decision-making, chiefly in Great Britain, and also to action and position-taking in some or all of the other states that by the beginning of 1969 had come to be members of the Commonwealth.

As to the selected issues, there has been effort to discern attitudes and pronouncements that have significance (from the standpoint of public international law) in parliamentary discussions, in executive pronouncements, in decisions of courts, in records of Commonwealth prime ministers' meetings, and in international forums such as those of the United Nations. All of the selected issues appear to touch in some measure upon human rights. Each issue seems likely to be, for some time, a continuing one. In a context such as that which Commonwealth relations provide, the singling out of questions of international law that are involved will conceivably serve the purpose of indicating in some measure the utility of that law as compared with the purely political measures and considerations that are relevant. Selection of issues has not been for the purpose of proving out any previously envisaged thesis, but rather for the purpose of noting the extent to which international law has figured in the process.

By an investigator whose past research has related principally to historical developments touching international law, there must be, in an approach to the study of contemporary events, recognition of all the problems which attend the basing of conclusions upon the study of developments that are in some measure still current. In the examination of the selected issues there has been special attention to primary sources, insofar as they were available. In the effort to evaluate some very recent and contemporary thought and action, however, there has been considerable use of press reports and editorial opinion. In the process the investigator has noted the relative frequency with which there seem to have been considerations of rights (under international law) of human beings as such, rather than as nationals of particular states.

The selection of particular issues (and of some but not all aspects of these issues) has been, in a sense, arbitrary. With respect to the issue of state succession it might be more apt to describe what has been selected as a *cluster* of issues rather than a single one. The special rapporteur of the International Law Commission, in a report presented at the commission's twentieth session, noted a natural tendency among writers and in state practice to use "succession" as a convenient term to describe any assumption by a state of rights or obligations previously applicable with respect to territory that had passed under its sovereignty "without any nice consideration of whether this is truly succession by operation of law or merely a voluntary arrangement of the States concerned." Each of the selected "contemporary issues" would doubtless merit more extended consideration.

In a period marked by the emergence of many new states, the subject of state succession has had the attention of both public and private organizations. The former include especially the International Law Commission, the latter the International Law Association. As is well known, a foremost scholar in this field is Professor D. P. O'Connell of Australia, to whose contributions there are frequent references in chapter 2.

Communalism, apparently more frequently considered as a sociological than as a legal concept, has given rise not only to internal problems but also to international ones, as the continuing United Nations Force in Cyprus (UNFICYP) will bear witness. Here, again, there has been in the present volume arbitrary limitation to developments of international significance in three selected states (Malaysia, Ceylon, and Cyprus) to the exclusion of communalism in other Commonwealth states, such as Mauritius.

Secession is a phenomenon normally occurring entirely within a state (such as, for the present purpose, the United Kingdom or Nigeria), but as in the case of Rhodesia's unilateral declaration of independence, there are legalities incident to de facto and de jure status as affecting relations with outside states. Chapter 4 also notes international legal questions that have arisen as to the authority of United Nations bodies and the legal basis for sanctions.

Migration problems have long figured in the course of Commonwealth history, but recently they have taken a new and somewhat more difficult form for the United Kingdom and have given rise to questions of the status of persons who are citizens of the "United Kingdom and Colonies." This issue has in turn opened practical questions as to law and usage applicable to international travel documents. For the purpose of comparison, chapter 5 considers briefly (as do chapters 2 and 6) some law and practice of the United States.

The issue of defense, as examined in chapter 6, has seemed to merit attention from the point of view of public international law in an era of rapid scientific development. Matters noted include interpretation and application of some prior-made Commonwealth (now international) commitments, and the legal connotation of such a term as "self-defense," as well as practical legal problems touching the jurisdiction over forces of one Commonwealth state that might be utilized for defense in another Commonwealth state.

The concluding chapter seeks to weigh the extent to which considerations of public international law have figured in public discussion of the several issues dealt with in the preceding chapters. In this process attention is drawn to the relative frequency with which there has been reference to human rights, even in a period which has seen but limited acceptance by states of the Human Rights Covenants as distinct from the Universal Declaration. Relationship of Commonwealth states' policies to a potential world community law has seemed to be envisaged in what has been adduced with respect to some of the selected issues.

The author has been the recipient of useful advice and assistance from various quarters. For the privilege of travel and study in various Commonwealth countries at different times over the past decade and a half he is most grateful. He acknowledges with high appreciation courtesies shown him by various institutions and agencies within the Commonwealth, including (to name only those in Great Britain) the Institute of Commonwealth Studies at the University of London, the Secretariat of the Commonwealth, the library at Chatham House, and the Library of the Royal Commonwealth Society in London.

Professor Ralph Braibanti, director of the Center for Commonwealth Studies at Duke University, has kindly encouraged the research for the present volume, and the Center has approved the inclusion of the volume in its Commonwealth-Studies series. Mr. John W. Halderman of the Rule of Law Research Center at Duke University and Professor Richard Preston of the Duke University Department of History have read an early draft of one portion of the manuscript and have made useful suggestions concerning it.

A grant from the Duke University Council on Research, and a supplement from the Duke University Committee on International Studies made possible the research and clerical work on the present volume. Mr. Kenneth Cherry, assistant editor of the Duke University Press, has made many helpful suggestions as to form and arrangement. Mrs. C. W. Ralston's assistance in the research, in the preparation of the manuscript, and in the decision of many questions as to the inclusion and arrangement of materials has been of the greatest value.

Publication of the study as one of the volumes comprising the Duke University Commonwealth Studies was made possible by funds provided for the Center for Commonwealth Studies by the Carnegie Corporation. For opinions expressed or conclusions reached, however, the author alone is responsible.

Robert R. Wilson

Durham, North Carolina
June, 1970

Contents

*To the memory of a
Canadian-born mother*

*International Law
and Contemporary Commonwealth Issues*

Perspectives

The Commonwealth now comprises developed countries with less than one hundred million people and developing countries with a combined population of about eight times that.[1] Attitudes and positions the associated states have taken in their relations inter se as well as in their dealings with non-Commonwealth states continue to be the subjects of much official and unofficial discussion. Issues that are involved and action upon them may help to illumine the essential nature of the Commonwealth association as well as elements of the public law that is relevant. The limitations of the latter, as well as its utility in the settlement of practical problems, become proper subjects of inquiry. The Commonwealth experience in this particular field of public law may conceivably have bearing upon the utility—or in some situations possibly the limitations upon the utility—of this law in the wider (international) community of states.

As a preliminary to a consideration of selected issues that have come to exist between Commonwealth states and that involve in some manner questions of public international law, it seems useful to consider the different possible perspectives from which Commonwealth states' practice may be viewed. It is in order to note (a) some opinions on the present stage of actual development in the Commonwealth as a base for law, (b) the apparent primacy of political questions as compared with legal ones, (c)

---

1. R. H. C. Steed, "The Trouble about the Commonwealth," *Commonwealth Journal*, IX (1966), 167–171, at 169. Cf. statement in the British House of Commons on June 1, 1965, by the secretary of state for Commonwealth relations, in which he noted that there were Commonwealth countries on five continents, that one person in four at that time lived in a Commonwealth state, and that the Commonwealth association was a "world in miniature." *Parl. Deb.* (C), 5th ser., vol. 713 (1964–1965), c. 1549.

the reception of public international law by newly emerging states, (*d*) some illustrative circumstances in which international law has been relevant in relations between Commonwealth member states, and (*e*) justification for selection of issues to be considered in subsequent chapters.

I

The essential nature of the Commonwealth continues to be the subject of both official and academic discussion. One view is that what now exists is simply a voluntary association without constitutional status, although monarchies within the system comprise a personal union.[2] The general development has given rise to the question whether there might come to be a new form of willing partnership, possibly one smaller than the present Commonwealth.[3] One observer has written under the title "There Is a Commonwealth, Whether We Formalize It or Not." [4] Another has described the Commonwealth as a concept often employed to keep Britain out of difficulties that might otherwise have proved awkward. Origins in the 1920's he regards as a matter of easing situations in South Africa, Ireland, and Africa which might have caused trouble for Britain; and the question has arisen whether the point has now been reached at which Britain actually loses rather than gains from Commonwealth connections.[5]

2. On the matter of nomenclature, see S. R. Methrotra, "On the Use of the Term 'Commonwealth,'" *Journal of Commonwealth Political Studies*, II (1963–1964), 1–16. In an address on "A Bridge between Continents and Races" before the Royal Commonwealth Society in Montreal, Lester Pearson is reported as having said that "one member of the Commonwealth even has an elected monarchy inside the Commonwealth with another monarch as Head of the Commonwealth" and to have added, "You can do practically anything inside this association." *Commonwealth Today*, no. 128 (1967), p. 2.

3. Hugh Tinker, "The Crisis in Commonwealth Asia," *Commonwealth Journal*, IX (1966), 113.

4. Dennis Harkness, in *Commonwealth Journal*, VIII (1965), 256–258.

5. J. D. B. Miller, "British Interests and the Commonwealth," *Journal of Commonwealth Political Studies*, IV (1966), 180–190, at 180, 182. A more critical viewpoint is set forth in an article "By A Conservative" in the *Times* (London), April 2, 1964, p. 13, under the caption "Patriotism Based on Reality, Not Dreams," which contains the statement that the Commonwealth "has become a gigantic farce."

In a speech at Lahore on November 29, 1968, Michael Stewart, secretary of state for foreign and Commonwealth affairs, said the Commonwealth was "a multi-

Somewhat in contrast, the first secretary-general to the Commonwealth has observed that it is in a state of "continuous creation" and that while there are relatively few "hard principles" there may be "useful habits"—one firm principle being that racial discrimination cannot be tolerated. He has emphasized that voting is on a basis of consensus and that there is no longer worry about questions of status. Describing the Commonwealth in still more optimistic terms, he has observed that "constitutional logicians" have often proved to be wrong—as, for example, in their saying that a member state in the group could not be neutral if Britain were at war.[6] That Commonwealth members have followed different courses of foreign policy is illustrated in Canada's dissociating itself from action of the United States in Vietnam, while Australia and New Zealand have supported to some extent with troops and equipment.

It is natural that Commonwealth states should have part in many international organizations. In an address before the Royal Commonwealth Society during its centenary year (centenary for the Royal Empire Society which later became the Royal Commonwealth Society) Prime Minister Wilson emphasized that the associated states "know each other." He added that he did not believe there was, outside the Commonwealth world, "any political, military, social or religious or other combination into which the Commonwealth does not extend, or with which it at least did not have contact," through the presence therein of one or more of its members.[7]

It is, of course, apparent that the Commonwealth may be studied from points of view other than the legal, and that in the legal point of view the variables may be so great as to make

racial society, sometimes stumbling a bit, sometimes wrangling a bit, but accepting from the start the vital principle of racial equality." In the whole work of trying to make mankind more civilized, he suggested, not only bilateral associations were needed, but common membership of many international bodies. "Among these international bodies," he said, "I rate the Commonwealth high." *Survey of British and Commonwealth Affairs,* III (1967), 19.

On recognition of the rule of law as a possible uniting element in the Commonwealth, see Robert Gordon Menzies, *Afternoon Light,* 4th ed. (1968), chap. 9, "A Critical Examination of the Modern Commonwealth," p. 968.

6. Arnold Smith, "The Commonwealth and Its Global Purpose," *Commonwealth Journal,* IX (1966), 53–58.

7. *Survey of British and Commonwealth Affairs,* II (1969), 582.

prediction hazardous. An authoritative historian has pointed out that in the realm of higher politics it is not possible to feel as much measure of assurance concerning what the Commonwealth has done or may do as it is in professional or social fields.[8] An Australian scholar has noted Sir Winston Churchill's use of the Commonwealth in the war years as a synonym for Britain's power and influence in the world at large in order to even the balance between Britain and the United States.[9]

It is possible to regard the Commonwealth as a device which seeks to carry over the heritage of the past into an era of political and cultural equality.[10] In this process it was natural that legalists should have had a considerable part. One publicist has expressed opinion that credit for coining and popularizing the very expression "Commonwealth of Nations" should go to the writers on international law.[11]

A possible development which some observers have envisaged, and which would seem to be appropriate and useful to the development of these now independent states, is the creation within the Commonwealth of jurisdictional ties that would make possible appeals from Commonwealth state courts not to the Judicial Committee of the Privy Council but to a separate appellate tribunal.[12] In reply to a questioner who had said that many countries in the Commonwealth (including those in the West Indies as well as Singapore and Malaysia) still showed an interest in setting up such a court of appeals, Mr. Hughes for the United Kingdom government said on January 25, 1966, that the latter was doing what it could to ascertain the considered views of other Commonwealth countries to see whether there was a basis from which the British government could make some progress.[13] In the same general context there was reference to "defence of

8. P. N. S. Mansergh, "The Commonwealth and the Future," *International Studies*, IX (1967), 1–12, at 12.
9. Miller, "British Interests and the Commonwealth," p. 18.
10. Thomas R. Adams, *Western Interests in the Pacific Realm* (1968), chap. 3, pp. 49, 50, 53.
11. Methrotra, "On the Use of the Term 'Commonwealth,'" p. 3.
12. On the role of the Judicial Committee at the time of the Rhodesian crisis, see chap. 4 below.
13. *Parl. Deb.* (C), 5th ser., vol. 720 (1965–1966), c. 935, and vol. 723 (1965–1966), c. 121.

the rule of law and the ideals of a multi-racial Commonwealth." [14]

In the relatively short period of time since the Commonwealth came to comprise states that are on a basis of substantial legal equality (as to their foreign relations as well as their internal government), there has been no lack of prediction that the strains may be too great for the member states in their peculiar association. Thus a Canadian observer, after referring to certain "rescue" operations by which members "have been pulled back from the brink of dissolution to the edge of comparative safety," has described the Commonwealth as a vehicle "unsuited to the road ahead," since it is "oversized and underpowered." As to why states still decide to join the Commonwealth, the same writer has suggested that "where so many have gone before it is harder all the time not to follow after." He points, however, to the fact that members have indulged freely and frequently in threats to leave the Commonwealth. [15]

II

Despite the not infrequent references to the public law that is in force between Commonwealth states (both in the form of rules that are grounded in custom and those in conventional form), it would appear that most of the questions arising between these states have been and in the future are likely to be questions of politics rather than law—a statement which would perhaps hold as well for relations between individual Commonwealth states and non-Commonwealth states. Yet the very fact of statehood implies legal rights and duties for the states which have attained this status, as have all the Commonwealth members. Some of the issues that arise between Commonwealth states, whether old or new members, naturally provide occasion for interpretation and application of international law and also municipal law. If viewed from the standpoint of either international or municipal law, the

14. Ibid.
15. James Eayrs, "The Overhaul of the Commonwealth: Too Much Play in the Steering," *Round Table*, no. 225 (1967), pp. 48, 49, 50.

new states did not come into existence within a vacuum. They exist in a community of states that are subject to law, however imperfect it may be and however lacking a final authoritative interpreter with obligatory jurisdiction for all questions that might arise. The purposes or motives for invoking preexisting law may be of primary importance, and positions taken by states in diplomacy or in the course of litigation will presumably be designed to promote the interests of the respective litigants.

Study of the manner in which international law has come to be a part of the municipal law of Commonwealth states has elsewhere been the subject of discussion, on a very selective subject basis.[16] A different type of approach, essayed in the present volume, looks to the relevance of public international law to comparatively large issues that have very recently confronted, and in large measure continue to confront, some or all of the states that are associated as Commonwealth members. These issues touch upon historical factors, the incidence of legal as well as political heritage, the effect of ethnic forces in international relations, the so-called right of revolution, migration of people as affected by acquired citizenship, and newer-style defense under the authorization of international organizations or through the agency of national contingents serving as agencies of the wider international community. In various contexts these issues raise questions of human rights as well as rights of states.

The changing nature of the Commonwealth, and to a considerable extent the changing situations in various ones of the states which compose it, cannot well be overlooked in even a brief inquiry into what these states have done with respect to international law. The Commonwealth may be viewed from various perspectives, and it has sometimes been viewed with considerable skepticism. There has been suggestion that instead of treating the Commonwealth as any kind of unit, "attention may have to be focused upon particular relationships—bilateral, trilateral, even

---

16. Robert R. Wilson, ed., *The International Law Standard and Commonwealth Developments* (1966), chap. 4. A brief overview, by the same author, under the title "The Commonwealth and International Law, 1907–1967," is in *American Journal of International Law*, LX (1966), 770–781.

quadrilateral—within a total Commonwealth context which may become ever more difficult to keep in mind." [17]

In the determination of legal rights and duties of Commonwealth states themselves and of their respective nationals, the fact of Commonwealth membership and specific commitments incident thereto become relevant, as, for example, under conditions wherein intervention is sought through public international organization. Thus when in 1965 and thereafter the matter of Southern Rhodesia's status was before the United Nations bodies, there was the question whether the Rhodesian problem was one within the domestic jurisdiction of Great Britain (as apparently had been claimed by British representatives at the United Nations for some years) and how the request for intervention or sanctions might alter a factual situation that had not undergone any change.[18] It was apparently thought by some that an answer might be found in the change that had taken place in the traditional rules of international law (concerning action that may be taken when there is a threat to the peace, a breach of the peace, or an act of aggression). A change that has occurred (in the traditional rules of international law) such as would allow or call for individual or collective state action taken against a particular state, after a finding by the authorized body in the principal international organization, would presumably legalize sanctions. States concerned and "called upon" would still be in the position, however, of considering the feasibility and expediency of steps authorized or called for, and in the process political concerns would be likely to have first consideration.

Aside from sanctionist roles, states may invoke or have recourse to international law in a variety of circumstances when their own particular interests are involved, whether these interests lie in maintenance of the status quo or in changing an existing

17. J. D. B. Miller, in review of W. B. Hamilton, Kenneth Robinson, and C. D. W. Goodwin, eds., *A Decade of the Commonwealth, 1955–1964* (1966), in *Journal of Commonwealth Political Studies,* VI (1968), 162.

18. The writer of an unsigned editorial in the *Rhodesian Law Journal,* V (1965), 52, suggested that no request could go to the International Court of Justice because Rhodesia was not a state within the meaning of art. 34, para. 1, of the court's statute; he submitted that Rhodesia appeared to be neither a state nor within the domestic jurisdiction of a state—which he described as a logical absurdity—and concluded that Rhodesia could not do anything about it.

situation.[19] Resort could presumably be had to law not for the sake of the law but in order to strengthen a state's position in protecting its own interests.

III

That the legal heritage of the newer Commonwealth members (that is, communities that are now states after having been colonies of Great Britain) includes a considerable ingredient of public law, as well as other law, would no doubt be generally acknowledged. A former attorney general of India—when referring to his country's heritage of Anglo-Saxon jurisprudence and noting that cessation of the jurisdiction of the Judicial Committee of the Privy Council, so far as India was concerned, had removed a channel that had continuously injected English law into Indian jurisprudence—has suggested that discontinuance of appeals to the Judicial Committee has removed a channel through which there had been continuous injection of English law into Indian jurisprudence. He has predicted, however, that decisions of the Judicial Committee, even when formal appeals have been terminated, will continue to have in India the persuasive force they had before Indian independence.[20] As to the body of international law, the question whether it is a part of municipal law of Commonwealth states, either through incorporation in state constitutions or through judicial rulings, continues to be a subject of discussion.[21] Given such inclusion, or even without constitutional

19. On types of circumstances that may lead states in general to invoke international law, see Stanley Hoffman's introduction to Lawrence Scheinman and David Wilkinson, *International Law and Political Crisis: An Analytical Casebook* (1968), pp. xi–xix.

20. M. C. Setelvad, *The Role of English Law in India* (1966), pp. 51, 57, 58, 73.

21. See chap. 4, "Reception of Norms," in Wilson, *The International Law Standard and Commonwealth Developments*, pp. 66–97. It is understood that as late as 1967 in the former Commonwealth state of South Africa the question of the relationship between national law and international law had not been settled. See statement by C. S. R. Dugard in *South African Law Journal*, LXXXIV (1967), 482–483.

As of 1963 (in the United Kingdom and the legal systems derived from it) there was said to be no general adoption or incorporation of international law, although there had been observance and application of particular customary or conventional rules of the law. J. E. S. Fawcett, *The British Commonwealth in International Law* (1963), pp. 18, 32–55.

incorporation or general judicial directive, it would seem to be in the interest of Commonwealth states to acknowledge and apply this law in municipal courts as well as in their foreign relations. The Blackstone doctrine that international law is a part of the municipal law of England does not preclude the passage of statutes that, for the purpose of municipal courts in England, are contrary to international law, but failure to incorporate the latter in municipal law does not mean inapplicability in diplomacy or in international forums. Situations may arise, however, in which the relevance of international law may be in question, and in the absence of obligatory jurisdiction accepted by the parties there is no assurance that questions arising will ever come before an international tribunal. Even if there is such obligatory international jurisdiction, a party litigant may contend that a rule invoked as international law cannot be shown to have become generally accepted or may contend that the matter in dispute is entirely within domestic jurisdiction. In the course of recent Commonwealth history the scope of such jurisdiction has received considerable attention.[22] Adherence to a broad conception of domestic jurisdiction would presumably have as one of its effects an emphasis upon political rather than legal bases in the settlement of international questions. It is of questionable value to generalize concerning the progress that has been made toward

22. Among recently published articles that are instructive on the matter are those by John M. Howell, including "The Commonwealth and the Concept of Domestic Jurisdiction," in the *Canadian Yearbook of International Law*, V (1967), 14–44, and "Implications of the Rhodesian and Congo Crises for the Concept of Domestic Jurisdiction," in the *Australian Journal of Politics and History*, XIV (1968), 358–372. In the first article the author concludes that little is to be gained by arguing for a wider or narrower interpretation of domestic jurisdiction, since it is more sensible to ask "what matters may need settling in the future, whether their settlement will have to be worked out on the international level, and whether the international jurisdiction that is needed will come fast enough to allow effective solution." In the second article Howell suggests that the two crises he has studied may mark a turning point regarding the reserved domain of states. "The period of the expansion of international powers to discuss and make resolutions supported by moral force," he anticipates, "may give way to increases in international control that resembles the transfer of powers from state to national government in a federal system more than a transfer from domestic jurisdiction to the jurisdiction of an international organ."

A Canadian publicist has observed, "Clearly, until the Prime Ministers Conference of 1960, successive Canadian governments had adhered to the time-honored policy in Commonwealth relations of non-interference in the domestic affairs of member states." Peter Hartnett, "Canada, South Africa and the Commonwealth," *Journal of Commonwealth Political Studies*, II (1963–1964), 36.

widening the scope of matters to which international law has come to apply. The contribution that Commonwealth states have made toward such widening would seem, however, to merit attention. As has been suggested elsewhere, "to the extent that . . . this law depends upon some sense of community (however short the present reality falls of being such a community) the background of recent Commonwealth history suggests a situation conducive to cooperation through legal arrangements that are wider than national in their application." [23]

One of the most perceptive historians of the Commonwealth has observed that "it has never been easy to foresee the history of the Commonwealth and those who have attempted to do so have usually been pretty wide of the mark." [24] He submits, however, that "for all the frustrations and intentions of past and present year," there is no doubt at least that "it was right to have attempted the experiment of multiracial Commonwealth and that despite frustrations and set-backs on balance it has contributed much over the past two decades to the resolving of colonial and racial issues and to wider international understanding." He suggests that it is in the realm of higher politics, as compared with professional and social fields, that it is possible to find such measure of assurance.[25] The realm of public international law would seem to be closer to the political than to the professional and social ones.

IV

The fact that an issue is primarily one in state policy and that it is principally political in nature does not necessarily mean that it

23. Robert R. Wilson, "Some Questions of International Law in Commonwealth Relations," in Hamilton et al., *A Decade of the Commonwealth*, pp. 172–193, at p. 19.

24. P. N. S. Mansergh, "The Commonwealth and the Future," *International Studies*, IX (July, 1967), 1, 2. Mansergh raised the question why, if Robert Borden could foreshadow in 1917 with reasonable accuracy the pattern of Commonwealth development, the same could not be done some five decades later. He submits that it is not only the increased number but also the variety of interests and viewpoints which make any forecast of the Commonwealth so problematical by comparison.

25. Ibid., p. 12.

is completely outside the domain of public international law. The concession of independence to a new state is, in a sense, an extension of public international law to the emerging community. For the present purpose the object is not to discover what has sometimes been called (or perhaps more frankly, miscalled) the "impact" of state practice upon international law, but rather to note the manner in which this law has been a factor in some public international relations of Commonwealth states. Instead of considering, state by state, positions taken and interpretations of particular parts of the law, it is proposed to look to the manner in which and the extent to which the law has figured in relation to specific issues Commonwealth states have faced. Restriction to "contemporary" issues does not preclude some consideration of the manner in which present issues have developed. It does limit attention, so far as that is feasible, to general principles or particular rules (whether in the form of custom or of conventional rules) that have been invoked as bearing upon the questions at issue. To proceed from the fact of an issue to the law that is claimed to be relevant is not to preclude some consideration of the manner in which issues have developed historically. General principles or particular rules (whether in the form of custom or of treaties) have bearing upon the particular issues to be noted. To proceed from the fact of the issue to the relevant law is not to discount the utility of a different approach, such as the recording of particular states' practices with respect to international law in general, or comparing the practice of states in a particular region in regard to that law.[26]

The very number and variety of states that are presently members of the Commonwealth tend to preclude a state-by-state approach to all the matters that would seem to merit consideration. Nor is it proposed to undertake an overview of all sources of the law relevant to the selected issues, particularly in view of the scattered sources that might be involved.[27] Issues selected from

26. See, for example, V. Maya Krishnan, "African State Practice Relating to Certain Issues of International Law," *Indian Journal of International Affairs,* XIV (1967), 196–241.

27. Cf. American Bar Association, Special Committee on World Peace through World Law, *The Rules of Law among Nations: Background Information* (1960), p. 30: "The sources of international law are widely scattered. To get the law

the experience of Commonwealth states in their relations inter se are not necessarily matters peculiar to those states, but they are regarded as matters of special concern to those states. The criterion for selection has been not merely the fact that issues affect many Commonwealth countries (as in the case of state succession) but also that there is relation to general human welfare (as in the matters of communalism and migration), to self-determination (as in the cases of secession), and to the termination or prevention of international or internal strife (as through use of an international military force in Cyprus).

That there would be differences in policy among the associated states that are now members of the Commonwealth on the broad contemporary issues that have been selected for attention is to be expected. Racist policies have come to be so widely condemned by this group of states that they can hardly be described as an issue—although the attempted Rhodesian secession has provided occasion for continuing disavowal and denunciation. Since South Africa's withdrawal from the Commonwealth there has been occasion for condemnation of apartheid to the extent that this would seem to have become a binding rule throughout nearly all of the Commonwealth. Usage on such basic matters as the claimed right of independence, except as to Rhodesia, has marked recent Commonwealth history. It is reported, for example, that when Prime Minister Wilson of Great Britain on December 16, 1965, spoke in the General Assembly of the United Nations on the subject of immediate granting of independence to miniscule territories, delegates from some twenty African states

---

one must get together and distill evidence accumulated from centuries of custom, international arbitral and judicial decisions, writings of experts, publicists and diplomatic treaties and many other sources. There is at the present time no adequate compilation of the above. If we are ever to have a world rule of law it is obvious that there must be a current and complete set of source materials of international law." Since this statement was published the International Law Commission has, as is well known, made considerable progress (as in its work on the law of treaties) toward the goal envisaged by the American Bar Association's Committee. Jurists from Commonwealth countries have contributed significantly to this effort as also to work of the Asian-African Legal Consultative Committee. On the latter, see the brief editorial comment by Robert R. Wilson, "A Decade of Legal Consultation: Asian-African Collaboration," *American Journal of International Law*, LXI (1967), 1011–1015.

walked out in protest against British policy in Africa.[28] General acceptance of norms of international law by the newly emergent states has not, on the other hand, precluded an increasing emphasis upon rights of natural persons as individual human beings and not merely as nationals of their respective states.

Commonwealth states' positions on what are considered in the following chapters as "contemporary" issues may in some cases be considered separately from steps taken by public international organizations. With respect to the Rhodesian secession, however, the extent to which Commonwealth states have used the forums of international organizations as a means of emphasizing their positions may have bearing upon their reception of international law in general.

On such a broad subject as state succession (involving the many matters that grow out of a change of sovereignty) and the bearing of international law upon decisions of national courts touching such questions as public and private property rights (and also nationality of persons), adherence to general principles has guided state policies. In this general area the concept of "common status" in the history of Commonwealth state relations has served a useful purpose, as there has been transition from the status of British subject to Commonwealth citizen—if the latter term is applied to anyone who has the nationality of any Commonwealth state. This does not constitute an issue of seriousness, since customary international law does not preclude a Commonwealth state's according to nationals of another Commonwealth state treatment more favorable than that accorded to other "foreigners," unless such action is contrary to treaty provisions (such as those specifying national or most-favored-nation treatment of such other foreigners).[29] Yet, as will be seen,[30] legislation of a particular state within the Commonwealth may give rise to technical questions touching, on the one hand, the right of a state to

28. Valentine Blakeney, "The Commonwealth in the United Nations," *Commonwealth Journal,* IX (1966), 11–12, 24. The Prime Minister's remarks on this occasion are reported in the Gen. Assy. Off. Rec., Plenary Meeting 1397, A/PV 1397.

29. See Robert E. Clute, in Wilson, *The International Law Standard and Commonwealth Developments,* pp. 100–113. See also pp. 260–262.

30. Chap. 5 below.

determine who shall have domicile within its territory and, on the other, the effect of common sovereignty (for persons living in states that are linked together in a personal union) or of long-established usage. For states that have accepted the covenants pursuant to the Universal Declaration of Human Rights there is also the question of the extent to which they may, in light of their international conventional commitments, deny such rights as entry and residence to their own citizens.

The Commonwealth has undergone a transition from a system in which there were at least some legal arrangements, as in matters of nationality and citizenship, based upon rules that were applicable only to the member states in their relations inter se. The Commonwealth collectively now comprises a group of states which, while maintaining with each other optional arrangements for cooperation in various areas of activity, are completely separate members of the family of nations. The body of rules now applicable to them includes the generally recognized rules of international law.[31] While it is natural to expect that their respective interpretations of that law will in some measure reflect the common heritage, that heritage has not had the effect of creating and continuing what might be called a common outlook. Accusations of colonialism and racism have tended, for example, to be made in some areas since the acquisition of independence by emerging states.

V

As is to be noted in more detail,[32] public international law is applicable and may be invoked under widely differing circumstances and for a wide range of subject matter. It will inevitably be applicable when there is a state succession—as under the so-called devolution or inheritance agreements among Commonwealth states. In certain other contexts the "Commonwealth ex-

31. On legal aspects of the transition, see, generally, J. E. S. Fawcett, *The Inter Se Doctrine of Commonwealth Relations* (1958) and *The British Commonwealth in International Law* (1963), passim.
32. Chaps. 2–6 below.

ception" clause in treaties may find application. As will also be seen,[33] questions have arisen, when a state succession occurs, as to the rights and interests of third states under prior-made treaties—i.e., those made by the predecessor state—as also questions of nationality and of property rights (both public and private).

Unlike the principal issues relating to state succession, that of communalism involves primarily relations between groups *within* certain newer states of the Commonwealth, but when seen from the point of view of international law and foreign policy they may furnish occasion for the invocation, in the course of international discussions, of basic human rights. In several Commonwealth states there have been grave tensions between ethnic groups; in one such case this has given rise to continuing efforts for peace through the agency of the principal world organization, with contingents of troops being supplied by outside states. With the exception of Turkey and Greece, the state having most direct interest in the outcome of the communal difficulties in Cyprus is the United Kingdom, of which Cyprus was formerly a colony. Some easing of the communal problems in Ceylon has been sought through treaty arrangement between Ceylon and India. In still another Commonwealth state, Malaysia, events of May and June, 1969, would seem to indicate that in that state communal riots are by no means things of the past.

Withdrawal of member states of the Commonwealth (such as Eire and South Africa) is violative of no principle of international law.[34] The purported secession of Southern Rhodesia from the principal Commonwealth state, Great Britain, has, in addition to underlining the difference between the legal status of Southern Rhodesia and that of the "dominions," provided occasion for invocation of international law. Constitutional questions as to the rearrangement of authority as between Great Britain and the community whose present leadership has, to use language em-

33. Chap. 2 below, secs. ii and iii.
34. The Union of South Africa, when approving in 1969 the report of the Conference on the Operation of Dominion Legislation, had expressly affirmed "the right of any member of the British Commonwealth of Nations to withdraw therefrom." *1969 Yearbook of the Commonwealth*, p. 2. The British leadership has emphasized that the status of Southern Rhodesia has been and continues to be less than that of a dominion.

ployed in the 1969 *Yearbook of the Commonwealth,* "purported" to sever legal ties with Great Britain are for the present purpose less relevant than are the developments at the United Nations concerning sanctions against Rhodesia. In national courts questions have arisen as to the de facto and de jure status of the Smith regime in Salisbury. The move, through balloting in June, 1969, to establish a republic has not been followed by other Commonwealth states' according recognition to the new regime. Legal bases for sanctions have been adduced not so much from traditional international law as from new international community law. Sanctions have been instituted against a community while, in British official opinion, it is still a part of Great Britain.

In the multiracial Commonwealth the migration of naturalized citizens from one Commonwealth state to another has traditionally given rise to such devices as the so-called White Australia policy. Since the withdrawal of South Africa from the Commonwealth there has perhaps been less widely publicized resentment of such policy. In the very recent past, however, the policy of Great Britain in its limiting migration of persons (including a considerable number of persons holding passports attesting citizenship of the United Kingdom and Colonies) has apparently occasioned much criticism in certain quarters. While for decades the general subject of intra-Commonwealth migration has been one for analysts of policy as well as for students of international law,[35] recent and current developments would seem to have occasioned reexamination of public law that is relevant and of the apparent legal effect of recent moves toward controlling intra-Commonwealth movements of people. In this area also there has been some invocation of human rights as international legal rights.

Collective defense and peace-keeping action comprise measures that rest upon a basis of treaty commitments to which some Commonwealth member states have become parties. Included have been commitments to protect such Commonwealth states as Malaysia and Singapore, and also multilateral commitments with

35. See Robert E. Clute's discussion in Wilson, *The International Law Standard and Commonwealth Developments,* pp. 121–125.

reference to NATO, SEATO, and ANZUS countries. It has also been natural to view this subject from the perspective of United Nations functions and Charter law. Incident to the general development there has been some occasion for clarifying the legal concept of "defense" and "self-defense." There has also been need for determining the jurisdictional limitations of a "host" state as to peace-keeping forces under authorization of the United Nations, regional organizations, or other conventional arrangements.

———

From whatever perspective it is viewed, the Commonwealth remains a dynamic, as well as a changing, concern. Perception of the limits within which it operates effectively has not been lacking. On the eve of the 1969 Conference of Commonwealth Prime Ministers in London, an Asian newspaper in a Commonwealth state carried an editorial containing the statement that

if the Commonwealth tries to behave as a miniature united nations, which has appeared to be the role in which some members see it, then politically it will suffer the same handicaps and be baffled by the same problems. Rhodesia is an example. The African states are entitled to a pledge that there will be no sell-out. To press for more would be unwise.[36]

The manner in which international law has figured in selected areas of the relations between Commonwealth states can conceivably illumine the public relations of these states and, even if limited to a few selected issues, may throw some light upon the utility of that law.

36. *Straits Times* (Malaysian ed.), Jan. 7, 1969. An editorial in the same newspaper on Jan. 15, 1969, described Tengku Abdul Rahman of Malaysia and Lee Kuan Yew of Singapore as convinced that the Commonwealth would suffer from a steadily diminishing relevance unless it renewed itself by discovering new objectives closer to the interests of a majority of its members. In the words of the editorial, "there yet remains the question of what the Commonwealth is to be, as distinct from what it should avoid being."
On the view that while in the past British statesmen have seen the Commonwealth as an instrument of influence and prestige, in the course of the Rhodesian crisis the Commonwealth was often a source of humiliation, see James Barber, "The Impact of the Rhodesian Crisis on the Commonwealth," *Journal of Commonwealth Political Studies*, VII (1969), 83–95, at 85.

· 2 ·

State Succession

At the beginning of 1969 there had come to be twenty-eight member states of the Commonwealth, collectively comprising about one-fourth of the world's population. Evolution of some of the older members from dominion status to their present statehood and circumstances of the emergence of the newer members have provided occasion for consideration of many matters touching international law that is applicable to state succession. Issues arising relate not so much to the completeness of independence in the practical sense as to the attendant legal rights and obligations of the newer states in many matters touching public interests of the predecessor state as well as those of third states. There has recently been extensive reexamination of general principles that are possibly applicable, as well as of particular situations giving rise to successor states' rights and obligations. The very terminology involved has become the subject of critical comment, although foreign offices of the Commonwealth states are doubtless more concerned with substantive rights and duties than with nomenclature.[1] State practice generally, and not merely that of succession from the United Kingdom, has provided occasion for comprehensive diplomatic studies and legal analysis, although the terminology involved may not be the subject of complete agreement.[2]

1. Cf. statement by J. Mervyn Jones, "State Succession in the Matter of Treaties," *British Year Book of International Law,* XXIV (1947), 360–375, at 362, to the effect that his article "was not dedicated to the reform of terminology."

2. Any investigator in this area must at the outset acknowledge his indebtedness to D. P. O'Connell, whose published works include chap. 1, "Independence and Problems of State Succession," pp. 7–41, in W. V. O'Brien, *The New Nations in International Law and Diplomacy,* Vol. III in the *Yearbook of World Polity* (1965); *The Law of State Succession* (1956); *International Law* (1965), Vol. I;

The very number and varying size (apart from the differing situations in which the newly emerged member states of the Commonwealth find themselves with respect to natural resources, security, and opportunity for viable existence) present issues for which traditional international law does not in all cases appear to provide ready answers. In a brief survey only a very selective choice of topics within the large subject of state succession becomes feasible. For the present purpose it is proposed to consider, from the point of view of public international law, the effect of state succession upon (*a*) treaties, (*b*) private rights, (*c*) public rights and duties, and (*d*) nationality of persons.

I

The value or even pertinence of some precedents appears to have come into question. In its Resolution 1902 (XVIII) of November 18, 1963, the General Assembly of the United Nations recommended that the International Law Commission, in its continuance of work on the subject of succession of states and of governments, should take into account views expressed in the Assembly and the comments which might be submitted by governments, with "appropriate reference to the views of States which have achieved independence since the Second World War." In the First Report on Succession of States and Governments in Respect of Treaties, the special rapporteur (Sir Humphrey Waldock) observed that some jurists "go so far as to suggest that the precedents of earlier years, such as the emergence to independence of the American colonies of Spain and Portugal or the territorial changes at the end of the First World

State Succession in Municipal Law and in International Law (1967), Vols. I and II. See also O'Connell's chap. 1, "The Evolution of Australia's International Personality," in the volume he edited, *International Law in Australia* (1965). Earlier studies include F. A. Vallat, "Some Aspects of State Succession," *Transactions of the Grotius Society*, XLI (1955), 123–135, and Lord McNair, *The Law of Treaties* (1961), part 7, "State Succession and Other Changes," pp. 589–691. A more recent analysis is that by R. Y. Jennings, "The Commonwealth and State Succession," in Robert R. Wilson, ed., *International and Comparative Law of the Commonwealth* (1968), pp. 27–39.

War, are of limited or no relevance for the solution of the contemporary problems of succession which have arisen during the United Nations era." [3]

The problem of succession to rights such as those under treaties may depend upon the particular situation of the successor state. As Lord McNair has pointed out, the acquisition of independence by the dominions was "a process rather than an event," and the Statute of Westminster, 1931, makes no mention of treaties, such mention not being necessary since the dominions had not prior to 1931 exercised treaty-making capacity. [4] The precise point reached in movement toward self-determination may be a factor, as was illustrated in the settling of the question of the statehood of India and Pakistan, the latter state having to apply as a newcomer for membership in the United Nations rather than inheriting such status.

As to state succession to treaties in general, account needs to be taken of the many different purposes treaties serve. A treaty of alliance, for example, would seem to be quite distinguishable from a boundary agreement. The resolving of problems growing out of the effect of succession upon the successor state would seem, normally, to involve recourse to international law but might conceivably rest upon specific (*ad hoc*) arrangements rather than generally accepted principles. [5] Perhaps equally relevant is the fact that there had been treaty-like agreements be-

3. A/CN.4/202, p. 9. In the same report the special rapporteur has observed that in municipal law the term "succession" tends to "carry the meaning of a legal institution which, given the relevant event, brings about by itself the transfer of legal rights and obligations." Municipal law analogies, he pointed out, "however suggestive and valuable in some connexions, have always to be viewed with some caution in international law; for an assimilation of the position of States to that of individuals as legal persons may in other connexions be misleading even when it is suggestive." There is the further statement that "in international law and more especially in the field of treaties, the great question is to determine whether and how far the law recognizes any cases of 'succession' in the strict, municipal law sense of the transfer of rights or obligations by operation of law." Ibid., pp. 12, 13. Cf. D. P. O'Connell's reference to "lofty enunciation or repudiation of abstract formulas" and his view that "the empirical and pragmatic approach, provided it is 'informed' by an adequate philosophy, is the only practical one, and it leads . . . down a path midway between the universal-succession theorists and the negative-succession theorists, and prompts an assimilation of the problems of change of sovereigns and of change of governments." O'Brien, ed., *The New Nations in International Law and Diplomacy*, pp. 9, 12.

4. McNair, *Law of Treaties* (1961), p. 648.

5. For a judicial indication that the absence of such arrangements led the United States Supreme Court to hold that international law was applicable, see *United States* v. *Percheman* (1833), 7 Pet. 51.

tween dominions before the end of World War II, as, for example, the Ottawa agreement which applied to the dominions inter se. Apparently the first bilateral treaty between dominions was that between New Zealand and Australia, signed in 1944.[6]

That successor states in the Commonwealth have in practice had considerable leeway in the matter of electing to have British-made treaties continue to apply to them seems to be clear from practice—although it might be difficult in some cases to discern whether acceptance was on the basis of free choice rather than legal obligation. Considering state succession in general (rather than obligations in treaty form), one observer, taking a teleological point of view, has suggested that the former British communities that have at length become sovereign states were in effect designed to be their own rulers, and that this design would imply eventual succession and such consequences as practice would seem to support.[7] It would seem that the new communities, having now become states, would in their own interest elect to keep in effect many if not all of the treaties which the previous sovereign authority had willed to make. A less benevolent view of policies that had preceded succession (and perhaps charges of imperialism in the policy of the former sovereign) might undergird an argument that the only treaties to bind the successor should be those which it expressly elected to have continued in effect for its territory and people. Since neither of the two extreme principles that have tended to be invoked in the past seems to be completely acceptable—(*a*) that all of the presuccessor-made treaties would apply to the successor or (*b*) that the successor has a "clean slate" and is bound by no commitments except those which it expressly accepts—practice seems to support a middle position, which takes into account the essential nature of each treaty and the benefits or burdens of each to the

6. See Trevor Reese, "The Australian–New Zealand Arrangement, 1944, and the United States," *Journal of Commonwealth Political Studies,* IV (1966), 3–15, who states that a "warm welcome" was accorded the agreement in the United Kingdom (p. 12).

7. Cf. Jennings, "The Commonwealth and State Succession," p. 39: ". . . the cases of succession, insofar as they are not to be explained as voluntary novations, illustrate no more than the need to recognize that a new state inherits the ordinary stock in trade of general international law and that this today consists at least as much in treaty as in custom. But since a treaty is still in the form of obligation rather than general law, this need has to be expressed in terms of succession."

successor state. In actual practice there has developed, in the relations of the new states in the Commonwealth, a system of clarifying intent as to prior-made treaties. This permits considerable election on the part of new states without voiding, insofar as they are concerned, all earlier (British-made) commitments that have been applicable to their respective territories. The so-called Nyerere doctrine would seem to deny prescriptive right to territories, even when it was based upon long-continued possession. The inference would be that instead of predecessor states (in the terminology of state succession) there could have been, in some situations, only occupations.[8] After the emergence of Israel as an independent state its government took the position that, in the matter of treaties, "on the basis of generally recognized principles of international law, Israel, which was a new international personality, was not automatically bound by the treaties to which Palestine had been a party." Applying the principle of novation, Israel denied that there was any automatic "elevation of a dependent territory to the status of a party to a treaty" merely because the treaty had previously applied to the territory. The state's position was that it had acceded "*de novo*" to some international conventions "regardless of whether Palestine was formally party to them or whether in some other way their provisions had been made applicable to Palestine." [9]

8. A fuller discussion is in W. B. Hamilton, Kenneth Robinson, and C. D. W. Goodwin, eds., *A Decade of the Commonwealth, 1955–1964* (1966), pp. 174–175. See also David R. Deener, "Colonial Participation in International Legal Processes," in Wilson, *International and Comparative Law of the Commonwealth*.

9. *Yearbook of the International Law Commission, 1950*, II (1957), 215–216. The communication also quoted (p. 214) from decision of the Supreme Court of Palestine in the case of *Al Shehadeh and Another* v. *Commissioner of Prisons, Jerusalem and Superintendent of Central Prisons, Acre*, [1947] 14 P.L.R. 461, which contained the following: "It is a well recognized principle of international law that changes in the government or in the constitution of a state have as such no effect upon the continued validity of the State's international obligations. . . . [W]e are unable to agree that the form of government that prevailed in the previous State is a relevant consideration in applying the principle of international law we have quoted. It seems to us immaterial whether that form of government was despotic or democratic, monarchical or republican or even that recent innovation known as Mandatory. The important question is whether legal sovereignty to enable it to enter into treaty negotiations was vested in the previous State. It cannot be doubted that the sovereignty, in so far as it affected treaty-making power, vested in the French Republic in the case of the Lebanon and in the Mandatory in the case of Palestine."

With this may be compared the position taken with respect to rights in a former trust territory comprising territory which is now that of an independent state in Africa. In a much-publicized statement in 1961 the prime minister of what was then Tanganyika made it clear, with respect to Belgian-acquired port facilities in Kigoma and Dar es Salaam, that status of the territory (when British authority succeeded German) was not that of a colony but that of a mandate and was later to be that of a trust territory —a community that was "not yet" able to stand by itself; it was made clear that a League of Nations mandate was a community "not yet" able to stand by itself; the later Charter of the United Nations plainly envisaged trusteeship for a limited period. The Belgians, the prime minister said, would have to give up the rights that had been granted to them by the United Kingdom, as these were not valid; the East African Services Organization would thereafter operate buildings and wharves and facilities on Tanganyika's behalf. There was proposal to compensate the Belgians for their investment after subtracting the amount which had already been paid to them by way of amortization of their investment, but all or part of the compensation which was due might be payable, not to Belgium, but to Burundi and Rwandi as Belgium's successors to rights in this area; distribution of the compensation, the prime minister indicated, might be a matter for arbitration.[10]

Apparently becoming well known as a means of settling questions concerning new Commonwealth states' being bound, after they become independent, by agreements that had previously applied to their territory and people under British rule is the so-called inheritance agreement. Frequently cited in illustration of this type of arrangement is the agreement concluded through an exchange of letters between Ghana and the United Kingdom on November 25, 1947. In broad language this provided that

(1) all obligations and responsibilities of the Government of the United Kingdom which arise from any valid international instruments

10. Tanganyika National Assembly, *Debates,* 37th Sess., 6th Meeting, Nov. 30–Dec. 2, 1961, p. 10. A more complete text of the prime minister's statement is quoted by the present author in Hamilton et al., *A Decade of the Commonwealth,* pp. 176–177.

shall henceforth, in so far as such instruments may be held to have any application, be assumed by the Government of Ghana; (2) the rights and benefits heretofore enjoyed by the Government of the United Kingdom in virtue of the application of any such international instruments shall henceforth be enjoyed by the Government of Ghana.[11]

That this technique represents practice rather than application of a binding rule of international law is supported by the view that international law does not embody a special rule concerning inheritance or lapse of treaties at state succession.[12] The manner in which the successor state has emerged and the extent to which, before succession, the new community has come to have part in the making of agreements that have been applied to it may affect the conclusion of arrangements that are to be applicable to the newly sovereign state. As is well known, the evolutionary process through which the older dominions passed as they moved toward complete independence provided bases for claims that as they approached autonomy they became parties in their own right to commitments which, while originally negotiated by Great Britain, had received the acquiescence of the overseas dominions.[13] Practice as to commercial treaties is instructive on this point. In the late nineteenth century there developed the practice of making automatic the application of the United Kingdom's treaties of this type to the colonies, with clauses looking to voluntary adherence by colonies (sometimes named) that wished to do this. The practice was apparently discontinued after World War II.[14] The dominions could "contract out" of commercial treaties, but this was apparently not true (at least at first) of political treaties.

11. 287 UNTS 234. Cf. the language in agreements with Ceylon, Nov. 11, 1947 (86 UNTS 25, sec. 6), with Burma (86 UNTS 25, sec. 6), with Nigeria (Cmnd. 1214), with Jamaica (Cmnd. 1918), with Cyprus (Cmnd. 1093), and with Trinidad and Tobago (Cmnd. 1919).

12. D. P. O'Connell, *State Succession in Municipal Law and in International Law* (1967), II, 6–7. The author also suggests that the criterion for isolating transmissible treaties "remains elusive" (p. 212).

13. *The Effect of Independence on Treaties,* a handbook published under the auspices of the International Law Association (1965), p. 111.

14. D. P. O'Connell, *International Law in Australia* (1965), pp. 4–5. The same writer notes that the Irish Free State, classified as a secessionary rather than a successor state, did not concede mechanical devolution of United Kingdom treaties, and that it registered this opinion with the United Nations. See judicial holding referred to in n. 35 below.

Professor O'Connell has pointed out that after the Versailles Peace Conference even political treaties were not to be binding upon the older dominions without their concurrence or consent. Evolution was to proceed through the period of the inter se cooperation to that of full statehood, and this affected treaty commitments as well as other attributes of fully independent states—some, but not all, of which retained the monarchical form of government under the same monarch.

The case of India and Pakistan may be considered a special one, since in that instance of partition the process which resulted in the creation of two new states was due to steps taken by a "constitutional superior," to use Professor O'Connell's description.[15] Succession to membership in the principal world organization accrued to only one of the new entities, and, as noted above, Pakistan was found to be in the position of having to seek membership (rather than inheriting it) in the United Nations.

Not all the instances of state succession in the Commonwealth as affecting preexisting treaties have involved devolution of treaties from the United Kingdom to other (new) Commonwealth states. Thus Zambia, upon becoming a separate state, issued a declaration on its succeeding to treaties to which Northern Rhodesia had been a party. The wording set forth that the list of treaties inherited would be those to which the new state would succeed "in virtue of customary international law," [16] and the assumption apparently was that some of the treaties of Northern Rhodesia might have lapsed. There was no devolution list, no listing such as Ghana had utilized, and no procedure exactly comparable to that which Tanzania had followed in the matter of inheriting treaties. The presumption was that "in virtue of customary international law" some of the treaties might no longer be applicable to Zambia, but the international law standard to be applied was not spelled out in the form of rules. As Professor O'Connell has pointed out, the Zambian declaration has been

15. *State Succession*, I, 8.
16. O'Connell (ibid., II, 115) has concluded that by virtue of international law some of the treaties had lapsed. In this instance there was no Zambian devolution agreement, questions being left for settlement on the basis of international law, with notice to be given.

followed by Guyana and by Barbados, and the question arises whether mere silence on the part of other parties to the preexisting agreements would constitute novation.[17]

Questions concerning succession to treaties arose when Malaya became independent in 1957, when Malaysia was formed in 1963, and when Singapore ceased to be a part of Malaysia in 1965. By an agreement dated August 7, 1965, relating to the separation of Singapore, there was provision (in Article IV) for "relinquishment of sovereignty and jurisdiction of the Government of Malaysia in respect of Singapore." By Article VIII,

> With regard to any agreement entered into between the Government of Singapore and any other country or corporate body which has been guaranteed by the Government of Malaysia, the Government of Malaysia hereby undertakes to negotiate with such country or corporate body to enter into a fresh agreement releasing the Government of Malaysia of its liabilities and obligations under the said guarantee, and the Government of Singapore hereby undertakes to indemnify the Government of Malaysia fully for any liabilities, obligations or damage which it may suffer as a result of the said guarantee.[18]

Another device is that of devolution by legislation of the predecessor state. In what was an example of its kind as late as 1965, the Parliament of the United Kingdom passed the Indian Independence Act, 1947,[19] following it with the Indian Independence (International Arrangement) Order, 1947, which apportioned between India and Pakistan treaties to which undivided India had been a party—with provision that treaties not having an exclusive territorial application would devolve upon both of the dominions. The order thus became the law of each of the new

17. Ibid. There was apparently no devolution agreement, questions being left, as the quoted language indicates, to be governed by international law and notice to be given.

18. *State of Singapore Government Gazette,* Aug. 9, 1965, as reproduced in *International Legal Materials,* IV (1965), 935. As to earlier Malaya-Malaysia commitments, the delegate from Malaysia to the United Nations had said in plenary session of the Assembly on Oct. 4, 1963: "The international obligations of the old Federation of Malaya continue to be honored by Malaysia and all external relations by the Federation of Malaya and continued by Malaysia." A/PV 1228, p. 67.

19. 10 and 11 Geo. 6, c. 30.

states, and the effect has been described as similar to that of a devolution agreement.[20]

Ceylon was the subject of a devolution agreement in 1947, on the basis of which the state has claimed that it was a party to the Opium Convention of 1925 and the Narcotic Drugs Convention of 1931.[21] To other international conventions, including the Dangerous Drugs Convention, 1957, Ceylon adhered; as to international organizations involving membership status, the plan which the United Nations had adopted for Pakistan was applied to Ceylon.[22]

It is of course possible that a treaty concluded by the United Kingdom and which was not made in contemplation of application to a successor state, such as a British dominion, would eventually be applied to a state which was a successor state. This was apparently the case with the Treaty of Amity, Commerce and Navigation of 1825 between Argentina and the United Kingdom, which by its terms had been applicable, so far as the United Kingdom was concerned, to His Majesty's subjects "in Europe." In 1953, by agreement between Pakistan and the Argentine Republic the treaty was made applicable to Pakistan. This might in

20. *The Effect of Independence on Treaties*, p. 197.
21. Ibid., p. 198.
22. Ibid., p. 196. In the case of Cyprus, art. 8 of the Draft Treaty Concerning the Establishment of Republic of Cyprus, 1960, between the United Kingdom, Greece, and Turkey of the one part and the Republic of Cyprus on the other, provided: "(1) All international obligations and responsibilities of the Government of the United Kingdom shall henceforth, in so far as they may be held to have application to the Republic of Cyprus, be assumed by the Government of the Republic of Cyprus. (2) The international rights and benefits theretofore enjoyed by the Government of the United Kingdom in virtue of their application to the territory of the Republic of Cyprus shall henceforth be enjoyed by the Government of the Republic of Cyprus." Cmnd. 1093.
In an instruction to the American consul general at Nicosia before the actual signing of the treaty quoted above, the Department of State had occasion to say, concerning the impending change in the status of Cyprus, that "in every instance to date when new states, formerly bound by United Kingdom treaty obligations, have achieved their independence, they have subsequently indicated their adherence thereto. Nevertheless, it should be borne in mind that in the absence of applicable treaty provisions, there is no conclusive ruling covering the continuation of the application of international agreements in the case of newly-independent states. The character of the act by which a dependent or semi-dependent state originally becomes bound by a treaty, the circumstances under which such area becomes an independent state, and the nature of the treaty in question, all are factors in determining whether the new state is to remain bound by treaties formerly applicable to it." Marjorie Whiteman, *Digest of International Law*, II (1963), 993.

a sense be considered a new international agreement between Argentina and Pakistan, the original language of the instrument being, in effect, incorporated by reference in the agreement between Pakistan and Argentina. Five years later the Argentine government declined to complete a comparable arrangement (on the basis of the 1825 treaty) with India which would have had the effect of establishing extradition commitments between India and Argentina.[23]

The view that state practice in the Commonwealth supports the principle of "clean slate" (so far as acceptance of the treaties of the parent or predecessor state may be concerned) [24] may be considered in relation to the fact that devolution agreements have maintained continuity and that at least they influence the reactions of other states or of international organizations. Such agreements have been referred to by the United Nations, for example, in explanation of its listing some British treaties as applicable to successor states. There has been achieved in the Commonwealth an "almost universal tradition" of attempting to maintain continuity of treaties through devolution agreements.[25] As was suggested by a member from the United Kingdom when the International Law Association's Committee Report was under consideration in 1966, despite divisions on important issues affecting the authority and effectiveness of international law, state practice reveals a remarkable degree of consistency.[26] The committee's recommendations stressed the advantages to be derived from achieving a maximum degree of continuity in treaty relations; they also looked to the adoption by international organizations of procedures to enable states that are willing to continue as

23. U.N. Legislative Series, *Materials on Succession of States* (ST/LEG/-SER.B/14), pp. 6–8.

24. A. P. Lester, "State Succession to Treaties in the Commonwealth," *International and Comparative Law Quarterly*, 4th ser., XIII (1963), 475–507, at 506. Contrast K. J. Keith, "State Succession to Treaties in the Commonwealth. Two Replies," in the same quarterly, 4th ser., XIII (1964), 1441–1450, who submits (p. 1445) that on the basis of practice, there is "probably a rule of international law that newly-independent States, having seceded peacefully and constitutionally, remain bound by multilateral law-making treaties which applied to their territories before independence."

25. O'Connell, *State Succession*, II, 373.

26. International Law Association, *Report of the Fifty-Second Conference Held at Helsinki, Aug. 14th to Aug. 20th, 1966* (1967), p. 570.

parties to multilateral organizations to obtain the benefits thereof.[27]

In the absence of the usual type of inheritance or devolution treaties there may be a policy, such as that which the United States has followed with respect to certain new Commonwealth states, of arranging for continuance in force (between the United States and the new states) of treaties the United States previously had with the United Kingdom. Thus an exchange of letters between the United States and Botswana effected the continuance in force for twenty-four months of eight listed instruments,[28] and there was a similar exchange with Lesotho as to six listed agreements.[29] The United States had previously signed with Ghana an agreement listing prior (British-made) treaties which were to continue in force between Ghana and the United States. There was also assent by the United States, as a matter of policy, to the continuance in force of the Bermuda Air Service Agreement relating to Jamaica, Trinidad and Tobago, and Pakistan; the Department of State is reported as having stated that it undertakes "with due regard for practical considerations" to determine which of the bilateral agreements of the parent country with the United States should be covered by the new state's general acknowledgment.[30]

There would appear to have developed in the Commonwealth a *tradition* looking to maintenance of the continuity of treaties, but with due regard for the consideration, in individual cases, of the legal rights and interests of predecessor states, the successor states, and third states. The coherence of policy involved as to state succession will doubtless continue to be a concern of foreign offices generally, and the experience within the Commonwealth in situations in which treaty issues have arisen would seem to suggest the need for rational bases for settling legal questions. There has been reiteration of the point that traditional international law leans rather strongly against succession to treaty obligations and rights; aside from novations, cases of accession in the

27. Ibid., p. 585. 28. TIAS 6165.
29. TIAS 6192.
30. Correspondence from the Department of State, as quoted in O'Connell, *State Succession*, II, 369.

Commonwealth are thought to illustrate that a new state "inherits the ordinary stock in trade of international law." As the writer just quoted points out,

since a treaty is still in the form of obligation rather than general law, this need has to be expressed in terms of succession. In addition it has to be recognized also that treaties which were negotiated by or with a government before its independence was fully recognized, but in contemplation of its realization eventually, should continue in effect not because there is a case of succession of states but rather because there is *pro tanto* succession of governments.[31]

The enormity of practical, administrative tasks that may attend the determination of what British-made treaties have come to be in force for newer states that are now members of the Commonwealth has been suggested by an officer whose function it has been to supervise research to determine which of the British-made treaties have continued to apply to Canada. Six years after initiation of this supervision, the officer could write that even an older Commonwealth country such as Canada had not up to that time been able to decide which treaties continued to apply.[32] If this is true of Canada, it is unlikely that all of the newly independent states of the Commonwealth will be able to work out their heritage of British-made treaties easily and quickly. A former policy adviser to Tanzania has suggested that "from the point of view of a developing country, one's initial reaction . . . is to say that no treaty rights or obligations are inherited by newly independent states." He submits that the idea of a general proposition of "no succession" has come under hot attack from "the academic community which is always interested in expanding the body of international law" and from civil servants in certain international organizations.[33] Yet if international law does not include a special rule concerning inheritance or lapse of treaties at a state succes-

31. Jennings, "The Commonwealth and State Succession," p. 39.
32. Hugh J. Lawford, "Some Problems of Treaty Succession in the Commonwealth," a paper read before a regional meeting of the American Society of International Law at Greenville, North Carolina, on April 25, 1967. Professor Lawford suggested that account should be taken of the practical problems involved for the new state and that "academic international lawyers might well consider a period of self-denial from the devising of new theories of state succession."
33. G. P. Verbit, "State Succession in the New Nations," *Proceedings of the American Society of International Law* (1966), pp. 119–124, at p. 120. See also his comment that "the new states are already suspicious of international law when they become independent" (p. 122),

sion, there is, on the other hand, as Professor O'Connell has found, a denial of a recognized doctrine that treaties automatically lapse upon independence in the absence of *immediate* assertion of their continuance in force.[34] Mere reference to customary law in connection with the determination of treaty inheritance may conceivably acquire greater significance if practice comes to undergird sufficiently the principle that there should be *examination* of every treaty which was originally made by the United Kingdom and ultimately invoked in favor of (or in a demand upon) one or more of the independent states of the Commonwealth. Such facts as the Irish Free State's refusal in the 1950's to concede mechanical devolution of treaties that had been made by the United Kingdom, as also Ireland's withdrawal (by notice) from certain British-made treaties, provide illustration of developing practice.[35]

Particular situations that have developed in different Commonwealth states have provided occasion for renewed effort to lay down some basic principles or rules that might reasonably be applied to the inheritance of treaty commitments. The Committee of the International Law Association has in its recommendations on the general subject stressed the advantage of having a "maximum degree of continuity in treaty relations" and recommended that public international organizations should devise "appropriate procedures to achieve the maximum continuity." Former colonial entities are, in the report, "urged to secure publication of lists of their treaties and to improve the means of access to original treaty texts." The stated objective is that uncertainty be reduced to a minimum and that technical assistance should facilitate the preparation of treaty lists.[36]

34. O'Connell, *State Succession*, II, v.
35. Ibid., pp. 122, 123. Cf. *Murray* v. *Parkes*, [1942] 2 K.B. 123, particularly the statement of the chief justice at p. 128: "It cannot be supposed that the United Kingdom Parliament by this Act [the Irish Free State Constitution Act, 1922] intended to deprive persons resident in the newly constituted Dominion of their British nationality. . . . The removal by the Statute of Westminster in 1931 of any restriction upon the power of the legislature of the Irish Free State to pass legislation, whether repugnant or not to an Imperial Act, did not either expressly or by implication provide for any separation, described sometimes as the right to secede, from the British Commonwealth of Nations. Nor at any time, so far as I am aware . . . has it ever been declared in terms by the government of Eire, that the so-called right to secede has in fact been exercised."
36. International Law Association, *Report of the Fifty-Second Conference.*

Reviewing, in 1966, the law of succession to treaties, a Canadian specialist noted that during the nineteenth and early twentieth centuries, "the general rule was that treaties continued to apply to a new government élite only where a political change was characterized as a change of government," but that even then "doctrinal rigidity gave way somewhat to overriding policy considerations." Favoring the view that all kinds of multilateral conventions that are nonpolitical should continue, he applied this particularly to technical treaties, such as those relating to communications. While bilateral instruments, such as those for alliance, should normally not survive a state succession, it has been suggested that multilateral conventions of all kinds other than political ones should continue, the multilateral conventions usually having been worked out to serve the needs not of one group of states but of a more general community, and the making of such multilateral treaties being "among the most promising methods for the development of international law." While admitting that there may be problems in categorizing treaties, the same author does not regard these problems as insuperable.[37]

The Bases Agreement which the United States made with the United Kingdom in 1941 and which has, with the emergence of Trinidad and Tobago as an independent state, been continued through agreement between the new state and the United States [38] presents a question of categorization. The classification of this treaty as dispositive has been the subject of considerable discussion; one author has submitted that the action is an acknowledgment that a bases agreement, being a dispositive one, is not necessarily inherited by a state from its predecessor.[39]

Much of the literature on state succession to treaties touches assumptions, interpretations, and classification of treaties accord-

37. G. V. LaForest, "Toward a Reformulation of the Law of State Succession," *Proceedings of the American Society of International Law* (1966), pp. 103–111, at pp. 106, 109, 110.

38. Exchange of letters, Aug. 31, 1962. On the background of this agreement, see Claude S. Phillips, "International Law and Questions before the Congress of the United States, 1941–1945," doctoral dissertation, Duke University, 1954.

39. Thomas Franck, "Some Legal Problems of Becoming a New Nation," *Columbia Journal of Transnational Law,* IV (1965–1966), 13–27, at 23. Cf., on the general subject, comments by Robert Delson, *Proceedings of the American Society of International Law* (1966), pp. 111–117.

ing to their subject matter, to other rights of a successor state with respect to its predecessor, and (if the instrument is a multilateral one) to other party states that may be in interest. There has obviously been, and doubtless will continue to be, careful consideration of usage in general in the effort to relate developing practice to international law. There remains for the new states, in the meantime, the practical task of determining, at least tentatively, what preexisting treaties there are that should or might be examined in the light of practice. The making of a list of possibly inheritable treaties may be a difficult one for new foreign offices with limited staffs and may take much time. Even a listing of those treaties possibly in force may be difficult. In the meantime there may be resort to what has been called the Nyerere doctrine —a device which seeks to continue treaties in force for a limited time, until the successor state has had opportunity to study them and to decide which ones it elects to keep in effect for itself. This was the course followed by Tanganyika (before the birth of Tanzania) as also by such Commonwealth states as Uganda, Kenya, Malawi, Botswana, and Lesotho.[40]

Even older dominions may have problems that are related to the inheritance of treaties. A Canadian scholar has recently pointed out that Canadian experience indicates that there may be difficulty even in securing an authentic text of a treaty that may be in question, as well as difficulty of determining the possible application of a treaty from its title or even from an examination of the

40. In its judgment in the case of *Molefi* v. *Principal Legal Adviser* (Jan. 15, 1969) the High Court of Lesotho referred to the Lesotho government's willingness to have bilateral treaties validly concluded by the United Kingdom on behalf of Basutoland continue in force, on the basis of reciprocity, for twenty-four months from the date of independence unless abrogated or modified by mutual consent. In a communication to the secretary general of the United Nations the Lesotho government said that at the end of a twenty-four-month period it would "regard such of these treaties which *could not by the application of the rules of customary international law* be regarded as otherwise surviving, as having terminated." Lesotho High Court Judgment CIV/APPN/68; *International Legal Materials*, VIII (1969), 585; emphasis added. As to multilateral treaties, the government of Lesotho proposed to review each of them individually and to indicate to the depositary in each case what steps it wished to take in relation to each such instrument "whether by confirmation of termination, confirmation of succession or accession." Ibid. A useful and instructive summary of problems involved and of the "opting in" theory is that by Jonathan Mallamud, "Optional Succession to Treaties by Newly Independent States," *American Journal of International Law*, LXIII (1969), 782–791.

text itself. He questions whether there can be a working rule which forbids the invoking of a treaty against a new state unless it can be shown that the new state has been notified, or otherwise knows, that the treaty has previously been in force for it.[41] It has been estimated that Great Britain has been party to well over ten thousand treaties, perhaps fifteen thousand if treaties with tribal chieftains and local rulers are taken into account.[42] The magnitude of the task of a new state in its determination of what treaties it will acknowledge as having continuing effect for it may place a heavy burden upon new foreign offices. On the other hand, it is possible to envisage the problem as smaller than the very number of treaties would suggest. Assertion of the relatively small dimensions of the task has emphasized that a large number of the treaties can by their provisions be terminated by a party in any case, aside from any question of succession; in this view a new state's attempt to negotiate a convenient solution of treaty questions is likely to meet with sympathy from third states; and a rule of law is required "only for the residuary and occasional case."[43]

The very number of state successions in the Commonwealth by or soon after the middle of the twentieth century has provided occasion and need for careful reexamination and reevaluation of practice and for reconsideration of principles that are claimed to be applicable. Newer states of the Commonwealth would appear to have provided in their practice some precedent that may well be useful, as practice, in the consideration of relevant legal questions in the larger international community. While the International Law Commission in its 1969 Vienna Convention on the Law of Treaties made clear in its Article 79 that provisions of the articles in that report were without prejudice to any questions that might arise in regard to a treaty by reason of a succession of states,[44] the Asian-African Legal Consultative Committee (which has representatives from a number of Commonwealth member

41. Hugh J. Lawford, "The Practice Concerning Treaty Succession in the Commonwealth," *Canadian Yearbook of International Law*, V (1967), 3–13, at 13.
42. Ibid., p. 8.
43. Jennings, "The Commonwealth and State Succession," p. 33.
44. U.N. Doc. A/CONF.39/27, May 23, 1969.

states and which exchanges observers with the International Law Commission) has competence wide enough to include the effect upon treaties of a state succession.[45] In 1968 there was a first report to the United Nations General Assembly by the special rapporteur on succession of states and governments in respect of treaties.[46] There have also been Secretariat studies on succession of states to multilateral treaties.[47] Issues concerning legal aspects of succession to treaties seem likely to engage the attention of international legalists in general and of legal advisers to Commonwealth foreign offices for many years to come. It is inevitable that questions of policy may affect actual resolution of legal questions. As far as the effect of state succession upon treaties is concerned, that of the Commonwealth experience, insofar as it can be gauged in 1969, would seem to have been a moderating one of avoiding arbitrary unilateral procedures and looking to the effect (of rights asserted on the basis of international law) upon the general international community as well as upon the interests of successor, predecessor, or third states that are parties to the treaties concluded by predecessor states.[48] Practice supports a

---

45. The relatively wide scope of the Consultative Committee's authorization is noted in the present author's comment, "A Decade of Legal Consultation: Asian-African Collaboration," *American Journal of International Law,* LXI (1967), 1011–1015.

46. Z/CN.4/202.   47. A/CN.4/200, Add. 1, 2.

48. Referring to an inquiry of September 20, 1968, the Canadian Department of External Affairs replied in part as follows: "The question of state succession in the matter of treaties is a highly complex one which is receiving a great deal of attention at the present time from international lawyers. Within the Commonwealth it is the traditional view amongst the older Commonwealth countries that the older British dominions had inherited all the treaty rights and obligations arising out of treaties concluded by the U.K. and applying to the dominions. However, since World War II this approach has been questioned by some of the newer members of the Commonwealth and some international lawyers go so far as to claim that newly sovereign states are free to accept or reject virtually all treaty obligations incurred on their behalf by the metropolitan power prior to independence." *Canadian Yearbook of International Law,* VI (1968), 275–276.

In connection with an enquiry concerning Newfoundland treaty succession, the Legal Division of the Canadian Department of External Affairs wrote that "the view of the Government on the question of Newfoundland treaty succession has in the past been that Newfoundland became part of Canada by a form of cession and that consequently, *in accordance with the appropriate rules of international law,* agreements binding upon Newfoundland prior to Union lapsed, except for those obligations arising from agreements locally connected which had established proprietary or quasi-proprietary rights, and Newfoundland became bound by treaty obligations of general application to Canada." Ibid., p. 276; emphasis added.

conclusion that insofar as succession to treaties is concerned neither of the two opposing principles—that of the "clean slate" or that of "general succession"—can be regarded as expressing present international law. Within the past decade an observer could say that international law was "singularly undeveloped, uncertain, and, it must be said, comparatively unstudied" when consequences of the emergence of a new state were under consideration.[49] A successor state is not apt to seek inheritance of a treaty that could reasonably be labeled "political" but may find it quite in its interest to cooperate with other members of the international community as to instruments designed for the general welfare of the participant states.[50] In general, Commonwealth states' approach to settlement of issues arising in this general connection would seem, if not productive of international law, at least to have set precedents that may in time affect the actual growth of that law.

II

Perhaps less publicized than devices employed in the Commonwealth for the purpose of determining the effect of succession upon prior-made treaties of the predecessor state have been questions raised as to the effect of state succession upon property rights, particularly those that relate to private property. Whether in terms of simple property rights or "acquired" or "vested" rights, there has been occasion for bilateral discussion as well as for consideration by the principal world organization. In 1948 the secretary general of the United Nations submitted to the International Law Commission, when it was conducting a survey of the whole body of international law with a view to choosing topics for codification, a memorandum on the principle of respect for private property rights which contained the following:

49. R. Y. Jennings, *The Acquisition of Territory in International Law* (1963), p. 12.
50. O'Connell (*State Succession*, II, 222, 224) has referred to rules developed by Australia and New Zealand concerning multilateral conventions having their origin in the nineteeth century, also to an understanding between Ghana and Ceylon as to treaties administered by the United Nations.

That principle has never been seriously challenged. It has been given frequent and authoritative judicial recognition. The Permanent Court of International Justice affirmed it emphatically with regard to what many considered as the border line case of private rights of public origin, created with a view of destroying cultural and economic values identified with the very being of the successor State. Yet while the principle of respect for private rights forms part of international law, there is no adequate measure of certainty with regard to its application to the various categories of private rights such as those grounded in the public debt, in concessionary contracts, in relations of government service, and the like. Arbitral practice has affirmed exceptions to the general principle, as, for instance, to the obligations of the predecessor State in the matter of tort. But these exceptions do not necessarily follow a general principle of law, and their validity has been challenged. Similarly, the exception with regard to the public debt contracted for purposes inimical to the successor State may require clarification.[51]

Protection of the private property rights of persons has frequently been the subject of provisions in bilateral treaties. Thus the United States in its policy through treaties of friendship, commerce, and navigation has included rather specific provisions to assure that there will not be uncompensated expropriation of the property of its citizens and companies and has, on its part, reciprocally agreed to protect nationals of the other parties to such treaties.[52] Early in its history, the United States Supreme Court had occasion, after Spain's cession of Florida to the United States, to assert in strong terms the principle of respect for private property. In words that have been much quoted, Chief Justice John Marshall said that

the modern usage of nations, which has become law, would be violated; that sense of justice and right which is acknowledged and felt

51. Memorandum submitted to the United Nations, A/CN.4/1, Nov. 5, 1948.
52. The background of law and practice is the subject of chap. 4, "Property Protection," in Robert R. Wilson, *United States Commercial Treaties and International Law* (1960), pp. 95–125. Following the inclusion in Art. XVII of the Universal Declaration of Human Rights of wording on the subject of individuals' rights to own property "alone as well as in association with others," the United States proposed the inclusion of similar provisions in the Draft Covenant on Economic, Social and Cultural Rights. Judicial rulings such as that in the *Sabbatino* case (376 U.S. 454, decided in 1964) have not marked a change of policy as to basic advocacy of respect for private property rights; in that case there was a ruling as to the proper forum in which the legality of an act of state might be questioned.

by the whole civilized world would be outraged, if private property should be generally confiscated, and private rights annulled. The people change their allegiance; their relation to their ancient sovereign is dissolved; but their relations to each other, and their rights of property, remain undisturbed.

Referring to the particular article of the treaty which provided that prior grants of land should be confirmed to the persons who had before conclusion of the treaty been in possession of the land, the Chief Justice held that even without this express stipulation the titles of individuals would remain as valid under the new government as they were under the old.[53] In the more than a century since this pronouncement, the principle of protection of

53. *Percheman* case, 7 Pet. 51 (1833), pp. 86–87, 88. There was reference to the *Percheman* ruling in a case decided in India in 1958 (27 I.L.R. [1963] 32). The High Court of Bombay ruled that a successor state was not bound by the obligations of the predecessor state, holding it to be a well-settled rule of international law that "a successor state, by whatever process the succession is effected, whether by conquest, by merger, by agreement or by treaty is not under any obligation to recognize the liabilities of the former State, and unless the obligations have been so recognized the municipal courts of the successor State are not competent to enforce that liability against the successor State." The court distinguished the case before it from the *Percheman* decision, saying that in the former the claim was made against the State of Bombay and did not arise out of conflicting claims between two citizens regarding their private property. There was reference to *Urmeg Singh* v. *State of Bombay*, A.I.R., S.C. 540.

In a case involving a claim against the State of Israel by one who had been a member of the Palestine Police Court for more than twenty-two years, the Palestine Supreme Court, sitting as the Court of Civil Appeals, noted the District Court's statement that if the claimant's right to a pension had not been recognized prior to the establishment of the State of Israel, the situation would not be any different. "It has been decided many times in the past," the District Court had said, "that the Government of Israel is not the successor of H.M. Government and the conclusion of this is that the Government of Israel is not bound by any obligations which the British Government took upon itself." *Richuk* v. *The State of Israel*, 28 I.L.R. (1963) 442, at 445. The Supreme Court said the case must be returned to the District Court for amendment of pleadings and for further evidence as to whether agreement had been concluded between the parties. Ibid., p. 446.

In a case before it in 1961 the Pakistan Supreme Court said that it advisedly used the expression "practice of States," as there appeared to be no settled rule of international law governing the succession of states. The case related to a certified appeal coming to the Supreme Court from the judgment and order of a Division Bench of the High Court of West Pakistan. It involved an order of a Single Judge of the Chief Court of Sind. The appellant was a company registered in London which had entered into contracts with the respondent firm, the latter carrying on business in Karachi. In the course of its ruling the Supreme Court quoted from the Agreement as to Devolution of International Rights and Obligations upon the Dominions of India and Pakistan. *Yangtze* (*London*) *Ltd.* v. *Barlas Bros.* (*Karachi*) *and Co.*, 34 I.L.R. 27, at 33. See also quotation from the decision at p. 48 below.

private property, as related to international law, has been considered in various contexts, contexts that have, of course, not always involved state succession but rather the right of investors to receive (or states of which they are nationals to receive) from the country of investment adequate compensation for private property that is taken by states. The standard has often been considered in such terms as "prompt, adequate, and effective," but attention has been drawn to difficulties that may be encountered if there is argument for "appropriate," "reasonable," or "just" compensation as a matter of international legal policy in deprivation cases.[54] One view that has been advanced is that customary international law is uncertain or that it calls for something less than full compensation.[55]

Discernment of international law as to private property rights of persons in an area that has undergone state succession may involve specific commitments of the successor state, apart from invocation of general principles. Some examples from recent history of the Commonwealth will illustrate. The Terms of Union of Newfoundland with Canada (1949) provided for the treatment of patents for inventions issued under the laws of Newfoundland prior to the union of Newfoundland with Canada as if these patents had been, by their terms, issued under the laws of Canada. There was to be continued application of the laws of Newfoundland as if the union had not been effected. Likewise trade-

54. Burns H. Weston, "The Taking of Property—Evaluation of Damages: A Comment," *Proceedings of the American Society of International Law* (1968), pp. 43–46. On the need for adoption by the international community of a uniform system of property valuation, see unsigned note "Real Property Valuations for Foreign Wealth Deprivations," *Iowa Law Review*, LIV (1968), 89–114, at 112–114.

55. Weston, "The Taking of Property." See also remarks of Hans Baade in discussion which followed (*Proceedings*, p. 47). Professor Baade drew attention to regional customs and the position of countries involved in a taking. Another participant pointed to a relevant resolution adopted by the International Bar Association in 1966. This resolution set forth, as "among the legal principles which are applicable in determining a State's responsibility for its conduct respecting foreign investments and commitments made by the State in dealing with foreigners," that "property of a foreign national shall not be taken in any case by a State if such taking is discriminatory or if it is in violation of a treaty or contract; nor shall such property be taken in any other case by a State except for a public purpose and then only upon payment of prompt, adequate, and effective compensation." *Eleventh Conference of the International Bar Association* (1966), pp. 8–9.

marks registered under Newfoundland law prior to the date of union were to be treated as if the union had not been effected.[56]

In a volume published in 1956 Professor O'Connell expressed the view that "the principle of respect for acquired rights in international law is no more than a principle that change of sovereignty should not touch the interests of individuals more than is necessary." He took the position, however, that while there was no general immunity from appropriating legislation, the legislation in order to be justified must be accompanied by recognition of the equities involved; if the successor state legislates to alter or cancel acquired rights there must be compliance with the minimum standards of international law through the granting of new titles of equivalent value.[57] In a volume published more than a decade later the same scholar observed that

if the legal system survives . . . State succession, then these rights are as effective after the event as before it. The problem that then arises is whether the successor State may act to alter them, and the answer to the question depends upon whether the rights are vested in nationals of the successor State or in nationals of other States. If vested in the

---

56. *British and Foreign State Papers*, CLIII (1949), part 1, 130, 136. British courts have, with relative frequency, had occasion to rule as to the effect of state succession upon private property rights. In the course of this there has at times been reference to international law. Thus in *Cook* v. *Sprigg* [1899] A.C. 572, Lord Halsbury, giving judgment of the Judicial Committee of the Privy Council said: "It is a well established principle of law that the transactions of independent states between each other are governed by other laws than those which municipal courts administer. It is no answer to say that by the ordinary principles of international law private property is respected by the sovereign which accepts the cession and assumes the duties and legal obligations of the former sovereign with respect to such private property within the ceded territory. All that can be properly meant by such a proposition is that according to the well-understood rules of international law, a change of sovereignty by cession ought not to affect private property, but no municipal tribunal has authority to enforce such an obligation." *British International Law Cases*, II (1965), 282. A quarter of a century later, in *Vayjesingji Joravarsingji* v. *Secretary of State for India* [1924] L.R. 51 I.A. 357, it was stated in the judgment that "any inhabitant of the territory can make good in the municipal courts established by the new sovereign only such rights as that sovereign has, through his officers, recognised. Such rights as he had under the rule of predecessors avail him nothing. Nay, more, even if in a treaty of cession it is stipulated that certain inhabitants should enjoy certain rights, that does not give a title to those inhabitants to enforce these stipulations in the municipal courts. The right to enforce remains only with the high contracting parties." *British International Law Cases*, I (1964), 634.

57. *The Law of State Succession* (1956), pp. 101–102. See also, by the same writer, "Secured and Unsecured Debts in the Law of State Succession," *British Year Book of International Law*, XXVIII (1951), 204–219.

former, they are protected only to the extent to which the successor State's constitution guarantees private rights. . . . If vested in the latter, they are protected to the extent to which international law protects any alien property.[58]

The latter part of this statement (concerning international law) does not of course preclude commitments in bilateral treaties such as the United States has made with some Commonwealth states, as, for example, with Pakistan.[59] If the other party (i.e., the party other than the United States) should be divided and yet has not lost its international personality, treaty obligations of the kind here envisaged would presumably continue to apply to the retained part of the territory, although it is conceivable that there might be an interpretation to the effect that the reduction of territory would be such a change as would comprise a terminating factor. The practice of the United States of including in such bilateral treaties clauses giving to each party the right (with notice) to terminate the treaty, as also a compromissory clause giving a right to either party unilaterally to refer a question of interpretation to the International Court of Justice, would seem to provide an international legal basis on which to seek termination. It seems unlikely, however, that a new state, emerging from an existing Commonwealth state by reason of territorial change and resulting state succession, would necessarily inherit obligations in the circumstances here envisaged.[60]

In still another situation, not unknown in the Commonwealth, entities that have under colonial rule been possessed of separate treaty rights and duties and that unite to form a dominion may continue to have applicable to them the provisions which the United Kingdom had made in the past. Thus when the Australian colonies became parts of the Commonwealth of Australia, there was apparently no abrogation *ipso facto* of treaties that had been previously applicable to individual colonies in Australia, the King remaining as the contracting authority for each part of the Em-

---

58. *State Succession in Municipal and International Law* (1967), I, 237.
59. See Art. IX of the treaty of friendship and commerce, which entered into force on February 12, 1961. TIAS 4683; 12 UST 111.
60. Cf. O'Connell, *State Succession*, I, 185, 186. See his statement concerning vested rights, in Public Officers Agreement 5.

pire, and the federation arrangement having been under his sovereignty.[61] When Burma became independent, the United Kingdom concluded a treaty with the new state which provided for devolution to the provisional government of all liabilities, contractual or otherwise, to which the preindependence government in Burma had been subject.[62]

Various judicial decisions in the successor states of the Commonwealth have related to obligations of these successor states growing out of contracts with private parties. Thus in *Dalmia Dadri Cement Company* v. *Commissioner of Income Tax, Simla,* the High Court of Pepsu held that, with respect to the contractual obligations of the ceding state, it was for the new state to consider and decide which of these obligations it was prepared to have devolve upon it and which ones it was prepared to repudiate.[63]

Numerous kinds of private property rights may be affected in some way by the fact of a state succession. The relatively large number of successions involving developing states of the Commonwealth has provided occasion for weighing the issues involved and the working out of reasonable bases for settlement of them. It is conceivable that some judicial rulings and some devolution arrangements have been made *de lege ferenda* without necessarily implying that the provisions reflect existing (in the sense of universally accepted) international law. Yet it would appear that consideration of general principles of law as well as of practice has marked this era of Commonwealth development. The transition from Empire to separate Commonwealth states, not all of these being members of the still existing personal union under the Crown, has provided frequent occasion for the reexamination of traditional principles, however difficult it may have been to discern universally applicable rules. In the process there would seem to have been, as the process of including additional new states as

61. In 1927 the British Foreign Office informed the United States that a convention of 1899 which by its terms was not to apply to any of the "colonies or foreign possessions" of Great Britain was thought to apply to the Irish Free State. Hackworth, *Digest*, V, 370.

62. British Treaty Series no. 16 (1948), Cmd. 7360, art. 2; 70 UNTS 183, 190.

63. All I.R., Pepsu ser., 3, 4, 5, 6, 18 (vol. 42, C.N.2); 21 I.L.R. (1954) 51; reproduced in part in Whiteman, *Digest of International Law*, II (1963), 820. Cf. McNair, *The Law of Treaties*, p. 468.

full members in the Commonwealth has continued, constructive reexamination and testing of doctrine and practice concerning the effect of state succession upon prior-acquired rights of private parties.

III

To the very general term "public relationships" may be subsumed various matters touching the effect of state succession upon rights and duties of predecessor states as such, as distinguished from effects upon their respective peoples. An informed observer has cautioned against lofty enunciation of abstract formulas and has observed that postsuccession problems are "novel, important and urgent." [64] Some novelties may have attended arrangements that have marked the recent evolution of the Commonwealth, and the nineteenth-century doctrine of succession has been described as "notably lacking in cogency for mid-twentieth-century purposes." [65] The manner in which the newly independent states of the Commonwealth have emerged, and the fact that some older members had, as dominions, even before their complete independence attained legal personality for the purpose of determining their own treaty rights and duties, would need to be taken into account in any complete estimate of the effect upon the developing law of nations.

As in the case of the effect of state succession upon preexisting treaties and upon acquired private rights, there might be need in a complete analysis for critical reexamination of familiar terminology. In this context there has been criticism of the continued use of such a term as "servitude" and the suggestion that instead of employing this concept derived from Roman law there might well be more attention to the actual *localization* of a previously made treaty in determining the effect of a state succession.[66] There has apparently been, in the study of effects that state

---

64. D. P. O'Connell, "Independence and Problems of State Succession," in W. V. O'Brien, ed., *The New Nations in International Law and Diplomacy* (1965), pp. 7–41, at p. 9.
65. Ibid., p. 10.   66. Ibid., p. 4.

succession has upon public as well as private rights, endeavor to find practically applicable doctrines that are appropriate for contemporary phenomena. Some of the proposals offered may be brief but not completely self-interpreting, such as the proposal that public archives at a state succession should be transferred to "that State which acquires the assets to which they relate." [67] Perhaps the most frequently cited ruling by an international court concerning the right of a predecessor state to dispose of public territory within its boundaries before the cession actually took place is that of *German Settlers in Poland*.[68] The special circumstances in this case would seem to justify the court's ruling; unless precluded by provisions of a treaty on this point, it would seem that a state which is about to divest itself of a portion of its territory may, up to the time of transfer, cede what has previously been public property to private persons.[69]

Practice in relation to such new Commonwealth states as Ceylon, Malaya-Malaysia, and Cyprus (and formerly South Africa) provides illustration of a predecessor state's retaining, in its public capacity, some type of control over property and facilities in the successor state. Before South Africa's withdrawal from the Commonwealth the Simonstown naval base had by an agreement of June 30, 1955,[70] been transferred to South Africa, but with the provision that its facilities would be available to the Royal Navy in peacetime, that it would be usable by the Royal Navy in peacetime, and that its facilities would be usable, in any war in which the United Kingdom should be involved, by the Royal Navy and by the allies of the United Kingdom. This has been thought to mean that even if South Africa had been a neutral, the base would have been available to Great Britain and its allies.[71]

For nearly a decade after Ceylon attained dominion status the United Kingdom had, by understanding with that Commonwealth state, rights as to the Trincomalee naval base and an air base at Katunayake.[72] Upon its attainment of independence Ma-

---

67. D. P. O'Connell, *International Law* (1965), I, 450.
68. P.C.I.J., Ser. A, no. 9.
69. Cf. *Percheman* case, cited in n. 53 above.
70. Cmd. 9520.
71. F. A. Váli, *Servitudes in International Law*, 2nd ed. (1958), p. 223.
72. Cmd. 7257 (the 1947 agreement). See also chap. 6, n. 9, below.

laya concluded with Great Britain an arrangement concerning the establishment, maintenance, and use of bases and facilities in the territory of the new federation.[73] In the case of Cyprus there was agreement as to British retention of "sovereign bases" on the island [74]—Cyprus, although it is a republic, being included as among Her Majesty's "dominions and possessions" within the meaning of some statutory enactments.[75] With the exceptions set out in Annex B of the treaty and certain property rights described in Annex E, section 1, paragraph 2, "all property of the Government of the Colony of Cyprus" was, on the date of the entry into force of the treaty, and subject to the Constitution of the Republic of Cyprus, to become the property of that republic.[76] There was further provision to make clear that "property" was to mean property, whether movable or immovable, tangible or intangible and rights of every description.[77] The communal situation in Cyprus in relation to the effect of state succession upon public property is reflected in the following provision of the new state's constitution:

1. Any movable or immovable property, or any right or interest thereon, which, immediately before the date of the coming into operation of this Constitution, was vested in, held by, or registered in the name of, the Colony of Cyprus or any other person or body, for and on behalf of, or in trust for, any school, or other body or institution which come by or under the provisions of this Constitution, within the competence of the Communal Chambers shall, as from that date, be vested in, and be held by such person, body or authority as provided by a law of the respective Communal Chamber and subject to such terms and conditions as such communal law may provide:
Provided that no such law shall direct that any such property shall vest in, or be held by, the communal Chamber itself.[78]

Recent practice in the Commonwealth has provided examples of the devolution of various types of public property. With the partition of India and formation of the new state of Pakistan, public lands theretofore vested in the viceroy of the undivided state, referred to officially as "land vested in His Majesty for the purpose of the Governor-General in Council," became public

73. Cmd. 263.
75. See also chap. 3, pp. 84–85 below.
77. Ibid., sec. 4(a).
74. 382 UNTS 8, art. 1.
76. 382 UNTS 8, Annex E, sec. 1.
78. Cmd. 1093, art. 197, p. 169.

property of the new state of India. Land located outside what had been British India was to become the joint property of the two dominions; there was further provision that public land in an Indian state, if that state acceded to one of the two dominions, would become public property of that dominion.[79] A basic decision touching succession was that India should remain a "constant international person" with continuing membership in international public organizations such as the United Nations, while Pakistan was considered a new state, and the matter of its relations to the principal world organization remained to be settled.

Illustrative of judicial holdings pertaining to state succession, as they may be viewed in light of international practice as well as international law, is a decision of the Supreme Court of Pakistan (Appellate Division) to the effect that the Indian Independence (Internal Arrangements) Order, 1947, did not and could not provide for the devolution of treaty rights and obligations that were not capable of being succeeded to by a part of the country which had been severed from the parent state and established as an independent sovereign power "according to the practice of States." In the course of its ruling the Court said:

> We advisedly use the expression "practice of States" in this regard for there appear to be no settled rules of International Law governing the succession of States. But as far as it can be gathered the consensus of opinion among international jurists seems to be in favor of the view that as a general rule a new state so formed will succeed to rights and obligations arising under treaties specifically relating to its territories, e.g., treaties relating to its boundaries or regulating the navigation of rivers or providing for guarantees or concessions but not to rights and obligations affecting the State, as such, or its subjects, e.g., treaties of alliance, arbitration or commerce.[80]

The constitutions of new Commonwealth states have sometimes included rather brief provisions concerning the devolution of public property. Thus the Constitution of the Federation of Malaya, 1957, contained in its article 166(1) the following:

79. See more detailed statement in O'Connell, *State Succession*, I, 220–221.
80. *Yangtse (London) Limited* v. *Barlas Brothers (Karachi) and Company; Judgment of 6 June, 1961* (Civil Appeal no. 139 of 1960), cited above, p. 40n.

Subject to the provisions of this Article, all property and assets which immediately before Merdeka Day were vested in Her Majesty for the purpose of the Federation or of the colony or settlement of Malacca or Penang, shall on Merdeka Day vest in the Federation or the State of Malacca or the State of Penang, as their case may be.

The Constitution of Malaysia, 1964, contained in its chapter 4 provisions concerning public property of the new federation.[81] With the separation of Singapore in 1965 there was provision that property that had been Singapore's before Malaysia Day and that had become property of Malaysia on that day should again become property of Singapore.[82] This aspect of the effect of state succession, since it relates to public rights, to property, and to jurisdiction, would seem to touch less upon human problems than does the effect of succession upon nationality of persons, to which matter attention may now be directed.

IV

Of all the relationships that have come to be associated with the peoples of the Commonwealth and that have given rise to questions concerning international law, perhaps the one which has had to do with status of the individual in relation to the state, i.e., the link of nationality, has had greatest attention. This link at first bound all British subjects, under the broad classification of persons owing allegiance to the monarch.[83] When, after World War I, the self-governing dominions became members of the League of Nations, there was occasion for their respective peoples to have a status distinct from that which other communities had within the Commonwealth. A judicial holding in Australia shortly after the end of World War II was to the effect that

81. Amos J. Peaslee, ed., *Constitutions of Nations,* rev. 3rd ed. (1965) II, no. 2.

82. Annex B to an Agreement Relating to the Separation of Singapore from Malaysia, *International Legal Materials,* IV (1965), 940.

83. On the general subject, see Robert R. Wilson and Robert E. Clute, "Commonwealth Citizenship and Common Status," *American Journal of International Law,* LVII (1963), 566–587; also Robert E. Clute, "Nationality and Citizenship," in Wilson, *The International Law Standard and Commonwealth Developments,* chap. 3, pp. 100–136.

naturalization in Australia did not cause the person naturalized to be a British subject in Great Britain.[84] Yet the concept of a common status continued in effect for application in relation to other matters, such as the extradition of fugitives, the use of letters rogatory, and the recognition of foreign judgments—procedures which continued upon the basis of imperial acts. The Statute of Westminster had for one of its purposes to keep these statutes in force in each dominion unless and until they should be repealed by the legislature of such dominion. The present consideration of the effect of state succession upon nationality will be limited to nationality of individual persons, excluding nationality of claims or of vessels.

An important step toward eventual abandonment of the concept of common status was the passage of the Canadian Citizenship Act of 1946; by this legislation all persons who were British subjects under the law of any other Commonwealth state were to be recognized as such in Canada. Subsequently there was passage of the British Nationality Act of 1948, and a White Paper explained that the act gave effect to the principle that nationals of self-governing countries of the Commonwealth possessed status as citizens of their respective states and also status in the Commonwealth as a whole.[85] This looked to the general arrangement whereby each member state of the Commonwealth would in legislation define its own citizens, the latter also being regarded as continuing to be British subjects. The paper envisaged that what was described as the "common clause" would serve the purpose of recognizing clearly the separate identity of Commonwealth member states and of enabling a Commonwealth member state that had occasion to negotiate to define with precision the natural persons on whose behalf it might be negotiating. The British Nationality Act of 1948 set forth that the status of British subject was to have, for the purpose of this legislation, the same meaning as Commonwealth citizen.[86] While not all Commonwealth member states followed with passage of legislation similar to that of Great Britain, apparently no Commonwealth member

84. *Markwald* v. *Atty. Gen.,* [1920] 1 Ch. 348.
85. Cmd. 7326.   86. 11 and 12 Geo. 6 (1948).

state regarded British citizens or subjects as aliens in the full sense of that term. The White Paper further set forth that creation of the dual status of citizen of a Commonwealth country and British subject would have the advantage of

giving a clear recognition to separate identity of particular countries of the Commonwealth, of clarifying the position with regard to diplomatic protection and of enabling a Government when making treaties with other countries to define with precision who are the persons belonging to its country and on whose behalf it is negotiating. Such a system also enables each country to make alterations in its nationality laws without having first, as under the common code system, to consult the other countries of the Commonwealth.[87]

Since the present purpose is not to trace the history of legislation but rather to note briefly the background of present legislation and to see wherein legislative policy has touched issues bearing upon public international law, the question arises whether in Commonwealth practice there has been conformity to any general principles of law applicable to both predecessor and successor states. As at least a partial background for a claim of restriction upon states in this general area there is the ruling of the International Court of Justice in the *Nottebohm* case to the effect that in order for an individual to acquire by naturalization the citizenship of a state there must be a "genuine link" between him and the naturalizing state.[88] The question of the effect of state succession upon nationality of persons living in the community which is to become independent may of course be settled by an undertaking between the predecessor state and the potential successor state, or by legislation of the former, such as the Burma Independence Act, 1947.[89] In the case of India, Pakistan, and Ceylon, respectively, no enactments of the same type were necessary since these were in the status of dominions. There was,

87. Cmd. 7326.   88. 1955 I.C.J. Rep. 4.
89. 11 and 12 Geo. 6, c. 3, sec. 2. This legislation contained the following:
"2(1) Subject to the provisions of this section, the persons specified in the First Schedule to this Act, being British subjects immediately before the appointed day, shall on that day cease to be British subjects:
Provided that a woman who immediately before the appointed day is the wife of a British subject shall not cease by virtue of this subsection to be a British subject unless her husband ceases by virtue of this subsection to be a British subject."

however, legislation to cover the case of British-protected persons. By statutory provisions these might continue to be British subjects; the legislation indicated classes of persons who were potentially citizens of the respective successor states.[90] As to newer states, such as Nigeria, Tanganyika, Sierra Leone, Kenya, Zanzibar, Malawi, Zambia, and Malta, persons resident there who before independence were citizens of the United Kingdom and Colonies would cease to be such citizens if by law of the respective new states they became citizens of such states.[91] The effect of such legislation was apparently to restrict the change of nationality of persons to individuals of indigenous or semi-indigenous character. Professor O'Connell has drawn attention to the fact that there were no legislative enactments that would have deprived anyone of citizenship because of the transfer of the Cocos Islands and Christmas Island to Australia, or the incorporation of Penang and Malacca into Malaya, or the birth of the new state of Singapore.[92]

If in legislation of the type referred to there was no mention of rules of international law *ipsissimis verbis,* there was considerable evidence in the lawmaking of consideration for the individual human beings themselves, and perhaps recognition in principle of the Universal Declaration of Human Rights in its statement that every individual has the right to a nationality and that no one shall be arbitrarily deprived of his nationality nor denied the right to change his nationality.[93] International law does not lay down rules that would be applicable to every situation with

90. The statute also set forth procedure by which persons ordinarily domiciled in designated (British-controlled) territory outside of Burma might by declaration elect to remain British subjects. By further provision, certain classes of persons under the above-mentioned sec. 2 who should neither become (nor become qualified to become) citizens of the independent state of Burma might retain the status of British subjects.

91. Nigeria Independence Act, 1960, 8 and 9 Eliz. 2, c. 55, sec. 2; Tanganyika Independence Act, 1961, 10 and 11 Eliz. 2, c. 1, sec. 2; Sierra Leone Independence Act, 1961, 9 and 10 Eliz. 2, c. 16, sec. 2; Kenya Independence Act, 1963, 10 and 11 Eliz. 2, c. 54, sec. 2; Zanzibar Act, 1963, 11 Eliz. 2, c. 55, sec. 2; Malawi Independence Act, 1964, 11 Eliz. 2, c. 46, sec. 2; Zambia Independence Act, 1964, 11 Eliz. 2, c. 65, sec. 3; Malta Independence Act, 1964, 11 Eliz. 2, c. 86.

92. *State Succession,* I, 522.

93. Art. 15. The International Covenant on Civil and Political Rights provides (art. 24, para. 3) that "every child has the right to acquire a nationality." See also chap. 7, n. 9, below.

respect to the effect of a state succession upon nationality, and practice in the Commonwealth beginning about the middle of the twentieth century has left open the possibility that after a state succession the new (successor) state may, as in the case of India, lay down broad principles concerning the acquisition of its citizenship. A section of the Indian Constitution bases citizenship on domicile, and another section contains rules as to the effect upon citizenship of migration from India to Pakistan or migration from Pakistan to India.[94] Upon the completion of a state succession, it will be for the new (successor) state to decide who shall be its nationals subject to the rights (under international law or treaties) of resident aliens, and except insofar as it may have made commitments to the predecessor state as to the predecessor state's citizens or "protected persons" who choose to remain in the territory of the successor state. While the right of an individual to have a nationality and to change his nationality is widely accepted as a human right, it has in the past been possible to have noncitizen nationals—as, for example, was formerly the case with American Indians in the United States.[95] South Africa's withdrawal from the Commonwealth in 1960 apparently did not cause the people of that state to lose their status as British subjects, and this situation was apparently not changed until later. Until the end of 1965 a South African citizen might through registration be assimilated to a Commonwealth citizen in the United Kingdom and Colonies.[96] One effect of the "common status" principle was that a British subject who was a citizen of one Commonwealth state but resident in another Commonwealth state might be held to obligations in the latter—i.e., obligations to which an ordinary alien (one from a non-Commonwealth state) might not be held.[97] Such an individual might also be permitted by law to vote or, if the law in the Commonwealth state of residence so provided, be required, under penalty, to vote. Such voting would not preclude

94. Constitution of India, part 2, secs. 5, 6.
95. Robert R. Wilson, "Gradations in Citizenship and International Reclamations," *American Journal of International Law*, XXXIII (1939), 146.
96. O'Connell, *State Succession*, I, 522.
97. See Clute, "Nationality and Citizenship," in Wilson, *The International Law Standard and Commonwealth Developments*, p. 110.

his voting in the Commonwealth state of which he was a citizen.[98]

In the case of a partial succession in the Commonwealth state, as also in the event of a territory's being transferred from the United Kingdom to another Commonwealth country, there would appear to have been a practice of avoiding legislation concerning any change of citizenship; examples have been the transfer of the Cocos Islands and Christmas Island to Australia and the creation of the State of Singapore.[99]

———

From even a very limited survey of the literature and of practice in the Commonwealth relating to state succession in the period since the passage of the Statute of Westminster, it would appear that there has not been rigid adherence to either of the two broad principles commonly associated with the emergence of newly independent states. The so-called universal theory, by which rights and duties generally followed the succession, and what has sometimes been called the negative or clean slate theory have not, in any case, been the stated bases for general policy. The second of the two theories would seem to have had greater influence, since the practice of the United Kingdom has been to allow considerable leeway to the new states in their consideration of what rights and duties would attend their transition to independence. The varied circumstances under which successions have occurred within the Commonwealth in the period since World War II would perhaps have made it impracticable for the United Kingdom to adhere rigidly to either of the two mentioned principles. Instead, there has been a pragmatic approach which has avoided restrictive classification of entities and has had regard for the special circumstances in each case. In fact, some of the areas for which Great Britain previously had responsibility apparently did not go through the traditional forms of state succession. In the case of the former mandate for Palestine and the emergence of the State of Israel with the termination of the mandate in 1947 there has been support for the view that, by

———

98. Ibid., and Clive Parry, "International Law and the Conscription of Non-Nationals," *British Year Book of International Law*, XXXI (1954), 437–452.
99. O'Connell, *State Succession*, I, 522.

virtue of Israel's Declaration of Independence in 1948, "a new international personality was created, which was not, internationally speaking—the successor of the Mandatory Government, so that Israel started with a clean slate and was only bound by such of the former international obligations affecting her territory as she might accept." [100]

As to the growing number of instances in which communities formerly under the sovereignty of Great Britain have in the recent past come to be independent in the international law sense, and as to which there has been state succession in the full international law sense, the relevant issues have been approached in a pragmatic manner, and the lingering ties which exist between Great Britain and those of its former colonies that have now become independent states appear to rest upon arrangements to which such new states have assented.

Determination of whether a particular treaty of Great Britain binds a state that has now emerged from dominion status to full independence apparently presents no insuperable legal problem, for in a sense these older members of the Commonwealth have long controlled their own destinies so far as agreement to be bound by treaties is concerned, and their continued adherence to commitments which they have long since elected to have applicable to them is a natural deduction. This, however, does not overlook the fact that foreign offices may not have adequate staffs or work with perfect efficiency, and that determination as to continuance in effect of "old" treaties may sometimes require considerable study.

The device of "devolution" or "inheritance" agreements, apparently begun with respect to some of the newer Commonwealth states in Africa, has provided a means of allowing newly independent states of the Commonwealth to opt for continued application to themselves of "old" treaties. It represents a practice which, together with the United Nations plan for the registration of treaties with the Secretariat, may have the effect of at least

---

100. Sir Arnold McNair, *The Law of Treaties* (1961), p. 654. This view was believed by McNair to be correct "on the assumption that treaties creating local obligations" required separate consideration.

clarifying the wills of the respective successor states. The traditional rule of *pacta servanda sunt* is not destroyed by reasonable
consideration of the position of the new states and their respective policies, as well as the attitudes of the predecessor state and
of third parties. In the case of areas that were former mandates,
consideration of the succession questions arising might be consistent with the view that some questions need to be settled in light
of the larger (international) community's interest.

In matters of succession affecting private rights, there has apparently not been disregard of a long-established doctrine of
international law, but practice has permitted consideration of
special situations and of such conditions as individuals' removal
from the territory of the successor state. The secretary-general of
the United Nations, in a memorandum to the International Law
Commission (whose proposals were under consideration at an
international conference at Vienna in 1969), has referred to private rights in connection with state succession as something the
validity of which has never been seriously challenged, while
conceding that there is no measure with regard to its application
in all categories of private rights.[101]

As to the present effect of state succession upon public rights as
distinct from private, there would seem to be no international law
rules that would preclude special arrangements between predecessor and successor states. The nature of the public rights acknowledged or retained would seem to be important in reaching
decision as to some such rights. The turning over to the successor
state of ordinary public property would appear to be normal
practice. On the other hand, the United Kingdom, while granting
independence to some of the emergent new communities, has
retained, at least temporarily, important rights in the form of
"sovereign bases," as in Cyprus.[102] In certain other situations, for
example in Ceylon, bases retained for a period have ultimately

---

101. Prior to 1969 the International Law Commission's discussions (of the
effect of state succession in respect of rights and duties resulting from sources
other than treaties) had elicited views as to the effect upon private property
rights. *Year Book of the International Law Commission, 1968*, I, "Summary
Records of the Twentieth Session," 105–130. See, for example, at p. 114, the
critical reference by Mr. Rosenne to the special rapporteur's mention of "traditional" international law of state succession as affecting private rights.
102. See p. 47 above.

been allowed to come under control and ownership of the states in which these British rights had formerly been maintained. In the subcontinent of Asia public lands, previously state property of the United Kingdom, were apportioned to India and Pakistan. In 1963 Great Britain took steps to arrange the turning over to Malaysia of public property that had previously belonged to Malaya. After Singapore ceased to be a part of Malaysia, there was British legislation for the return to Singapore of public property that Great Britian had previously turned over to Malaysia.[103]

The human (as well as state) problem of nationality as affected by state succession has apparently been regarded in the Commonwealth as a major one, and one in which there should be regard for the will of the individuals affected. It has been said that international law does not provide a rule as to what persons should, as citizens, compose a successor state. Yet the International Court of Justice has underlined the principle that there should be a "genuine link" between the individual and the state whose nationality he has procured.[104] There would seem to have been, in the determination of the effect of a state succession upon nationality of persons since World War II, continuing regard for individuals' own choice in the matter. There has also been, as a holdover from the period when the concept of a "common status" was more in evidence, some practice by the principal Commonwealth member states of exacting duties, such as military service, from a noncitizen "British subject" in its territory.[105]

The issue of state succession in the Commonwealth, as it has

---

103. See n. 82 above.   104. 1955 I.C.J. Rep. 4.

105. This is illustrated in the drafting of Irish citizens, resident in the Great Britain, for military service in the latter country. More directly relevant to international law is the decision of the Australian High Court that the drafting of aliens was contrary to international law but that the national court could not disregard the statute which authorized such drafting. *Politis v. The Commonwealth and Another; Kandolitis v. The Commonwealth and Another.* 7 Commonw. L.R. 60 (1945).

The legal status of particular racial groups in Commonwealth countries other than the United Kingdom was the subject of judicial decision in the *Japanese Canadians* case, in which the Judicial Committee of the Privy Council held that Canada could deprive the persons concerned of their status as British subjects only insofar as the law of Canada was concerned, but that the legislation under consideration would deprive them of their status as British subjects *only* insofar as the law of Canada was concerned. *Co-operative Committee on Japanese Canadians v. Attorney General for Canada* A.C. (1947), p. 87. Cf. decision in *Musson and Musson v. Rodriguez,* 1955 I.L.R. (1960), p. 60, and *Sudali Andy Asary v. Van den Dreeson,* 1952 I.L.R. (1957), p. 61.

figured in the four selected fields, would appear to have been met with considerable regard for public as well as private rights, and with regard for international community interests as well as for individual state interests. Collectively considered from the legal point of view, practices in the Commonwealth have emphasized what Sir Arnold McNair has referred to as the "geography of international law." [106]

106. Foreword to O'Connell, *International Law*, I, vi.

· 3 ·

Communalism

Sizable problems arising out of ethnic groupings have marked the evolution of certain states which are members of the Commonwealth. That international legal principles and rules have figured in the development has been increasingly apparent as more and more of the former British possessions have become independent states.[1] Occasions for (and in some instances obstacles to) the invocation and interpretation of international law may conceivably be more effectively illumined if account is taken of racial, religious, and linguistic factors (as well as political, military, and economic ones) that have affected states' policies in their foreign relations. With the taking into account of such factors, foreign policy and the legalities involved become more understandable as the outward expression of domestic forces. In the multiracial Commonwealth, communalism in what are often described as "plural" societies invites special attention from the point of view of the effect upon international legal relations.

Communalism implies distinctive alignments of people on ethnic, religious, or linguistic bases. Most governmental problems arising from such groupings will presumably be political or constitutional, i.e., internal ones. That there may also be effect upon international relations is indicated by the repercussions to President de Gaulle's public statements in Quebec in 1967—even if, as in the case of Quebec, the distinctive groupings there be regarded as on a basis essentially cultural.[2] A less publicized indica-

1. An examination, on a highly selective basis, of some of the matters involved has been undertaken by the present author and associates in *The International Law Standard and Commonwealth Developments* (1966).
2. See *Preliminary Report* of the Royal Commission on Bilingualism and Biculturalism, Ottawa, Feb. 1, 1965. In its report dated Oct. 8, 1967, the com-

tion of concern about communalism in a Commonwealth state was the setting up in the Commonwealth state of Guyana of a Department of Race Relations under the Ministry of Education "with the object of overcoming the racial Schisms, exacerbated by the recent history of civil disturbances." [3] The achievement of independence in Mauritius (reportedly a contested issue) in March, 1968, was attended by "severe racial animosities and fears," with most of the inhabitants preferring to be identified as Hindus, Creoles, or Muslims rather than Mauritians.[4] That con-

---

mission submitted that it was "important for Canada to maintain strong and vigorous links in the chain of French language and culture across the whole country. We believe furthermore that 'equal partnership' for Francophones necessitates a change of policy, from offering the minimum of education in their mother tongue to offering the maximum."

Referring to the French-Canadian renaissance and the balancing of this with a strong federal Canada, the then president of the Montreal Branch of the Royal Commonwealth Society suggested that from 1963 onward the Crown stood for the symbolic and political foresight of a French minority on an English-speaking continent, the Crown not being an oppressive symbol but a guardian of the integrity of a French-speaking remnant. He referred to the "Fulton Formula" to the effect that the Constitution cannot be amended in some instances without the consent of at least two-thirds of the provinces having 50 percent of the population of Canada. This formula, it was submitted, must not be allowed to provide for a built-in veto by a single province where no federal constitution could admit such "permanent entrenchments" to be extended for languages, schools, federal House and Senate representation, in religion and private law. Maxwell Cohen, "The Queen and the Constitution of Canada," *Commonwealth Journal,* VII (1964), 271–272.

3. *Guyana,* a publication issued by the Reference Division, British Information Service (1966), p. 17.

4. Dispatch of Joseph Lelyveld, *New York Times,* March 19, 1958, p. 16. Independence celebrations in March of 1969 were preceded by communal riots, and twenty-six persons lost their lives. The prime minister of Mauritius, Sir Seewoosagur Ramgoolam, is reported as deploring racialism and having fought against it most of his political life. Patrick Keatley, "Jewel of the Indian Ocean," *Guardian,* May 27, 1969, p. 9.

Illustrative of legislation against communalism in a large Commonwealth state were bills introduced (and subsequently enacted) in India in 1961. One of these made it an offense (punishable by imprisonment) to promote enmity or hatred between different religious, racial, or language groups, castes, or communities, or to commit acts that were prejudicial to the maintenance of harmony between such groups and likely to disturb public tranquillity. Another measure laid down penalties for attempts to appeal to religious, racial, caste, communal, or linguistic sentiments for electioneering purposes. In the same year there was in New Delhi a convention of some six hundred Moslems who considered problems growing out of communalism. *Keesing's Contemporary Archives,* XIII (1961–1962), 18399.

The Law of Elections and Elections Petitions in India, 3rd ed. (1962), contains (sec. 123[3], p. 569) wording to the effect that the object of the subsection is to introduce the principle of nondiscrimination between different castes, communities, and religions, which is laid down in the Constitution of India, the subsection merely carrying into effect in the sphere of the law of elections articles.

flicts incident to the disharmony of religious groups may be serious even in a very advanced country was illustrated in events in Northern Ireland in August, 1969.

International rights and duties may be invoked in the demands of outside states for the protection of ethnic groups, whether these demands be on the basis of humanitarianism, bilateral treaty commitments or on the broader plane of universal human rights. The commitments which a state makes to other states in treaty form—as, for example, on the subjects of entry, establishment, business, or missionary activity of admitted aliens—may naturally be affected by the granting state's particular situation with respect to the relative size and nature of distinct ethnic or religious groups already within the state.

In the evolution toward self-government and independence of entities that now comprise newly independent states within the Commonwealth there has apparently been, in general, frank recognition of the problems communalism has presented. As early as 1928 a special commission appointed to consider one aspect of the subject included in its report the following general statement, which, while looking to the situation of a particular unit in the Commonwealth, would seem to have applicability to more than one Commonwealth entity:

One of the most difficult problems in connection with the formation or alteration of constitutions for the various overseas countries of the Empire is that of communal representation. The populations are made up of diverse elements, often with fundamental racial and religious

---

15, 16, 29, and 325 of the Constitution. There is judicial statement that, having regard to the association of words "caste, race and religion" with the word 'community' the meaning of the latter must be restricted to include only a body which has been formed, organized, or has come into existence "on the basis of caste, race or religion or any other factors contributing or leading to the division of the nation." For an interpretation of sec. 123(3), see *Khilumal Topandas* v. *Arjundas Tulsidas,* 1959 Raj. 280; I.L.R. (1959) 9 Raj. 245.

On the point that communal problems based on religion, languages, and race are commonplace phenomena and that the tendency toward large associations of peoples based upon geographical contiguity, supposed advantages, or recent political history, has met with but mixed success, see Herbert Feldman, "The Communal Problems in the Indo-Pakistan Subcontinent: Some Current Implications," *Pacific Affairs,* XLIII (1969), 145–163, at 160.

differences. Even within the same racial or religious community caste distinctions may be responsible for rigid division of classes. These diverse elements and distinct classes, even if not antagonistic to each other, are in more or less separate compartments, this resulting in a lack of homogeneity and of corporate consciousness which makes it difficult to achieve any national unity of purpose. Communal representation was devised with a view to assisting the development of democratic institutions in countries of different races and religions and in the hope of eliminating the clash of these various interests during elections. It was expected to provide, peacefully, an elective legislative assembly which would have a fair representation of the different elements in the population and would also tend to promote unity. Unfortunately, the experiment has not given the desired results, but has had, if anything, the opposite effect. The representatives of the different communities do not trust one another, and communal representation has not helped to provide a uniting bond or link. The minority communities are fearful that any preponderance of governmental power held by another community will inevitably be used against them and are keenly on the alert for signs of discrimination.[5]

The manner in which and the extent to which communalism has affected developments within the Commonwealth touching public international law would doubtless merit a much wider inquiry than the very limited one here essayed, which relates to elements of communal phenomena as they have affected the external relations of three relatively small states of the Commonwealth. The choice, for this purpose, of Malaysia, Ceylon, and Cyprus rather than more populous members of the Commonwealth such as India, Pakistan, or Nigeria, or of a small state such as Mauritius, does not of course imply that greater practical importance necessarily attaches to practice in the selected states. Comparisons aside, practice in the three selected states during the relatively short period of their independence would seem to provide evidence of communalism that may be viewed in the light of its apparent effect upon the foreign policies and law of the respective states. A concluding section comprises such generalizations as seem to be justified, not necessarily by experience in the Commonwealth in general, but at least by that in the three selected states.

5. *Report of the Special (Donoughmore) Commission on the Constitution of Ceylon,* Cmd. 3131 (1928), pp. 90–91.

I

There is no *single* pattern of communalism in the three states. Developments in Malaysia invite special attention by reason of the particular racial groupings, constitutional arrangements that have apparently been directed to the protection or favoring of one racial group, relatively rapid change from Malaya to Malaysia, and thereafter the short-lived federation with what is now the separate and independent state of Singapore.

Writing in the mid-1960's, one observer, while noting that there had been some indication of Chinese nationalism in Malaya before World War II, pointed out that the Chinese community's life was dominated by external issues. He referred to the split in the Malay community—as between traditionalists and modernists; while Malay nationalism before the war had been neither very popular nor very effective, there came to be among the Malays a growing political awareness.[6] In the developing Commonwealth there was apparently an increasing interest in Malaya's assuming a place as a united and enlightened country in a manner appropriate to its economic and strategic importance.[7]

6. K. J. Ratnam, *Communalism and the Political Process in Malaya* (1965), p. 13. In the course of debates in the British Parliament concerning policy for Southeast Asia the point was made that when Siam transferred to the United Kingdom all rights of suzerainty, protection, administration, and control which it possessed over the four northern Malay states, this made these states in effect dependencies of Great Britain, but the British government in effect "abjured any right of absolute ownership" and made treaties with the rulers, "exchanging the right to administer for the right to advise." There was reference to the fact that as early as 1904 the Malay rulers had objected to foreign Asiatics being appointed to State Councils and subordinate service; regulations were altered so that administration should be carried out by Malays and Europeans. The speaker added that the Chinese and Indians "were admitted to the Malay States on British advice and if the Malay is edged out of the administrative field it will cause considerable dissatisfaction and bitter resentment." *Parl. Deb.* (L), 5th ser., vol. 138 (1945–1946), cc. 930, 931 (remarks of Viscount Marchwood). In the course of the same debate Viscount Addison, answering a question concerning the establishment of privileged minorities, said that the scheme aimed "to give better opportunities for the native population"; he said that he had no doubt that the Malays would take full advantage of the scheme. "It is our earnest desire," he said, "that they shall" (p. 941).

7. On official British concern after World War II, see statement in Cmd. 6724 (1946): "International relations as well as the security and other interests of the British Commonwealth require that Malaya should be able to exercise an influence as a united and enlightened country appropriate to her economic and strategic importance."

After surmounting the Communist menace which Malaya faced from 1948 to 1961, the citizens of the state which had come into being on Merdeka Day in 1957 were still far from being completely unified. The Malay element tended to be rural and agricultural, the Chinese to be urban.[8] The Indian Tamils tended to be associated with labor, many of them having been brought into the country by the British for work on the rubber plantations. The communal feeling of non-Malays has been described as extranational in origin and content.[9] The educational problem has been called the key difficulty in Sino-Malay relations.[10] One observer of the region, in a volume published in 1966, suggested that the danger from communalism in Malaysia might not be imminent and that the two principal cultures of the country were coming together in the educated middle class which comprises Malays, Chinese, Indians, Dusuns, Ibans, and others.[11] This does not overlook the fact that, in terms at least, some constitutional arrangements within the state would still seem to be weighted in favor of Malays. Nor can it be easily reconciled with the bloody communal fighting in Kuala Lumpur, such as occurred in May and June of 1969.

If a plural society is described as comprising two or more communal groups, it is possible to have one of these groups officially singled out for preferential treatment. The Constitution of the Federation of Malaysia, which became effective in September, 1963, continued the plan of preferential treatment of Malays and aboriginal peoples of the Malay Peninsula as this has been provided for in the Constitution of the former Federation of Malaya.[12] The Malaysian Constitution, while asserting the equality of persons before the law (section 8) and asserting freedom of

8. For a more detailed statement on the two communities, see Ratnam, *Communalism and the Political Process in Malaya,* pp. vii, 2–9.

9. K. G. Tregonning, *Malaysia* (1966), pp. 11, 12. The same author observed (p. 81) that Malaysia was virtually without a nonracial party.

10. See Wong Purcell, in Wang Gungwu, ed., *Malaysia: A Survey* (1964), p. 191.

11. Tregonning, *Malaysia,* pp. 10–12.

12. For discussion, see S. M. Huang-Thio, "Constitutional Discrimination under the Malaysian Constitution," *Malaya Law Review,* VI (1964), 1–16; this writer submits that article 153 of the Constitution did not really benefit the bulk of the Malay population.

religion (section 11), provides that Islam is the religion of the federation (section 3). Section 153 makes it the responsibility of the Yang di-Pertuan Agong to safeguard the position of the Malays. In section 160 a Malay is defined as "a person who professes the Muslim religion, habitually speaks the Malay language, conforms to Malay custom and: (a) was before Merdeka Day born in the Federation or in Singapore or born of parents one of whom was born in the Federation or in Singapore, or is on that day domiciled in the Federation or in Singapore; or (b) is the issue of such a person." State law may control or restrict propagation of any other doctrine or belief among persons professing the Muslim religion.[13]

As a possible rationale for discrimination (or in the case of aborigines, protective discrimination) enjoyed by Malays, there has been reference to the fact that they form an economically depressed community. Malaya has been described as a "rich, under-populated, and an important strategic centre" with a population that is "a mixture of races from three other territories all larger, all poorer, and all more over-populated than Malaya is ever likely to be." [14] Constitutional arrangements have permitted persons of the Malay race not born in Malaya to acquire citizenship without subjection to the literacy test required of other immigrants.[15] Privileges of Malays have also extended to land-holding, civil service positions, and licensing for certain trades and businesses.[16]

Before the formation of Malaysia (in 1963) the Constitution of Malaya had provided for preferential treatment of Malays in that

13. As to legal effects of this and of other factors in the history of the region, see L. C. Green, "Malaya/Singapore/Malaysia," *Canadian Yearbook of International Law*, IV (1966), 3–42, at 18, 19.

14. T. H. Silcock, *Towards a Malayan Nation* (1961), p. 9.

15. Ibid., p. 14.

16. In *Ghazali* v. *Public Prosecutor* (A.Cr.J. [Ong J.], March 21, 1964; Ipoh, Criminal App. no. 126 of 1963), *Malayan Law Journal*, XXX (1964), 156, the High Court at Ipoh ruled that an entry on a taxi driver's license to the effect that the vehicle could be driven only by a person of the Malay race was not a valid condition; but by law a licensing board might grant licenses only to persons of that race until such time as there should be "effective participation of Malays in the road transport industry." Cited after F. A. Trindade and S. Jayakumar, "The Supreme Head of the Malaysian Federation," *Malaya Law Review*, VI (1964), 280–302, at 297.

the official language was to be Malay, although for a period of ten years, which ended on August 31, 1967, English might also be considered official. The Malaysia Act, which became law on September 16, 1963, can, as one writer suggests, "be spoken of as amending the Constitution of the Federation of Malaya; but it would seem to be more accurate to regard it as creating essentially a new constitution for a new nation, Malaysia." [17] The latter now includes the eleven component parts of Malaya in addition to Sabah and Sarawak. Left intact was the arrangement which apparently makes possible preferential treatment of Malays and the aboriginal peoples of the Malay Peninsula in their respective states. In Sabah and Sarawak "natives" were to have special privileges (Malays in Sarawak who are citizens apparently coming within this category). The government of Singapore was given power to promote the status of Malays, although the Constitution itself conferred upon the latter no special rights as to recruitment for the public services filled by recruitment in Singapore, or with respect to trading licenses or permits.[18]

The jurist who was for a time chief justice in Malaya and later lord president of the Federal Court in Malaysia referred, in a New Year's message after the emergence of Malaya but before the Federation of Malaysia became a reality, to the Constitution as "the outward form of the free spirit of the nation." [19] As to continued constitutional discrimination in favor of Malays, whatever justification there may have been from the point of view of the peculiar economic situation of the Muslims,[20] the possibility remained that the non-Muslim Malayans might be disadvantaged. Election of the legal head of the federation (the Yang di-Pertuan Agong) was in fact a Muslim ceremony; it was unlikely that the highest officer of the federation would be other than one of the Malay monarchs who elected the ruler. The fact

17. H. E. Groves, "The Constitution of Malaysia," *Malaya Law Review,* VI (1963), 245–275, at 245.
18. Art. 161. See also Huang-Thio, "Constitutional Discrimination under the Malaysian Constitution," p. 1.
19. Sir James Thomson, C.J., in a New Year's greeting printed in *Malayan Law Journal,* XXIV (1958), ii.
20. See Ungku A. Aziz, "Facts and Fallacies on the Malay Economy," *Straits Times* (Malaysian ed.), Feb. 28–March 5, 1957.

that some of the heads of states that comprised the federation were non-Muslims seemed to make it possible to distinguish between first-class and second-class rulers.[21] The Tengku of Malaysia was reported as having denied saying in 1965, however, that non-Muslims were "guests" in the country.[22]

One of the contributors to a symposium published in 1964 observed that communal feeling, latent before, had been aroused during World War II and the subsequent emergency in the country, so that practically every issue acquired communal implications; involved were policies concerning citizenship, languages, and education, and the only successful way of building an effective noncommunal party was thought to be through a federation of parties that were communal.[23] This was presumably the basis for Lee Kuan Yew's persistent emphasis upon the principle of "Malaysia for Malaysians" (as distinct from Malaysia for Malays) in the short period of years that Singapore remained in the federation.

Separation of Singapore from Malaysia apparently occurred only after there developed a conviction on the part of federation leaders that the situation was such that there could be no truly national policies that would be effective for the undivided group of states that comprise Malaysia. Whether the leadership of the federation took action that in effect meant the dismissal of Singapore from the federation, as some seem to have believed,[24] or whether Lee Kuan Yew took the step which effected the separation of Singapore from the other federated states, the withdrawal seems to have been regarded as largely due to the impossibility, or supposed impossibility, of an effective working relationship with the other states in the federation. The Tengku, Abdul Rahman, was reported as saying that it was his idea that Singapore should withdraw and become independent.[25]

21. Cf. Tregonning, *Malaysia,* pp. 78, 79.
22. *Straits Times* (Malaysian ed.), June 1, 1965.
23. R. S. Milne, "Politics and Government," in Wang Gungwu, *Malaysia: A Survey,* p. 328.
24. Wang Gungwu, in *Straits Times* (Malaysian ed.), Nov. 11, 1965.
25. *Straits Times* (Malaysian ed.), Aug. 10, 1965. According to the press, he also said that "when we took in Singapore we did so to prevent its becoming a second Cuba. But Singapore leaders have done nothing but talk politics, dream politics."

Shortly after the separation Lee Kuan Yew was said to have warned the managing director of Singapore's leading Malay-language newspaper against publishing articles that could arouse religious strife, and as having confronted the director with a statement signed by leaders of Singapore's religious bodies (Buddhists, Sikhs, Muslims, Christians, and Parsees) who had conferred on the subject. The statement reportedly set forth that the signers did not believe in or countenance unfair or unethical attempts to change a person's religious convictions.[26] The Singapore leader, himself a third-generation Singapore Chinese, was reported as having denied that he advocated partition of Malaysia if Chinese were not allowed to share in "ownership"; his avowed attack was upon those he called the "ultras" among Malay leaders, who wanted "to keep Malaya's feudal society intact within Malaysia."[27] Lee was in turn accused by Malays of using the racial issue to secure the support of non-Malays. One publicist has suggested that Lee obviously pressed too hard and that the Chinese had become more politically conscious than before, while the Tengku had not wished to have Singapore in the federation in the first place.[28]

26. *Times* (London), Oct. 1, 1965. While Islam is the religion of Malaysia, the Constitution provides that other religions may be practiced in peace and harmony in any part of the federation (art. 3[1]). On the position of the ruler as to religion, see *Commonwealth Office Year Book*, 1968, p. 232.

27. Reported in *New York Times*, June 4, 1965.

28. Richard Goold-Adams, "The Problems of Malaya and Singapore," *Commonwealth Journal*, IX (1966), 63–68. Abdul Rahman is reported to have said to the Federal Parliament of Malaysia on August 9, 1965, that there had been many differences between the federal government and the government of Singapore and that two courses were open—to take repressive action against the government of Singapore or to sever connections with that government. The Singapore leaders, he said, had allowed their personal glory to override the interests of the federal state. To the press, at a conference on the evening of the same day, Abdul Rahman said he had told Lee Kuan Yew that it was clear that there was no hope of compromise. The Singapore leader was reported as saying at a press conference that Malay would remain a national language that was compulsory for those seeking national employment, that Singapore was not a Chinese colony, nor a Malay country, nor an Indian country, but that it belonged to Singaporeans, and that he would take drastic action against any groups trying to stir up communal passions. Accusing Malay extremists of forcing Singapore out of the federation of Malaysia, he said the Tengku should have taken action against communal elements a year before that time; he (Lee) had been left no choice except to secede. There had been reported to the Federal Parliament an agreement between Singapore and the federal government on a joint defense council, on the federation's maintaining military bases in Singapore, and an understanding that neither the federation nor Singapore would make a treaty that would be detrimental to the other's independence and defense. *Keesing's Contemporary Archives*, XV (1965), 20891, 20892.

The effect of communalism in Malaysia, and of the state succession which resulted when a separate state of Singapore came into being, may not yet be fully apparent. Certain of the international repercussions to conditions and political changes in Malaysia are too well known to require extended consideration here. A result, for example, of the very formation of Malaysia in 1963 and of its admission to the United Nations and to Security Council membership was Indonesia's move to leave the United Nations —a move which seems to have had little if any lasting effect and to leave open the question whether Indonesia ever in fact ceased to be a member of the principal world organization.[29] The confrontation between Indonesia (under Sukarno) and Malaysia provided occasion for British concern, and this was not immediately alleviated when the separation of Singapore from Malaysia occurred. Concerning that separation, the Tengku is reported to have said that Britain, Australia, and New Zealand had shown "great disappointment." [30]

The development in general seems to have discouraged for the time being the dream, advanced by Macapagal, of "Maphilindo," which envisaged cooperation between Malaysia, the Philippines, and Indonesia. Since Malaysia had never been a member of SEATO, the separation of Singapore from Malaysia did not directly affect that regional arrangement. Nor did it necessarily affect cooperation through the Colombo Plan, which involves not only participation of Commonwealth states but also participation by some states not in the Commonwealth. In the interest of economic, cultural, and scientific progress there came into being in 1967 the Association of Southeast Asian Nations (ASEAN) to include Thailand, the Philippines, Malaysia, Singapore, and Indonesia. An earlier (1961) regional plan for an Association of Southeast Asia (ASA) apparently ceased to be feasible when the Philippines' claim to Sabah was advanced.[31] What was probably an important step toward regional cooperation through ASEAN

29. Cf. Egon Schwelb, "Withdrawal from the United Nations: The Indonesian Intermezzo," *American Journal of International Law,* LXI (1967), 661–672.
30. *Straits Times* (Malaysian ed.), Aug. 10, 1965.
31. *New York Times* (editorial), Aug. 9, 1967, p. 38. As of mid-July, 1968, the Philippine claim to Sabah was still at issue with Malaysia. Ibid., July 16, 17, 1968.

was the restoration on August 31, 1967, of full diplomatic relations between Malaysia and Indonesia, a year after these two
states had agreed to end some three years of armed confrontation.[32]

Not only Malaysia and Singapore but other entities in the
Southeast Asia region have presumably been affected by the
announcements in 1967 and 1968 that the United Kingdom
would terminate its present arrangements for defense in the general area in a phased withdrawal extending over several years.
There have subsequently been reports of Southeast Asian leaders
having indicated their respective countries' dependence upon
United States policy in the general region.[33] On another point of
possible importance in more than a geographical sense, an observer pointed out as recently as 1964 that Borneo was not a
Malay country in the "Malayian sense"—a fact which he considered it necessary to face "for the successful achievement and
survival of Malaysia." [34]

Communal factors—and their effect in the form of safeguards
for Malays along with the Malay language and religion (through
constitutional provisions and preferential treatment in the matter
of certain occupations) [35]—appear to have been basic in Singa-
pore-Malayan relations from 1963. These relations have now
come to be on an international (although intra-Commonwealth)
basis. Communal factors may, to a lesser extent, conceivably
affect Malaysia's policies in the developing international community in Southeast Asia. Events of May and June, 1969, when
communal riots in Kuala Lumpur followed the reported decision
of the alliance government not to include Chinese representatives, seemed, however, to indicate that communal emotions had
been heightened.[36]

---

32. Ibid., Aug. 31, 1967, p. 2.   33. Chap. 6 below.
34. T. Harrison, in Wang Gungwu, *Malaysia: A Survey*, p. 164.
35. Cf. the statement that the communal feeling of non-Malays is "extranational" in origin, that the Japanese occupation changed non-Malays from transient
to largely settled persons, and that the Malays had a new sense of their own importance and abilities. Ratnam, *Communalism and the Political Process in Malaya*,
pp. 28, 43.
36. *Economist*, May 17, 1969, p. 31, and May 31, 1969, p. 29; *New York
Times*, June 30, 1964, p. 9.

II

Communalism in Ceylon is relatable to that country's early history as well as to some recent international legal arrangements. The Report of the (Soulbury) Commission on Constitutional Reform in Ceylon, published in 1945, pointed out that what had come to be the "major community," the Sinhalese, could be traced back to invaders from India in the sixth century B.C. This community's age-long struggle with the principal minority community—the Tamils, who also came from India—was described in the report as "obscure." The Sinhalese adopted Buddhism, while the Tamils remained Hindus. Geographically, the Tamils became predominant in the extreme north of the island, where they were able to maintain some contact with their fellow Dravidians; the Aryan Sinhalese became cut off from their original home in northern India. Separate traditions and languages survived. By the time of the Soulbury Report Sinhalese numbering some four million and Tamils comprising some seven hundred thousand were descendants of early settlers on the island. In addition there were Moors (whose ancestors included Mohammedans who came as traders from the shores of the Persian Gulf in the eighth century A.D.). To the Dutch, who captured Colombo after Spain and Portugal became united under Philip II, is due the introduction into Ceylon of the Roman-Dutch law; the Burgher community by 1945 had come to comprise about thirty thousand persons.

The Dutch governor eventually surrendered Colombo and all Dutch territory in Ceylon to the British. The Soulbury Commission reported that the distinction between the Kandyan and Low Country Sinhalese had become blurred; of the approximately four million Sinhalese, about one third were said to be Kandyans. From India had migrated laborers, mainly Tamils, numbering from six hundred thousand to seven hundred thousand, and these had come to be distinguished from Ceylon Tamils. Of Europeans, there were an estimated ten thousand. Of the total population, the commission estimated, 61 percent were Buddhists, 22 percent were Hindus, 10 percent were Christians (8 percent of these being Roman Catholics), and 7 percent were Muslims. Divisions were based on location, religion, and occupation. The commission submitted that nationalism, "if it is to be a unifying force, requires the elimination of communalism from political life. It is also intolerant of external restraint. Democracy . . . demands for its free operation a wider tolerance in religion, an understanding of the conflicting claims of race and language and a willingness to compromise on major political issues after full and free discussion." [37]

The Ceylon Constitutional Order in Council, 1946, provided under "Legislative Powers and Procedures" that no law should

(a) prohibit or restrict the free exercise of religion,
(b) make persons of any community or religion liable to disabilities or restrictions to which persons of other communities or religions are not made subject, or
(c) confer on persons of any community or religion any privilege or advantage which is not conferred upon persons of other communities or religions, or
(d) alter the constitution of any religious body except with the consent of the governing authority of that body,

Provided that, in any case where a religious body is incorporated by law, no such alteration shall be made except at the request of the governing authority of that body. [38]

When Ceylon became an independent state in 1948, legislative power was restricted by a prohibition of communal or religious discrimination, but there continued to be a problem relating to communalism. The Official Languages Act of 1956 made Sinhalese the only official language. The following year the Federal Party, a leading Tamil political organization, announced that there would be a civil disobedience campaign. It demanded that the objectionable act be repealed and that there be equality of

37. Report of the Soulbury Commission on Constitutional Reform (1945), Cmd. 6677, pp. 5–7. Cf. Robert N. Kearney, *Communalism and Language in the Politics of Ceylon* (1967), p. 137: "The peoples of Ceylon have been divided into separate and exclusive communities differentiated by language, religion, culture, and myth of origin for at least a thousand years."
38. Sec. 29(2).

status with Sinhalese for the Tamil language, also an ending of the "colonization" of Tamil-speaking areas by Sinhalese-speaking persons. There was fear that there might be communal rioting such as there had been in the previous year. The working committee of the Sri Lanka Freedom Party proposed to recruit a hundred thousand persons to help in maintaining order, although the prime minister was reported as saying that this would be a youth movement rather than a paramilitary force. The president of the Federal Party said that his party would call off the civil disobedience campaign only if satisfactory action was taken by the government to restore the Tamil language to its rightful place. The leader of the party in power apparently took the position that all the other parties were opposed to a federal constitution and that the demand for repeal of the Official Languages Act was neither practicable nor conducive to the strengthening of friendly relations between Sinhalese and Tamils; the government leader disavowed any intention of converting Tamil areas into areas with Sinhalese majorities through planned colonization. At a press conference Mr. Banderenaike said that he was for a "reasonable" use of Tamil; there could be the right to educate in one's mother tongue through the university stage; Tamils might take civil service examinations in their own language but would not get permanent employment unless they acquired a sufficient knowledge of Sinhalese within two or three years; Tamils could correspond in the northern and eastern provinces of Ceylon (and would be permitted to transact their official business) in Tamil.[39]

The language matter again called forth opposition and demonstrations early in 1966. Army, navy, and air force personnel were called out; a state of emergency was instituted and a curfew imposed. An amendment to the criminal law prescribed seven years of imprisonment for racial and religious incitement.[40]

So far as international legal relations of Ceylon have been concerned with communalism, the Indo-Ceylonese agreement

---

39. Factual statements in this and in the preceding paragraph are based on *Keesing's Contemporary Archives*, XIV (1964), 20405.
40. *Encyclopaedia Britannica Book of the Year*, 1967, pp. 193–194.

signed August 30, 1964,[41] has probably led to more discussion of status, citizenship, and treament within Ceylon than any other international agreement to which Ceylon is a party. A considerable Indian community in Ceylon consists of persons mainly descendants of those who had migrated to Ceylon in the nineteenth and early twentieth centuries and who had come to work on the tea and rubber plantations. The estimated number of these persons at the time Ceylon became an independent state in 1948 was about 975,000. Of this number, it was agreed that 150,000 would have their future status determined by a future agreement. India was to receive back 525,000, plus their natural increase through birth, and confer citizenship upon them; Ceylon was to confer Ceylonese status upon the remaining 300,000, plus their natural increase (although there apparently has been some dispute as to the exact meaning of the wording on this). The parties were to have fifteen years from the date of the signing for carrying out the agreement—although there has subsequently been speculation that a longer period may be required. There has been later announcement of a plan to place on a separate electoral register persons of Indian origin who had been registered as citizens of Ceylon under the Indian and Pakistan Residents (Citizenship) Act, along with those to be received under the international agreement of 1964.[42] The question has arisen whether this plan of communal registration will perpetuate a sense of separatism and at the same time be a permanent source of tension between the communities in Ceylon.[43]

The 1964 (Sirimavo-Shastri) agreement has given rise to sharp discussion, some of it being on legal grounds. Tamil parties in Ceylon criticized the arrangement as shameless in its sacrificing the human rights and liberties of more than half a million workers. Involved were questions of whether stateless persons could be deported to India, whether persons affected by the arrange-

41. Appendix 2 (joint communiqué and exchange of letters, reproduced from *Indian Journal of International Law*, IV, 1964, 637–640).
42. Harnam Singh, "The Indo-Ceylonese Agreement of 1964: The Question of Separate Electoral Registers," *Indian Journal of International Law*, V (1965), 9–22.
43. Ibid., p. 16.

ment could remit their assets to India, and whether such persons could have access to courts of law in connection with determination of their status and their return to India. On the latter point the Ceylonese section of the International Committee of Jurists, in a letter to the Ceylonese prime minister, asserted that to deny access to courts would be a violation of one of the basic postulates of the rule of law, as adopted by the commission at its Rio de Janeiro conference.[44]

An even sharper criticism adduced general international law. Given the fact of the difference between the Ceylonese and the Indian positions on the citizenship of persons who lived for long periods of time in one country without formally acquiring that country's nationality, it was possible to argue that this would be a case not of repatriation but of involuntary mass migration and expatriation for the 525,000 persons.[45] There has been invocation of the Fourth Additional Protocol to the European Convention on Human Rights, and comparison of the projected Indo-Ceylonese plan with other instances of mass migration.[46] In a resolution of November 9, 1964, the Ceylonese Democratic Congress submitted that what was proposed was treatment of the Indian Tamils as a "commodity" rather than as human beings, in a move for the settlement of a political problem.[47] A further contention has been that general international law safeguards even nonnationals against indiscriminate mass expulsion.[48]

44. *Ceylon Daily News*, Sept. 1, 4, 1967. A useful editorial comment soon after the signing of the agreement is that by J. S. Bains, "Indo-Ceylonese Agreement: A Legal Analysis," *Indian Journal of International Law*, IV (1964), 522–526. For more detailed discussion see Urmila Phadnis, "The 1964 Indo-Ceylonese Pact and the 'Stateless' Persons in Ceylon," *India Quarterly*, XXXIII (1967), 362–407.

45. Kurt Rabl, "Involuntary Mass-Migrations as a Problem of International Law: Some Notes on the Indo-Ceylonese Issue," *Indian Year Book of International Affairs*, XIV (1965), 45–89.

46. Ibid., p. 51–66.

47. Ibid., p. 61. See also M. K. Muhammad Kunhi, "Indian Minorities in Ceylon, Burma and Malaysia," *Indian Year Book of International Affairs*, XIII (1964), 405–472.

48. In the course of discussion in the Ceylon Parliament, questions arose as to the design and meaning of the agreement, as well as the state of affairs at the time it was signed. Dr. Kalpage of the Senate read into the record from what Shastri had said in a letter about India's position. "Despite the heavy burden falling on us under the agreement, the agreement's main attraction for us was the consideration that those accepted as Ceylon citizens would become full-fledged Ceylon citizens and join the mainstream of Ceylon's civic life. The an-

Soon after the signing of the 1964 agreement questions arose in the course of parliamentary debates in Ceylon over the status of Indian Tamils concerning whom the agreement was made. These discussions have at times touched upon the whole background of policy concerning immigration to Ceylon. For example, it has been claimed that Indian Tamils were induced to come there on the distinct understanding that they would be given citizenship rights within the country as would any other citizens in Ceylon. In 1837 the Indian government had permitted such migration to Ceylon—to Ceylon only—with the understanding that the migrants would be given citizenship rights after a residence of five years. "They were British subjects in common with us," one speaker pointed out, "and they were British subjects before they came here"; the Donoughmore Commission had found no discrimination against Indians, or "at least they were made to believe so," and even the Soulbury Commission made the same observation.[49] Concerning the 1964 agreement, the same speaker continued, "the plantation workers were not consulted and they were treated as chattels. Over the next fifteen years, 525,000 will be bundled out of Ceylon with no respect for their feelings. These are all matters of procedure which may or may not be implemented." Ceylon's recent policy concerning Indian labor was described as having involved "a negation of human rights and liberties." Continuing, the speaker asserted that the government of India insisted upon complete equality with the rest of the inhabitants of the country to which the laborers emigrated. There was also reference to a dispatch of Lord Salisbury in 1875 to the

nouncement of Ceylon Government's intentions would, however, mean that Ceylon citizens of Indian origin would be unassimilable with the rest of the population and unlike other Ceylon citizens, entitled to influence only a very limited spectrum of Ceylon's political life. You have, of course, given expression to the hope that in time Ceylon citizens of Indian origin will be assimilated with the indigenous elements of the population. The lesson of history is that where a religious or ethnic group has been placed apart from the rest of the people and brought onto a separate electoral roll, not only has assimilation become so difficult but separatism has become intensified giving rise to disunity and conflict. We ourselves have had sad experience of this in the past." *Ceylon Parl. Deb.,* Senate, vol. 23, part 2, Nov. 28, 1966, to June 19, 1967 (1966–1967), c. 5254.

49. Ibid., vol. 21 (1964), cc. 424, 427 (remarks of Senator Dissanayake). For a more detailed account and a criticism of Ceylon's policy, see N. Radakrishnan, "The Stateless in Ceylon," *Indian Year Book of International Affairs,* XII (1963), 487–563.

effect that indentured persons who had completed terms of in-
denture should be "in all respects free men" with personal privileges not inferior to any other classes of British subjects resident
in the colony.[50]

On another occasion a Ceylonese Senator said:

. . . you get, from about 1920, the history of the difference between
the Tamils and the Sinhalese. To realize this you have only to read
through the four volumes of evidence that was given before the
Donoughmore Commission when the Tamil leaders opposed the grant
of universal suffrage. At the time the Sinhalese were to be given the
vote, the Donoughmore Commissioners were shocked at the state in
which the country was ruled. . . . They [commissioners] granted universal suffrage. . . . This was a bitter blow to the Tamil people. They
boycotted the State Council for the one reason that the Sinhalese were
getting universal suffrage.[51]

A *Report of the Committee on Citizenship by Descent* issued
in March, 1965, had been based on memoranda (reportedly more
than 1,300) and on oral evidence. The committee referred to
some matters which, while not coming within its terms of reference, were considered relevant to the matter of citizenship in
general. Included in the committee's report was the following
statement:

While there has been no suggestion that the authorities have acted
in the way they have done in bad faith, or with any racial or religious
bias, there was dissatisfaction that the authorities had shown no real
appreciation of the practical difficulties in the way of complying with
the demands for proof, and had adopted towards the indigenous people of this country a cold, unhelpful, and suspicious attitude in a
matter that affects them so vitally.[52]

As to international aspects of its assignment and the relevance
to general foreign relations, the Committee submitted that:

it was, perhaps, because of the anxieties caused by the presence here
of Indians (and Pakistanis) in large numbers and by the flow of illicit
immigrants, that the administration of the Citizenship Act had been
allocated to the Ministry of Defence and External Affairs, which is

50. *Ceylon Parl. Deb.*, Senate, vol. 21 (1964), cc. 430, 431.
51. Ibid., c. 5991. This statement was challenged by Senator Tiruchelvam.
52. Sess. Paper XVIII, March, 1965, p. 3.

the Ministry concerned with Indo-Ceylon matters and with the control of immigration. The attitudes of extreme caution . . . that may be proper, and are perhaps necessary, in dealing with illicit or sly immigrants, over-stays, etc., militate against the adoption of the realistic approach that is so essential in determining, or in dealing with, the inherent rights of the indigenous people of a country. The association under the same administrative authority of subjects that call for different methods of approach cannot, naturally, lead to happy results. A change in the present arrangement therefore is most desirable.[53]

In another paragraph of its report the committee considered that "until that Indian problem has been satisfactorily straightened out and adequate measures are adopted to check illicit immigration," the subject should be dealt with "by the Prime Minister, qua Prime Minister, as a residual function not assigned to any Ministry." [54]

Editorial comment on the report suggested that the difficulties experienced by nationals of minority groups in particular were due chiefly to the manner in which citizenship laws were administered. The committee recommended that a public official be authorized to accept such documents as Ceylon passports, certified extracts from an official register, or birth certificates. However, representations were made to the committee that nationals could not establish their status by producing these proofs, such documents being available only to those who had proved their citizenship; registration of births, it was suggested, had become compulsory only in 1897, and for a long time relevant regulations were not well observed. "The trouble," in one editor's opinion, was that officials seemed to "suffer from an excess of zeal for the letter of the law or are racist either in their own thinking or because they feel that such an approach commends them to communal-minded politicians in power." [55]

Before the Indo-Ceylonese agreement of 1964 there had been anticommunal legislation in Ceylon. Illustrative are two bills passed in 1961 designed to suppress communal propaganda, one of which made it an offense to "appeal to religious, racial, caste, communal, or linguistic sentiments for electioneering purposes,

53. Ibid., pp. 31–32.   54. Ibid., p. 32.
55. "Proof of Citizenship," *Times of Ceylon,* March 5, 1965.

and disqualified those convicted of this offence from voting or from membership" in the Ceylonese Parliament or in state legislatures.[56]

The fact that both India and Ceylon are members of the Commonwealth would seem to have become increasingly important in allaying any Indian threat to the Ceylonese. One observer has drawn attention to the fact that while Nehru previously had said that the "small national state" was doomed and that it might survive "as a cultural autonomous area but not as an independent political unit," [57] in 1949 Nehru disclaimed designs on Ceylon.[58] This has suggested the view that the Commonwealth link was seen by the Ceylon government during this period as affording, among other things, a measure of security against India. Yet the same writer has observed that "apprehension of India on various grounds has been a not-unimportant factor in Ceylon's attitude to India." [59] There appears, however, to be adequate basis for asserting that the questions which have been at issue between India and Ceylon concerning emigration, compulsory repatriation, and citizenship have not seriously affected or interrupted economic relations between these two Commonwealth members.[60]

There have, on occasion, been judicial pronouncements on the general subject of communalism. Thus the Judicial Committee of the Privy Council in 1953 found that certain Ceylonese legislation could not be said to make persons of the Indian Tamil community liable to a disability to which persons of other communities were not made liable and did not offend against section 29(2)(b) of the Constitution Order-in-Council, 1946. In an appeal from a judgment of the Supreme Court of Ceylon the tribunal said (in the headnote of decision) that it would "not be astute to attribute

56. *Keesing's Contemporary Archives*, XIII (1961–1962), 18399.
57. *The Discovery of India*, 3rd ed. (1944), as quoted in S. U. Kodikara, *Indo-Ceylon Relations since Independence* (1965), p. 34n., citing the *Hindu*, May 7, 1949, and the *Times of Ceylon*, April 27, 1949.
58. Kodikara, *Indo-Ceylon Relations since Independence*, p. 34n. See also Sir Ivor Jennings, *The Commonwealth of Asia* (1951), p. 133.
59. Kodikara, *Indo-Ceylon Relations since Independence*, p. 22.
60. Ibid., p. 182. On another matter of economic policy and law not directly relatable to the matter of communalism, see C. F. Amerasinghe, "International Law and Oil Expropriation in Ceylon," *Ceylon Journal of Historical and Social Studies*, VI (1963), 124–152.

to the legislature motives or purposes or objects" which were beyond its power. The Judicial Committee referred to the Indian and Pakistan Residents Act, number 3 of 1949, by which an Indian Tamil could through application obtain citizenship by registration and thus protect his descendants, provided he had a certain residential qualification. The migratory character of the Indian Tamils, rather than facts concerning them as a community, was found to be relevant to their suitability as citizens. In the course of its opinion the Judicial Committee said that "the community is not bound together as a community by its illiteracy, its poverty or its migratory character but by its race or its religion." [61]

As has been pointed out by analysts of the independent state of Ceylon the "militant popular nationalism" in that country did not develop until after the coming of independence and to this the sequel has been a period of tensions and conflict between Ceylonese ethnic and religious groups.[62] The matter of language appears to continue as a divisive force. As a member of the Ceylonese Senate pointed out in parliamentary discussion in 1966, "We are . . . one nation, one country, one state and two national languages." [63] Earlier in the debate another senator had observed that after Sinhala was made the official language not a single Tamil child had been allowed to learn the official language.[64] In this connection there was reference to the use in Switzerland of three official languages—or, if Romansch be included, four languages—an evidence of Switzerland's "insight and considerateness." [65]

It was but natural that in the course of discussion of the Indian Tamils and their status in Ceylon there should have been invocation of human rights. One writer submitted that Rajagopolachari

61. *G. S. N. Kodakan Pillai, Petitioner, and P. B. Mudanayake (Registering Officer), et al., Respondents, New Law Reports,* LIV (1952–1953), 433.

62. Robert N. Kearney, "Sinhalese Nationalism and Social Conflict in Ceylon," *Pacific Affairs,* XXXVII (1964), 125–136.

63. *Ceylon Parl. Deb.,* Senate, vol. 22, part 2 (1965–1966), c. 5901 (remarks of Senator Tiruchelvam).

64. Ibid., cc. 3755–3756, 3760 (remarks of Senator de Souza).

65. Ibid., cc. 6040–6042 (Senator Senanayake). The speaker also observed (c. 6041) that "for the first time in this country we have a National Government the component sections of which are all willing to co-operate with one another for the betterment of the Sinhalese as well as the Tamil-speaking races. Already one observes that these two races have started even to intermarry."

had accused Ceylon of a "near genocide policy"; while Indian labor had been a *sine qua non* for the very national existence of Ceylon, it was asserted that "in the political tussle between the Governor and the Sinhalese the poor Indians' interests were gambled away." [66] In this context the same writer referred to the decision of the United States Supreme Court in 1886 which

66. Radakrishnan, "The Stateless in Ceylon," pp. 489, 493. Some of the problems incident to the carrying out of the 1964 agreement were subjects of discussion in parliamentary bodies. Clause 8(3), for example, received special attention (see n. 48 above). There was read into the record a letter from Prime Minister Senenayake of Ceylon to the prime minister of India, which contained the following:

I do not think that I misrepresent the "Facts of History" when I state that Indian labour did not come to Ceylon to settle down permanently in this country but primarily to seize the opportunities for employment with the Coffee, Tea and Rubber plantations so generously offered. It is no reflection on Independent India that there was a time when a number of her sons were made, under an arrangement which a foreign power in India made with foreign capitalists in Ceylon, to leave India in search of employment and a fair livelihood abroad, nor can independent Ceylon be held responsible for the unsatisfactory conditions under which emigration took place then.

There is no justification therefore for the claim that Indian immigrant labour came to Ceylon "to settle down on equal terms with the indigenous population." The "special" privileges sanctioned by the Government of Ceylon were not so much "benefits considered necessary to attract immigrant labour" but really "conditions" demanded by the Government of India for the well being of her citizens in Ceylon and in view of which the Indian Government declared Ceylon as one of the countries to which emigration was declared lawful under the Indian Emigration Act of 1922.

Ceylon Parl. Deb., Senate, vol. 22, part 2 (1965–1966), c. 5380. Apparently the 1964 agreement is being carried out, if rather slowly. A press report from Colombo in 1969 was to the effect that, while the agreement provided for repatriation to India of 525,000 Tamils plus their increase through births, only 9,792 persons to whom this applied had left for India. It was also reported that only 1,000 Tamils had been granted Ceylonese citizenship (of the 300,000 plus increase by births, as contemplated in the agreement). Also reported was uncertainty whether the fifteen-year period would be counted from the date of the 1964 agreement or from the date of passage by Ceylon of its new citizenship legislation in 1968. Tillman Durdin's dispatch, *New York Times*, Aug. 10, 1969, p. 10.

In 1968 Ceylon's statute law was revised to permit conferring of nationality upon more than the number (reportedly twenty-five persons) upon whom nationality could theretofore be conferred in one year. In July, 1969, there was a press report that the government of India had informed the government of Ceylon, through India's High Commission in Colombo, that a recent rule which had been added to the Indian Citizenship Act, whereby Indian nationals who were away from India for over three years without valid Indian travel documents would cease to be Indian citizens, would not affect people of Indian origin covered by the 1964 agreement, and that there was no intention to interfere with the arrangement under that agreement. The press correspondent also referred to the relative speed with which Indian authorities had processed papers connected with the agreement and had processed arrangements to settle repatriates from Ceylon. *Ceylon Daily News*, July 9, 1969, p. 1, and July 12, 1969, p. 1.

struck down a law discriminating against Chinese.[67] Another writer has pointed out that when Nehru was about to go to Colombo for a prime ministers' conference in 1950, he was urged to raise the question of the Indian Tamils' plight in Ceylon.[68] In the opinion of the extremist Tamils, Sir John Kotewali's views were reportedly compared with the South African government's views with respect to Indian settlers.[69] There is no rule of customary international law which requires a state admitting aliens to confer its citizenship upon them, but the Universal Declaration of Human Rights and the covenants which followed would seem to envisage reasonable standards for the treatment of persons, whatever the basis on which they were originally admitted.[70]

III

While the effect of communalism upon the international legal relations of states has been manifest in the two preceding sections of this chapter, the case of Cyprus, which has perhaps been more publicized than the other two, appears in particular to have had more attention in the Western Hemisphere. It seems, moreover, to have provided more difficult problems for the principal world organization, as well as for regional ones. As early as August, 1964, Secretary of State Rusk was reported to have said that Cyprus was the most serious problem facing NATO.[71] A CENTO

67. *Yick Wo* v. *Hopkins*, 118 U.S. 356 (1886).
68. Kodikara, *Indo-Ceylon Relations since Independence*, p. 221.
69. Ibid., p. 227.
70. Art. 15 of the Universal Declaration asserts that everyone has a right to a nationality and that no one shall be arbitrarily deprived of his nationality nor denied the right to change his nationality. Cf. statement by R. St. J. Macdonald, in *Canadian Yearbook of International Law*, V (1967), 103, that the whole subject of human rights is bound up with ideology and that the implementation of human rights can never be guaranteed at the international level. See also some of the points raised in connection with migration to the British Isles when the applicant migrants are citizens of the United Kingdom and Colonies, chap. 5 below.
71. *New York Times*, Aug. 19, 1964. The Secretary of State described the problem of Cyprus as deep, stubborn, and dangerous. In a news conference on September 10 Secretary Rusk said the Cyprus situation presented "a distressing problem and has in it great elements of danger to the parties and members of NATO, three of them—in fact the three guarantor powers are all members of NATO." *Department of State Bulletin*, LI (1964), 428.

communiqué of April 21, 1966, expressed "deep concern" over the Cyprus conflict. The Commonwealth has a stake in Cyprus since, after attaining statehood in 1960, the new republic applied for membership in February of 1961 and was welcomed to the Commonwealth by action of the Commonwealth Prime Ministers' Conference on March 13, 1961. Even before this time, however, the question of Cyprus had presented formidable problems for the United Nations. The years from 1954 to 1958 were marked not only by strife on the island but also by efforts before the United Nations principal body looking to some reasonable settlement of the problems encountered.[72] Although the number of people directly involved in communal problems was much smaller than in the case of either Malaysia or Ceylon, the intensity of feeling and the difficulties encountered in the effort have caused the problem of Cyprus's future to be one of the most disturbing of the post-World-War-II period. Unlike either Malaysia or Ceylon, Cyprus has now for some years had a United Nations "presence" in the form of UNFICYP, with contingents from such "neutral" states as Eire and those in Scandinavia.

From a strict legalist's point of view, the most striking developments relating to Cyprus have been actions sought in the United Nations looking to conciliation on the island, and moves to release Cyprus from treaty obligations originally regarded as the condition of the state's independence. The continuing efforts to find some mutually acceptable arrangement of communal relations in Cyprus have encountered formidable obstacles, and the future of the country remains far from settled. The type of communal problem involved obviously does not lend itself to easy solutions or accommodations. From the point of view of public international law, the developments in and concerning Cyprus may be considered in relation to the legal basis of the state's independence, domestic jurisdiction matters, and the interpretation of relevant treaties (including the United Nations Charter and commitments of NATO states). Communalism is not only

72. For an account of this effort extending over the years 1954–1958, see Stephen G. Xydis, *Cyprus* (1967), passim. See also Thomas Ehrlich, "Cyprus, the 'Warlike Isle': Origins and Elements of the Current Crisis," *Stanford Law Review*, XVIII (1966), 1021–1098.

present but tends to pervade the entire system of domestic affairs and to affect any significant move in foreign policy.

The very constitution of the state rests upon the assumption that there can be separatism for the great body of matters that most directly affect the lives of individuals, and a common authority for the handling of some matters such as foreign affairs and defense. Legislative authority, other than that in the communal chambers, is by provision of the constitution to rest in the House of Representatives, whose fifty members are to be elected for a period of three years by universal suffrage. The constitution provides that the president (a Greek Cypriot) and the vice-president (a Turkish Cypriot) each shall have a veto, "separately or conjointly," on matters concerning foreign affairs, defense, and security. By provision of the Constitution, if either the president or the vice-president should consider a law to be discriminating against either the Greek or the Turkish community, the Supreme Constitutional Court might annul or confirm the measure or return it to the House of Representatives for reconsideration in whole or in part. There is for each of the two principal ethnic groups a communal chamber, which exercises authority in such matters as religion, education, cooperative societies, and "other questions of a communal nature."[73] A citizen of the state not being of Greek or of Turkish origin was required to opt for membership in either the Greek or the Turkish community. The communal chambers had the right to impose taxes on the members of their respective communities.

The workability of this constitutional plan came rather quickly into question after Cyprus achieved independence in 1960. Subsequently, it has been said that for the Greek Cypriots justice meant majority rule in a unitary state, while for the Turkish Cypriots, who comprise approximately 18 percent of the island's population, justice meant built-in safeguards, such as the Constitution was intended to provide, for their rights as a separate community.[74] The EOKA (Ethniki Organosis Kyprion Agoniston, or National Association of Cypriot Combatants) antedated the

---

73. Text of Constitution of Cyprus, Cmnd. 1093, pp. 91–174.
74. Cf. discussion in the *Daily Telegraph*, June 12, 1964.

breakdown of the Constitution. The achievement of *enosis* (union with Greece) became the announced goal of many Greek Cypriots, Cyprus having decided to join the United Nations in 1961 for a provisional period of five years. One British publicist writing early in 1965 reached the conclusion that the 1960 (treaty) limitations placed upon Cyprus should be relaxed and self-determination leading to *enosis* should be permitted. He questioned why the Greek Cypriots (composing the majority in that state) were deprived of their basic democratic right of self-determination—a right which the British had conceded, he said, to every other ex-colony, including those with far more difficult problems, such as Kenya and Ceylon.[75]

In March, 1965, a mediator, Galo Plaza, reported to the secretary-general of the United Nations that the Turkish Cypriot leadership regarded the two communities as distinct entities that were recognized as such by the Constitution of 1960, differing in status only insofar as the provision of the Constitution established such differences. Accordingly there would be no such thing as a "majority community" or a "minority community" in Cyprus. In contrast, it was fundamental to the Greek Cypriot argument that organization of the republic should be based on the existence of a majority capable of governing and a minority entitled to the protection afforded by a normal democratic system. The Turkish Cypriots, it was reported, wanted geographical separation of the two communities, along with a federal form of government; any formula looking to the continuation of Cyprus as an independent state must, according to this view, contain a guarantee against union with Greece and provision for protection of the safety and rights of the Turkish Cypriots as a community.[76]

As to the sovereign bases still held by the British in Cyprus, Cypriot President Makarios was reported as having said that these should be incorporated in the Republic of Cyprus as soon as possible; in the event of *enosis*, the future of the bases would become a matter to be raised by the Greek rather than the Cypriot government. Vice-President Küçük in a memorandum

75. Francis Noel-Baker, in the *Guardian*, Feb. 24, 1965.
76. Doc. S/6253, pp. 219, 222, 229, 236, 239, 245.

presented to the mediator had said that the Turkish Cypriots asked nothing more than their right to be free from threats as individuals and as a community and to be able to enjoy their basic human rights and preserve their communal interests.[77] On December 18, 1965, there was favorable action in the United Nations General Assembly by a sharply divided vote on a resolution to the effect that Cyprus was "entitled to enjoy full sovereignty and complete independence without any foreign intervention or interference." [78]

The subsequent course of events with respect to communal strife and attempts at settlement seems as yet to have provided no clear and mutually acceptable bases for avoidance of further communal strife or arrangements of views between the outside states principally concerned. One press report as late as August, 1967, was to the effect that events in Paphos and elsewhere indicated that Cyprus was in the grip of an "epidemic of race hatred." [79] Another press report indicated that the Cyprus government might be considering the easing of restrictions on the supply of "prohibited items" to Turkish Cypriots, while the Turks interpreted the government move as an "attempt to mislead world opinion." On the same day there was Greek Cypriot press suggestion that there were separatist problems elsewhere as a part of a partition trend throughout the world—with the observation that Cyprus should be allowed to maintain law and order, as the United States does, and reject outside interference in internal affairs, as Canada does.[80] The government of Turkey was reported as saying that it would never accept a Cyprus solution based on *enosis*, after a Greek spokesman had said that Greece was working toward that goal.[81] On the same general subject, a member of the Turkish Parliament was said to have observed, while on a private visit to Cyprus, that there could be no one-sided peace and no one-sided *enosis*. Soon afterward there was a report that

---

77. Ibid., pp. 226, 227.
78. Voting for the resolution (A/6166) were forty-seven states (including Cyprus and twelve other Commonwealth states—each of the latter being in Asia, Africa, or the Caribbean). There were five votes against, and fifty-four abstentions.
79. *Cyprus Mail*, Aug. 1, 1967.   80. Ibid., Aug. 4, 1967.
81. Ibid., Aug. 14, 1967.

Dr. Küçük, Turkish Cypriot leader, had said that the only way to solve the Cyprus problem was through Greek-Turkish dialogue; he reportedly rejected the establishment of a NATO base on Cyprus as a means of protecting Turkish rights on the island and observed that only through provision of a geographical basis for the constitutional rights of Turkish Cypriots could physical security be provided for them.[82] A few days later rumors were reported that Greece might be prepared to have the Turkish Cypriots receive two military bases with a total area of ninety-nine square miles.[83]

According to the press, the ex-mediator, Galo Plaza, said that the Cyprus problem could not be solved without Cypriot participation, and President Makarios's position apparently had continued to be that a Cyprus settlement hinged not on Greek-Turkish discussions but on the Cypriots themselves.[84] Shortly afterward there was a news report of a Canadian peace plan for Cyprus, which looked to the building up of United Nations forces and the reduction of Greek and Turkish forces.[85] An American newspaper editorial attributed tensions in Cyprus to "frenzied nationalism on both sides." [86] Meanwhile, the United Nations has continued the UNFICYP for short periods of time. There was a communication from Vice-President Küçük to the secretary-general of the United Nations, saying it was imperative that Turkish Cypriot representatives participate in the Security Council debate concerning the continued authorization for the United Nations Force in Cyprus.[87]

In June, 1968, leaders of the Greek community and of the Turkish community in Cyprus conferred in Nicosia, reportedly for the first time in four and a half years. Also present was the special representative of Secretary-General U Thant, Dr. Bibiano F. Osorio-Tafall of Mexico, who expressed the hope that at an early date and as a first step there could be a satisfactory modus vivendi between the two communities.[88]

82. Ibid., Aug. 19, Sept. 1, 1967.
83. Ibid., Sept. 10, 1967.
84. Ibid., Oct. 23, 1967.
85. Ibid., Nov. 23, 1967.
86. *New York Times*, Nov. 25, 1967.
87. *Cyprus Mail*, Dec. 14, 1967.
88. *New York Times*, June 25, 1968, p. 10. There was discussion of the problems of communalism—begun in Beirut in June, 1968, and later transferred to

While international law comprises a set of rules for application *between* states, situations within states may greatly affect the conduct of ordinary business between acknowledged public "persons" in the international law sense. To the statement of the traditional view of entities to which international law applies may be added the obvious affirmation that public international organizations as such may have attributes of personality which can come to have importance when these organizations have occasion to act in relation not merely to member states as such but also to the welfare of groups within states who are adversely affected by the actions of state authorities. Not as a superstate, or merely a device to promote peaceful relations between national states, but rather as a means of protecting groups of persons against violation of their basic human rights, the principal international organization has had occasion to be concerned because of disharmony between distinct ethnic groups within national states.

Communalism implies separateness of ethnic, religious, or lin-

---

Nicosia—between a Greek Cypriot leader (Cleridis) and a Turkish Cypriot leader (Denktash), these men being personal friends who were formerly together as law students in London. Ibid., June 28, 1968. A year later, however, there was a press report that a final solution of the Cyprus problem was nowhere in sight. *Cyprus Mail*, June 4, 1969. In the meantime there had been a press report that the three fundamental Turkish demands had included (*a*) the setting up of a state in which neither side would have supremacy over the other, (*b*) the Turks would receive rights in a regime of national autonomy in return for their abandoning the veto rights conceded to them by the 1960 agreements, and (*c*) the Turks would be given safeguards for life and property to prevent recurrences of the 1963 events. *New York Times*, June 28, 1968; *Cyprus Mail*, May 1, 1969, p. 3.

Turkey was reported as asking the United Nations to cancel its plans for a seminar on human rights which was due to be held in Cyprus in June, 1969, the basis for the request being that it might jeopardize the intercommunal talks then under way in Cyprus. *Cyprus Mail*, June 10, 1968, p. 1. A report of June 11, 1968, by the secretary-general to the Security Council had stated that continued peace was an essential condition for the success of intercommunal talks but noted that in spite of the relaxation of tension and the improved relations between the Greek and Turkish Cypriots, the situation in the island remained unstable. *U.N. Monthly Chronicle*, V (1968), 13. The Council in Resolution X/Res/254 (1968) urged the parties "to act with the utmost restraint and to continue determined co-operative efforts to achieve the objectives of the Security Council by availing themselves in a constructive manner of the present auspicious climate and opportunities."

At the end of June, 1968, Greek Premier Papadopoulos was reported as saying he would like to see an ultimate federation of Greece and Turkey. *New York Times*, June 30, 1968, p. 6. In August, 1969, at which time the UNFICYP stood at about thirty-six hundred men, a United Nations representative, Ralph Bunche, was reported as saying that a possible reduction of the force was being considered. Secretary-General U Thant reported to the Security Council that governments contributing troops or funds to the force were becoming more and more reluctant to do so, one reason being the slow progress of the intercommunal talks. *Cyprus Mail*, Aug. 19, 1969, p. 1.

guistic groups within a state, and the form it takes may vary considerably, both in origin and in later rivalry or antagonism. When situations develop in which outside states have special interests—either because of humanitarianism, ethnic ties, or common interests growing out of former imperial and colonial responsibilities or current Commonwealth ties—the existence and effects of communalism in a particular state may become a proper concern not only for states that are related to each other by ties such as exist in the Commonwealth but also for outside states. The doctrine of domestic jurisdiction does not necessarily preclude communalism's becoming a matter of valid concern to the international community.

In the case of the three states here briefly considered from the point of view of communalism as affecting their external legal relations, the situation of Malaysia illustrates the problems arising out of racial differences in a state where there is not overpopulation or lack of opportunity, but where permitted preferences in favor of a particular ethnic group have apparently had a considerable part in the breaking off of an element of the state in which the Malays were not numerically stronger. At separation of Singapore from Malaysia, the state succession apparently did not raise grave questions of international law and did not preclude a high degree of continued cooperation between these two Commonwealth states. On the other hand, as events in Malaysia in 1969 attest, it did not bring communal strife to an end.

Communalism in Ceylon has raised questions concerning citizenship as well as preferred languages. The former British colony came by the mid-1960's to have a very considerable problem by reason of the migration from the subcontinent of India to Ceylon of Indian Tamils who did not find themselves fully accepted into the political life of Ceylon. The language problem figured prominently in the development, but from the standpoint of strictly legal arrangements the greater question ultimately came to be that of the right of individuals to a nationality, either that of the state from which they had come or that of the state in which they came to live (or into which, for whatever reasons, they had been brought). In the context of basic human rights, as well as that of apparent inability to assimilate the individuals, there was question of the right of the "host" state to expel (or persuade the state of origin to receive back) these individuals. Arrangement on the basis of international agreement with the principal state of origin has apparently had support on the ground of humanitarianism more than of international law, although the latter is not in conflict with the arrangement. In the circumstances the manner in which the agreement will be carried out by the two states principally concerned seems likely to assume as much importance as the letter of the agreement itself. Involved is the declared principle that every individual has the right of nationality and the right to divest himself of an acquired nationality.

The Cyprus question has involved sharp intercommunal disagreement and strife. It also, in a manner quite different from the other two cases of communalism that have been noted, emphasizes how a problem such as this can engage the attention of (and perhaps baffle for a period of years) the international community and its principal international organization. In this case, long-existing racial problems, together with the involvement of neighboring states that have an interest based upon strong ethnic and religious ties, as well as security considerations, have been central. The United Nations has had a trial of its mediating capacity and of its legal authority to reduce the binding force of existing treaties that appear to some of the member states as unduly limiting the freedom of a fully "independent" state. Both public international organizations and individual foreign offices have found great difficulty in meeting the problem in Cyprus, where communalism has perhaps taken a sharper form than in any other country. The hope of peace between the two principal elements of the island's population depends in large part upon the capacity and vision of the state's communal leaders themselves, as well as of its directly concerned neighbors, to utilize peaceful means of dealing with deep-seated antagonism. It would seem that in the long run considerations of communalism must inevitably yield to those of peaceful accommodation of views in a world where it is difficult to localize any situation of strife in which ethnic ties, religion, and language figure so prominently as they do in the case of Cyprus.

· 4 ·

Secession

The Commonwealth possesses no paramount legislature. Its most viable machinery includes Commonwealth Conferences, in which all of the member states participate, and the Secretariat in London, which does not have the attributes of a ministry of foreign affairs. The Commonwealth has in the past served to promote some legal understandings among its members and in many ways to promote the member states' relations with each other. It lacks a single appeals tribunal that is still utilized by all the members, although some of them choose to avail themselves of their right to allow appeals to the Judicial Committee of the Privy Council. There is cooperation among the associated states in many fields, but it is essentially voluntary.

Yet even if the ties that exist between Commonwealth member states are dissoluble, there remains the possibility that, not merely through trade and cultural cooperation, but also through the peace-promoting machinery of international public organizations, their common rights and duties in relation to peace-keeping and the promotion of peace may come to rest in large part upon public international law. Insofar as the present-day Commonwealth is concerned, the ties are not merely regional ones. They would seem to imply on a global basis (throughout much of the world where the authority was once British) practical cooperation in the common interest.

Commonwealth ties are not indissoluble, as the withdrawal of South Africa in 1961 emphasized.[1] Withdrawal may be with or

1. On the point that "secession is a matter solely for the member concerned," see J. E. S. Fawcett, *The British Commonwealth in International Law* (1963), p. 87; Robert R. Wilson, "International Law and Some Recent Developments in the Commonwealth," *American Journal of International Law,* LV (1961), 440–444.

without acknowledgment by the remaining member states that the state withdrawing has not breached any legal commitments to the remaining states; as in the South African case, there can be strong resentment of the withdrawing state's policies.

Secession by part of a Commonwealth state from that state, however, may raise questions as to constitutional legality of the move, and at the same time questions of the duty of the principal Commonwealth state to restrain the seceding community because of the alleged conflict of that community's laws and policies with principles to which Commonwealth states and the greater part of the remaining international community have adhered and are committed to other states to support. Issues then arising may be much more complicated than a simple claim of the right of revolution would be. In full realization that large questions other than international legal ones may be involved in such a situation, it is proposed to consider here (*a*) some recent developments bearing upon the permanence or impermanence of Commonwealth membership, (*b*) the case of Rhodesia in terms of the constitutional law of Great Britain, (*c*) the same case from the point of view of international organization law, (*d*) some international legal aspects of the attempted secession in Biafra, and (*e*) the recent development concerning self-determination in Anguilla.

I

By the end of the seventh decade of the twentieth century it had become quite clear that there was no assurance of permanency of membership in the Commonwealth. Eire, as a republic, had long since ceased to be a member.[2] There had also been an

2. On the manner in which this was done, see A. G. Donaldson, *Some Comparative Aspects of Irish Law* (1957), pp. 22–94. The writer explains the disagreement between de Valera and the United Kingdom government over the legal position of Eire in the Commonwealth. In 1937 de Valera adhered to the view that Eire's continued relation to the Commonwealth was that of an associate and that it did not imply any allegiance; Ireland preferred independence to dominion status if the latter meant allegiance, and if Commonwealth membership implied commitment to assist in a war in which the United Kingdom was involved. Following passage of the Republic of Ireland Act, 1949 (12 and

example of membership on a temporary basis; on February 16, 1961, the Cyprus House of Representatives acted by a vote of forty-one to nine to accept Commonwealth membership for a trial period of five years, and the state's membership on that basis was apparently approved by the Prime Ministers' Conference meeting in London on March 8 of that year.[3] The first president of Cyprus was reported as saying at a reception in 1963 in celebration of the Queen's birthday that he believed the Commonwealth had a great role to play in international affairs and generally in the future shaping of the world.[4] Several years earlier the prime minister of Ghana had referred to the Commonwealth as "the only organic worldwide association of peoples in which race, religion, nationality and culture" were transcended by "a common sense of fellowship." No policies, he said, were imposed upon it from above, and it did not seek unity of policy; rather, the Commonwealth provided "a unique forum in which men of different culture and different approach" could sit down together and see what could be done to increase the economic and social well-being of themselves and their neighbors.[5]

---

13 Geo. 6, c. 41), the formal termination of Eire's membership in the Commonwealth became effective in Ireland. By United Kingdom legislation of the same year the part of Ireland theretofore "known as Eire" ceased to be a part of His Majesty's dominions but was not to be regarded as a foreign country. Northern Ireland was to remain a part of His Majesty's dominions until the government of Northern Ireland consented to a change. This gave rise to the question whether a republican form of government was inconsistent with Commonwealth membership, a question which has long since been answered in the negative. For a summary of the development, see Nicholas Mansergh, *Documents and Speeches on British Commonwealth Affairs, 1931–1952* (1953), II, 799.

On the legal origin of the Irish Constitution, see Leo Kohn, *The Constitution of the Irish Free State* (1932), p. 26. In a later volume another author notes issues which arise concerning the historic concept of sovereignty as applied to the sovereignty of the United Kingdom Parliament, a study of which, he submits, falls within the domain of the constitutional structure of the individual members of the Commonwealth rather than study of the Commonwealth as a whole. At the conclusion of his chapter on "Autochthony" it is suggested that "although traditionalists may regret the breaking of a legal link, which in practice means very little, nationalists will welcome a step which places their country's constitution and laws on a footing comparable with that enjoyed by the other comparable states in the world." K. C. Wheare, *The Constitutional Structure of the Commonwealth* (1960), pp. 88, 112, 113.

3. On statutory language which has been thought to imply the right to secede from the Commonwealth (solely at the will of the member seceding), see Fawcett, *The British Commonwealth in International Law*, p. 87.

4. *Cyprus Mail*, June 9, 1963, p. 1.

5. Kwame Nkrumah, "African Prospect," *Foreign Affairs*, XXXVII (1958), 45–53, at 50.

At the time of South Africa's becoming a republic and leaving the Commonwealth a spokesman of the Progressive Party expressed the view that it would be better to keep the Union of South Africa in the Commonwealth, since this would assist the state in working "back to Commonwealth standards." He asserted that the "overwhelming majority of South Africans" desired to belong to the Commonwealth.[6] On an earlier occasion the question had been raised whether prime ministers from states composing the Commonwealth could act, on a matter touching the dismissal of a state from the Commonwealth, only by unanimous vote.[7] The question was apparently not settled. In any case, practice seems to have confirmed the conclusion that neither short-time trial membership nor withdrawal at will of a member state is precluded. The Commonwealth is not a state, nor can there be (by act of a member state as such) anything analogous to "secession" from the group of states, as that term is ordinarily used in the terminology of political science and public law. In practice, however, a state's withdrawal from Commonwealth membership might be regarded as a kind of political secession, particularly if withdrawal be accompanied by the breaking off of diplomatic relations with the United Kingdom. In 1960 Prime Minister Menzies of Australia had occasion to say, in his Smuts lecture at Cambridge University, that Smuts's thesis that the sum was greater than the parts was proved by the Commonwealth itself. "We," the Australian leader said, referring to the Commonwealth, "are not a superstate." [8]

If the Commonwealth device means, basically, mere voluntary cooperation of the member states with each other, if neither monarchical nor republican form of government is a prerequisite for membership, and if a state can join for a term of years with complete freedom to renew or to terminate its Commonwealth participation after that time, it is not possible to regard the

6. Reported remarks of Zac de Beer, speaking in the name of the Progressive Party, as reported in the *Journal of the Royal Commonwealth Society,* III (1960), 218, 219.

7. See L. A. Sheridan, "The Changing Conception of the Commonwealth," *Year Book of World Affairs* (1957), pp. 236–256, at p. 255.

8. Remarks as reproduced in *Current Notes on International Affairs,* XXXI (1960), 260.

Commonwealth as an entity in the public international law sense. A discontinuance of Commonwealth ties would presumably present questions of treaty rights of the states concerned inter se, when the design of the treaties posited Commonwealth membership of the parties.

Aside from treaty ties between Commonwealth states undergirding cooperation within the system, or cooperative plans which involve Commonwealth states' participation along with outside states' participation (as does the Colombo Plan), there may be constitutional changes which entail inheritance of Commonwealth membership or, in some situations, the withholding of full Commonwealth benefits from a particular territory. Thus, on the eve of the Commonwealth Prime Ministers' Conference of 1964, Malawi, as a new state, obtained membership after the breakup of the Federation of Rhodesia and Nyasaland, while Southern Rhodesia did not inherit separate Commonwealth membership or the right to be separately represented at the 1964 conference.[9] Rhodesia's claimed right to declare its own independence was soon to become one of the most heated issues in the history of Commonwealth relations.

According to press reports, the Rhodesian leader's claim of a right to be invited to the 1964 conference rested upon the fact that his country as "Southern Rhodesia" had had such rights and privileges before these rights and privileges were surrendered to the Federation of Rhodesia and Nyasaland and that, with the breakup of the latter federation, Southern Rhodesia would reacquire rights and privileges of Commonwealth membership which it had before the formation of the federation.[10] Thus, while the subsequent action taken by the Ian Smith regime in its unilateral declaration of independence was an attempted secession from the United Kingdom, it was also in a sense a secession from the

9. In the final communiqué the prime ministers "recognised that the authority and responsibility for leading her remaining colonies to independence should rest with Great Britain." Cmnd. 2441, p. 5. See comment in Robert R. Wilson, "Commonwealth Prime Ministers' Conference of 1964," *American Journal of International Law*, LIX (1965), 571.

10. *Times* (London), April 21, 1964; the statutory background is in 1 and 2 Eliz. 2, c. 30, An Act to Provide for the Federation of Southern Rhodesia, Northern Rhodesia and Nyasaland, July 14, 1953, and Eliz. 2, c. 34, Rhodesia and Nyasaland Act, 1963 (Dissolution of the Federation).

Commonwealth. Seen from the point of view of the larger international community, the legal aspects of the development, as distinguished from the political, invite attention from the point of view of international law. Occasions which there have been for the invocation, interpretation, and application of that law—as distinct from the purely historical and political aspects of the development (relating to the estrangement of Rhodesia not only from Commonwealth member states but from many other states) —continue to merit attention.

II

The factual background of the legal and political questions which have arisen between Rhodesia and the United Kingdom is too well known to justify more than brief mention here. Not primarily the general impact there has been upon Commonwealth relations, but the principal issues that have touched and that still touch upon public international law, may be briefly noted.

As early as July, 1964, the position of the United Kingdom and of the respective Commonwealth countries in relation to the political status of Rhodesia began to take shape. At their meeting in London that month the prime ministers of the Commonwealth welcomed the decision of the British government that, as in the case of other territories, a condition of the grant of independence would be that there should be sufficiently representative institutions in the country concerned; there should also be convened an Independence Conference, and the leaders of all parties in Rhodesia should be permitted to attend. The object of such a conference would be to have the independence of Rhodesia "within the Commonwealth" at the earliest practicable time and on the basis of a majority rule; there was a further appeal for the release of all detained African leaders. Toleration, mutual understanding, and justice were emphasized, as was the creation of a feeling of confidence in the minority community in Rhodesia that their interests would be protected. The British prime minister, while giving assurance that attention would be accorded to what the other prime ministers had said, drew attention to the fact that the government of Southern Rhodesia was responsible for internal affairs in that territory and that the granting of independence was a matter for decision by the British Parliament.[11] On a later occasion (June 1, 1965) the secretary of state for Commonwealth Relations had referred in the British House of Commons to a charge that the United Kingdom government was treating Rhodesia differently from the way the British had treated any former colonial territories when they were on their way to independence. The secretary referred to the fact that Rhodesia was the only territory for which Britain had had responsibility that had enjoyed "the penultimate stage of constitutional development before independence." He mentioned in this connection that Rhodesia had exercised full internal government for a period of forty-two years. The Rhodesian government had not been staffed or controlled by the Colonial Office, and the police force, armed forces, and administration had all been under control of the Rhodesian government.[12]

After further communication (particularly that of November 7, 1965, between the British and Rhodesian governments) looking to the setting up of a royal commission to consider the questions at issue, the effort failed by reason of the parties' disagreement on the content of the proposals which the royal commission should canvass, and also, apparently, on the question whether the report of the commission should be on a basis of unanimity. On November 23 the British prime minister informed the House of Commons that the 1961 Constitution of Rhodesia had broken down and that it had been replaced by a so-called new constitution. The prime minister also said that while Ian Smith and his colleagues "purported to be a Government" and had replaced the 1961 Constitution by a "new so-called Constitution," the House must accept the fact that the Constitution of 1961 had already broken down as a result of the ordinances and decrees signed in Salisbury on November 10, "which amounted to the destruction

---

11. British Information Service, T. 18 (July 16, 1964); Cmnd. 2441.
12. *Parl. Deb.* (C), 5th ser., vol. 713 (1964–1965), c. 1558.

of all safeguards for the rule of law, for human rights in the 1961 Constitution and earlier legislation." This, the prime minister made clear, did not mean that the British government had abrogated the former Constitution; it remained the law of Rhodesia, along with the laws made in the preceding week under the powers created by the Southern Rhodesia Act, 1965.[13]

The Commonwealth Prime Ministers' meeting at Lagos on January 11 and 12, 1966, was apparently the first meeting of this group called to deal exclusively with a single political issue. Subsumed to this issue were the ending of the rebellion, assistance to Zambia, the future of Rhodesia under "constitutional rule," economic measures against the "illegal regime" and "the question of Commonwealth assistance in training Africans in Rhodesia." There was a review of measures that Commonwealth and other countries had taken against the "illegal regime" in Salisbury up to the time of meeting. The possible use of force against Rhodesia was discussed, and it was "accepted" that such use would not be precluded if it should be necessary to restore law and order. The British prime minister stated that on the basis of expert advice available to him the cumulative effects of economic and financial sanctions might bring the rebellion to an end within a period of weeks,[14] but there was apparently some misgiving on the point. In the course of discussion attention was drawn to the prime ministers' statement, first made in 1964, that "for all Commonwealth Governments, it should be an objective of policy to build in each country a structure of society which offers equal opportunity and non-discrimination for all its people, irrespective of race, colour or creed." The Commonwealth, it was emphasized, should be able to exercise constructive leadership toward democratic principles so as to enable the people of each country having different racial and cultural groups to "exist and develop as free and equal citizens." Recalling their 1965 communiqué concerning "one man, one vote," the prime ministers emphasized that this principle should be applied to Rhodesia.[15]

Late in 1965 and early in 1966 there were discussions which,

13. Ibid., vol. 721 (1965–1966), c. 248.
14. Cmnd. 2890.
15. See reaffirmation in final communiqué of the 1966 Prime Ministers' Conference, Cmnd. 3115.

while relating principally to constitutional rather than international law, at points touched upon international obligations.[16]

The British prime minister emphasized that the only legal authority capable of granting independence to Rhodesia was the British Parliament, acting on legislation introduced by the British government. Without this, "any so-called declaration of independence not carrying with it the authority of the British Parliament would be illegal and invalid." The British government condemned the "purported declaration of Independence" by the "former Government of Rhodesia" as an "illegal" act and one which was "ineffective" in law. Acts for the purpose of giving effect to the declaration would be treasonable. The governor in Rhodesia and other ministers of the Rhodesian government had been informed in Rhodesia, the prime minister said, that they had ceased to hold office and were private persons.[17]

On November 12, 1965, there was introduced in the British Parliament a bill to make further provision with respect to Rhodesia.[18] On the question of citizenship as affected by the course of action taken by the Salisbury regime there was a statement in the British House of Commons by the attorney general, as follows:

It is proposed to amend the British Nationality Act of 1948 so as to make it easier for loyal Rhodesian citizens to obtain citizenship of the United Kingdom and Colonies; and to amend the Fugitive Offenders Act, 1881, so as to prevent the return of alleged fugitive offenders to Rhodesia unless the Secretary of State or other person issuing the warrant for his return is satisfied that it is not inexpedient that the fugitive should be so returned, having regard to the present circumstances.[19]

On November 16, the secretary of state for foreign relations, in answer to a question in the House of Commons, said concerning the constitutional situation with respect to Rhodesia:

Between 1923 and 1961 the British Government had the power of disallowance of any law passed by the Southern Rhodesian legislature and the Constitution also required certain Bills principally those dis-

16. See n. 19 below.
17. *Parl. Deb.* (C), 5th ser., vol. 720 (1965–1966), cc. 349, 353. In the course of the discussion there was passing reference to the fact that the Rhodesians had quoted some language from the American Declaration of Independence.
18. Ibid., c. 522.   19. Ibid., cc. 514–515.

criminating against Africans, to be reserved for Her Majesty's pleasure. Under the 1961 Constitution the power of disallowance is restricted to laws which affect Southern Rhodesian Government stock issued under the Southern Rhodesian Stock Acts or which are *inconsistent with international obligation* relating to Southern Rhodesia. The power to amend the Constitution by Order in Council is confined to a limited range of provisions, principally those dealing with the Governor and only certain Bills amending the Constitution are liable to be reserved.[20]

In the course of the same discussion the spokesman observed that the "scope of powers vested in the British Government by the Constitution does not, of course, affect the ultimate responsibility of this Parliament and the British Government for Rhodesia." On the same day the prime minister referred to the way in which the 1961 Constitution of Rhodesia had been "twisted out of recognition while still being appealed to as being enforced." This, he said, was "why we were anxious, if there were to be independence, that the Constitution should be fully entrenched and safeguarded against tricks of that kind." [21]

For the purpose of focusing attention upon such elements of international law as are relevant, not (presumably) the political talks on board H.M.S. *Tiger* and later H.M.S. *Fearless,* but certain judicial holdings are pertinent, along with pronouncements by high administrative officers. Certain accused persons in Rhodesia failed in the General Division of the High Court. There was occasion both in that court and in the Appellate Division to go at some length into the status of the ruling regime in Rhodesia. The chief justice found that

the status of the present Government is that of a fully *de facto* government, in the sense that it is in fact in effective control of the territory, and this control seems likely to continue. It cannot, however, be said that it is yet so firmly established as to justify a finding that its status is that of a *de jure* government.

The present Government having effectively usurped the governmental powers granted Rhodesia under the 1961 Constitution can now lawfully do anything which its predecessors could lawfully have done, but, until its new constitution is firmly established and thus becomes

20. Ibid., c. 931. Emphasis added.   21. Ibid., c. 935.

the *de jure* constitution of the territory, administrative and legislative acts must conform to the 1961 Constitution.[22]

The chief justice referred at various places in his opinion to international law. At one point he submitted that the

expressions "*de jure* government" and "*de facto* government," like the word "sovereignty," are capable of having many meanings, and . . . it is essential that the sense in which these expressions are used is understood and defined. Both expressions are ones which are generally used more in international than municipal law, but I can see no reason why an international law definition should not be used by a municipal court, because it would seem that, if a government conformed to an accepted international law definition of either a *de jure* or a *de facto* government, then *a fortiori* it should be recognised as such by a municipal court.[23]

A member of the Appellate Division of the court, Macdonald, J.A., made this reference in his opinion to international law in relation to English legal theory:

According to the principles of international law and, indeed, according to legal theory in force in most civilized societies, the modern territorial state which forms the basic unit of the international community is in itself a legal entity. As a legal entity it embodies all the institutions within its boundaries including, in particular, and without regard to the form which it takes, the institution of government. The failure of English law to subscribe to this generally accepted theory does not mean that Britain is not a state but only that English law has failed to bring legal theory into line with constitutional reality, with the result that in England the monarch represents and embodies the state whereas in most civilized societies the state embodies, as one of its attributes, the government administering its affairs, be it a monarchy or any other form of government. It is this peculiar and unusual concept of the "state" in English law which gives rise to the "strange shifts and circumlocutions and inelegancies of legal thought and language," of which Sir William Holdsworth speaks.[24]

The president of the Appellate Division of the court, Sir Vincent Quenèt, while agreeing that the Smith regime had de facto status, took the position that it had also acquired internal de jure

22. *Madzimbamuto* v. *Lardner-Burke, N.O. and Another, N.O; Baron* v. *Ayre N.O. and Others, N.O.*, S. Afr. L.R., II (April–June, 1968), 284.
23. Ibid., p. 314.   24. Ibid., pp. 382–383.

status. Judge Macdonald viewed the regime in Salisbury as having both de facto and de jure status in the sense that it was the only law-making and law-enforcing government "for the time being" within the state of Rhodesia, and he regarded Rhodesia as having become a de facto republic.

Such views were not persuasive at Westminster. There the secretary of state for Commonwealth affairs expressed in the House of Commons the view that "nothing that has taken place so far makes it necessary for Her Majesty's Government to reconsider their attitude towards the validity of current Rhodesian legislation or the status of the illegal régime." He observed further that none of the five judges had argued that the Smith regime should be given recognition, whether de facto or de jure.[25]

Both in the General Division and in the Appellate Division of the High Court of Rhodesia there was need to examine the effect of political developments in Rhodesia. In the course of his opinion, the chief justice said, concerning the applicable law:

An English court sitting in England must acknowledge the omnipotence of the British Parliament, however wide is . . . "the gap between omnipotence in theory and impotence in fact." A Rhodesian court sitting in Rhodesia as a 1961 Constitution court would be bound to acknowledge the omnipotence of the British Parliament, both in Britain and in Rhodesia, though it could not fail to recognise its impotence in Rhodesia. Such recognition must impel such a court to desist from the attempt to carry on its functions because these can only be carried on if it recognises the potency of the present Rhodesian Government. Without this recognition there could be no rule of law in Rhodesia but only chaos. If the judges grant this recognition and continue to carry on their functions they can only do so as a court other than a 1961 Constitution court. In the circumstances, there may well be a "conflict of laws." The law of Rhodesia as determined by an English court in England may be one thing, while the law of Rhodesia as determined by a purely Rhodesian court in Rhodesia, may be another. Examples of such conflict of laws are to be found in the English and American decisions decided during the later stages of the American War of Independence. Acts in America which an English court sitting in England would regard as treasonable, an American court sitting in America would not, and *vice versa* acts which an American court

25. *Parl. Deb.* (C), 5th ser., vol. 757 (1967–1968), c. 1068.

would regard as treasonable, an English court would not. Compare, for example, such cases as *Ogden* v. *Folliot* (1790) 100 E.R. 825 and *Respublica* v. *Chapman* I Law. Ed. 33. The position is well summed up in the case of *Inglis* v. *The Trustees of the Sailor's Snug Harbour,* 3 Peters 99 at 125, 7 Law. Ed. 617.[26]

The Rhodesian chief justice submitted that the issue was not on what chance the appellants had to succeed if they should have their case before the Judicial Committee of the Privy Council but was on what benefits they would derive if they were successful. He stated that no judgment would be of value inside Rhodesia, for there it would be wholly ineffective. In the course of the hearing on the application there had been submitted to the court an affidavit which stated that the regime in control in Rhodesia would not recognize a Privy Council decision, since the 1965 Constitution neither permitted nor recognized the right of such appeal, and that to grant the application would be an act of gratuitous cruelty.

Two days after the refusal in Rhodesia of the application for appeal to the Privy Council a statement by the Commonwealth Office in London contained the following:

The status of Rhodesia, the illegality of the regime and the invalidity of its acts are unambiguously stated in the Southern Rhodesia Act 1965 and the Southern Rhodesia Constitution Order 1965 made under it. The views expressed by the Rhodesian courts cannot be regarded as conclusive. The final appellate court for Rhodesia is the Judicial Committee of the Privy Council and it is for them ultimately to lay down what the law is. Since the legal issues involved are now subject to appeal, the authority to be attached to the decision of the Rhodesian courts must be regarded as provisional only. Accordingly, persons in Rhodesia must not rely upon it as a justification for committing acts which would otherwise be legal. In particular, any person who takes part in the carrying out of a death sentence without the confirmation required by law as eventually declared by the Privy Council will bear the gravest personal responsibility.[27]

Acting on advice of the commonwealth secretary, the Queen exercised the prerogative of mercy for three men who had been

26. *Archion Ndhlovu and Thirty-one Others, Appellants, and The Queen, International Legal Materials,* VII (1968), 1346.
27. *Survey of British and Commonwealth Affairs,* II (1968), 376.

condemned in Salisbury. In the House of Commons there was a statement that solicitors acting in behalf of these men had lodged petitions to the Queen and that on the same day application had been made to the Privy Council. As the commonwealth secretary explained, he was advised that, "though the constitution of Rhodesia delegates the Royal Prerogative of Mercy to the Governor to be exercised on Her Majesty's behalf, this does not empty Her Majesty of her Prerogative, which she may exercise on advice of the Secretary of State, though the cases in which it would be appropriate to do this are very rare." On March 5, 1968, the commonwealth secretary again emphasized in the House of Commons that the regime in Rhodesia was illegal and that its acts were invalid.[28] On the same day, petitions from the three condemned men in Rhodesia having been rejected in Rhodesia, the men were executed.

The course of political events that followed the unilateral declaration of independence had by 1969 produced but limited additional evidence that would bear directly upon customary international law (as distinguished from constitutional law and from international organization law) that was applicable. The legal status of Rhodesia and its government continued to be much under discussion. In the British House of Commons on June 17, 1968, Sir Elwyn Jones, attorney general, said that the British government was committed to a policy of restoring constitutional rule in Rhodesia, not merely because the regime in that country was in rebellion against Great Britain, but because the British government could neither wisely nor honorably underwrite the rebellion's objectives; at the same time, he indicated, the struggle must be waged by peaceful means because the British government believed that the use of force would be wrong. In the course of the debate Commonwealth Secretary Thomson said that assertion of independence by the European minority in Rhodesia—comprising, as he pointed out, 5 or 6 percent of the whole Rhodesian nation—had raised issues that went much further than constitutional legality; the rebellion was distinguishable from

28. *Parl. Deb.* (C), 5th ser., vol. 760 (1967–1968), c. 232.

other rebellions as being for the perpetuation of tyranny rather than for its abolition; and it supported the proposition that "95 per cent of the population of Rhodesia should be deprived of their rights for as far ahead as one could see." He described the Rhodesian problem as reflecting one of the great and explosive issues of world affairs, the problem of race and color. It was an issue, he submitted, on which, for both moral and material reasons, Britain could not afford to be on the wrong side.[29]

Ian Smith was reported in the House of Lords on June 17 and 18, 1968, to have said frankly that he did not believe in majority rule, that he could not agree to entrenched clauses or to any sort of guarantee that he would not alter the constitution afterward against the Africans. Lord Alport, formerly a high commissioner in the Federation of Rhodesia and Nyasaland, who had visited Rhodesia on behalf of the British government in June, 1967, expressed the opinion that as long as the Smith regime was in control in Rhodesia there was no possibility of successful negotiations. Smith, he said, was dominated by the Rhodesian Front hierarchy and had no power to negotiate an agreement that would be acceptable politically by the existing government in Britain "or by any British Government." The speaker at the same time expressed the view, which he said was based on his own contacts in Rhodesia, that a majority there, comprising nonpolitical Europeans and Africans, wanted a settlement and were prepared to pay the price for it.[30]

The Judicial Committee of the Privy Council, which had granted an appeal to Mrs. Stella Madzimbamuto in an action in behalf of her husband, an African detained by the Smith regime, delivered its judgment on July 23, 1968.[31] This was to the effect that the government in control of Rhodesia was a "usurping" one, whose purported law-making or administrative acts could have

29. *Parl. Deb.* (C), 5th ser., vol. 759 (1967–1968), cc. 1407–1408.
30. *Parl. Deb.* (L), 5th ser., vol. 293 (1968), cc. 328, 549, 553. In June, 1969, Sir Humphrey Gibbs offered his resignation as governor of Rhodesia. Michael Stewart, at the Foreign and Commonwealth Office, said that the government would, of course, "stand ready to resume links whenever there are people in Rhodesia who share our principles and with whom we can talk. It will remain our policy to work for an honourable settlement when that comes." *Guardian Weekly*, June 26, 1969, pp. 1, 3.
31. P.C. App. no. 13 of 1968.

no legal effect; the High Court in Rhodesia was found to have been in error in determining that the regime in Rhodesia could make any legally valid orders. Referring to "*de facto* government" as among the descriptive terms that had been applied to the illegal regime in Salisbury, the committee's opinion characterized these as "conceptions of international law" which "in their Lordships' view are quite inappropriate in dealing with the legal position of a usurper within the territory of which he has acquired control." There was no further reference in the judgment to international law as it is relatable to national law.[32] There was one dissenting opinion, that of Lord Pearce, who concurred with the other members of the Judicial Committee to the extent of finding that the regime in Salisbury was not a lawful one and that it was not legal for the judges of the Rhodesian High Court to acknowledge as valid the setting up of an illegal regime in defiance of the 1961 Constitution under which the judges of the High Court had been appointed. At the same time Lord Pearce found the continued detention of Mr. Madzimbamuto to be acceptable by the courts as valid. This latter conclusion rested upon the view that the Southern Rhodesia Act of 1965 and the orders that were made under it left it possible for judges to apply a "limited doctrine of necessity" under which they were able to allow validity, within certain limits, to some acts done by those who had actual control in Rhodesia.[33]

32. On the general relationship, particularly as it has been a factor in Commonwealth states, see Robert R. Wilson, *The International Law Standard and Commonwealth Developments* (1966), pp. 68–74.

33. The individual opinion apparently did not draw, in this connection, implications that would touch directly upon international law. The "implications" referred to were presumably general ones or those relating to constitutional law.

As Kelsen has pointed out in discussion of the recognition of states, while it is usual in theory and practice to distinguish between de facto and de jure recognition, the significance of the distinction is not quite clear, although in general it is assumed that de jure recognition is final, while de facto recognition is provisional and may be withdrawn. *Principles of International Law*, 2nd ed., rev. and ed. Robert W. Tucker (1966), p. 397. The same writer has said (p. 396) that legal recognition of a *state* can only be unconditional.

Within a few weeks after the Judicial Committee's judgment had been given, there was a ruling by the Appellate Division of the High Court of Rhodesia, at the conclusion of which the chief justice said:

1. A Rhodesian court should, as far as possible, respect any ruling of the Judicial Committee of the Privy Council on any point of law, as having the highest persuasive value.

2. The Judicial Committee of the Privy Council ruled on its first "main question" that the Southern Rhodesia Constitution Order 1965

(S.I. 1965–1952) has full legal effect in Rhodesia. This ruling makes it legally impossible for any judge or public servant appointed under the 1961 Constitution to carry on as a Judge or public servant serving under that constitution, because he cannot do so without, at least, acquiescing in infringements of "the Order in Council." If a judge or public servant decides to continue to remain in office, he can only do so by accepting the situation in Rhodesia as it is today. He cannot honestly claim to remain as a Judge or public servant serving under the 1961 Constitution.

3. The Judicial Committee of the Privy Council embarked on the factual inquiry whether or not the present Government of Rhodesia was a lawful government. This being so, it is equally competent for a court appointed under the 1961 Constitution to embark on a similar inquiry.

4. The test which the Judicial Committee adopted for determining whether or not a revolutionary government had become a lawful one was stated thus: "The essential condition to determine whether a constitution has been annulled is the efficacy of the change."

5. The Judicial Committee of the Privy Council stated that "the British Government acting for the lawful Sovereign is taking steps to regain control and it is impossible to predict with certainty whether or not it will succeed," and consequently concluded "that the usurping Government now in control of Southern Rhodesia cannot be regarded as a lawful Government." This particular ruling was a ruling on a question of fact, and was based on the facts as they existed when the Appellate Division of the High Court prepared its judgment, which was at the end of last year.

6. Such a ruling of fact must depend on the facts as they exist at the time when the ruling is made. In a revolutionary situation the facts are subject to change during the course of the revolution.

7. On the facts as they exist today the only prediction which this court can make is that sanctions will not succeed in overthrowing the present government and restoring the British Government to control (in the sense of its former authority), and that there are no other factors which might succeed in doing so.

8. It is clear from the judgment of the Judicial Committee of the Privy Council that while a court appointed under the 1961 Constitution may enquire into the lawfulness of the present Government and may rule it to be unlawful, such a court has no jurisdiction to rule that the constitution by virtue of which it owes its existence has ceased to exist and is no longer the lawful constitution. A Court sitting under the 1961 Constitution may not, therefore, rule that the present Government is a lawful one.

9. If a judge appointed under the 1961 Constitution comes to the conclusion that the 1961 Constitution has been annulled by the efficacy of the change, his jurisdiction in terms of the 1961 Constitution comes to an end, and he can adjudicate no further as a court under that Constitution. In these circumstances, the judge is faced with two alternatives: either (1) to leave the Bench without adjudicating at all on the matter, or (2) to carry on and adjudicate as a new court. The judge's choice here is whether he stays or goes.

10. Because of this court's finding of fact that the British Government will not regain control, and also because of the ruling of the Judicial Committee of the Privy Council that the Southern Rhodesia Constitution Order in Council 1965 has full legal effect in Rhodesia, it is no longer possible for a judge of the High Court to continue to sit as a court under the 1961 Constitution.

11. The judges of the High Court are, therefore, now faced with the agonizing decision of deciding whether they will go or carry on as judges in the new situation in which they now find themselves.

12. The choice now before the judges is this: Is it better to remain and carry on with the peaceful task of protecting the fabric of society and maintaining law and order as a Court, other than a 1961 Constitu-

In view of the failure of the new regime in Rhodesia to attain recognition by any considerable number of outside states, together with the continued application of sanctions by the British and other governments, it might be premature to try to evaluate the international legal effects of what has transpired in and concerning Rhodesia. In light of progress apparently made toward more effective organization of the international community, the international legal implications of what has happened in and concerning Rhodesia need to be gauged, not solely from the British or the Commonwealth position concerning the regime in Salisbury, but also from pronouncements of, and actions taken by, the principal world organization. Although the Commonwealth is not itself an international person,[34] states composing the Commonwealth have found in the United Nations a means of bringing collective pressure upon Rhodesia. In the course of this development, questions both legal and political have arisen.

III

The shifting of attention from actions taken by, and pronouncements of, the British government to discussions in the

tion court, or is it better to go, even though going may (to quote Lord Pearce) cause "chaos and work great hardship on the citizens of all races and incidentally damage that part of the realm to the detriment of whoever may be ultimately successful"?

13. In the circumstances, it is better for the judges to carry on as a court in the new situation.

14. The new situation in which the judges now find themselves is this: (1) The British Government will not regain control of the Government of Rhodesia; (2) The Judicial Committee of the Privy Council has ruled that a local court cannot sit as a *de facto* court under a *de facto* government.

15. In this situation this court, if it carries on at all, can only carry on as a court taking cognisance of the fact that the present government is now the *de jure* government and the 1965 Constitution the only valid constitution, which this court now proceeds to do.

16. This being so, I consider, the judge of the trial court was right in his conclusion that the indictment, which alleged a contravention of an Act passed by the present government, did disclose an offence, and he was right in his rulings on all the points of law reserved.

In the circumstances, the appeal must be dismissed.

Rhodesia; Judgment of Appellate Division of High Court in *Ndhlovu and Others* v. *The Queen*, Judgment no. A.D. 138/68, Aug. 15, Sept. 13, 1968. S. Afr. L.R., IV [1968], pp. 535–537.

34. Cf. Fawcett, *The British Commonwealth in International Law*, p. 88.

United Nations General Assembly and the Security Council provided opportunity for various national points of view to be expressed. The outlook of the United States government found
expression in a Department of State publication which provided
a factual background and a brief summary of the constitutional
status of Rhodesia.[35] It drew attention to the fact that the 1961
Constitution of Rhodesia limited the Crown's power to reject
constitutional amendments to acts affecting the position of the
sovereign or governor, international relations, and obligations
taken under certain government loans of Southern Rhodesia.
It also pointed out that the Crown could reject under certain
procedures any changes in the several "entrenched" clauses of the
Constitution, the latter having been designed primarily to protect
rights of Africans; there was a lengthy declaration of rights and
provision for a constitutional council to protect such rights. After
noting what had transpired in Rhodesia since November, 1965
(the declaration of independence, the British prime minister's
statement that the only way Rhodesia could become independent
was by an act of the British Parliament, that a unilateral declaration by the Rhodesians would be an open act of defiance and
rebellion, and that it would be treasonable to take and give effect
to such a step), the Department of State publication listed the
steps which the United States government had taken. These
included the recalling of the United States consul general from
Salisbury, the reduction in size of the American Consulate staff in
Rhodesia, the placing of an embargo on arms and ammunition
exports to Rhodesia, notifications to American companies that the
United States recognized the legal authority of the British order
in council prohibiting the exportation of tobacco and chromite
from Southern Rhodesia, the nonrecognition of Rhodesia by the
United States, and a total embargo on oil from the United States
to Rhodesia. The Department of State publication also noted that
the British government had withdrawn its high commissioner
from Rhodesia but had made it clear that the British government
would not use force to end the rebellion.

One fact that was adduced in support of the claimed right of

35. *Department of State Bulletin,* LVI (1967), 366–377.

the new regime in Rhodesia to assert its own independence was that Whitehall had never administered the government in the country nor provided guns or forces for its defense. Between 1935 and 1953 the Rhodesian prime minister had sat "as an equal" in the meetings of the prime ministers, first of the empire and later of the Commonwealth. The prime minister of the federation (of Rhodesia with Nyasaland and Northern Rhodesia) had taken his place until the dissolution of the federation in 1961. Thereafter Rhodesia's two associates sat with the other Commonwealth prime ministers, but Southern Rhodesia's prime minister was excluded because of the dispute which had arisen.[36]

When the United Kingdom refused to concede independence to the Rhodesians without a liberalization of the franchise, and after the unilateral declaration, the other Commonwealth states followed in refusing to recognize the new regime.[37] The previous legal and administrative relationship of Southern Rhodesia with the United Kingdom was the subject of discussion by both jurists and administrators. Legislation dealing with certain matters was subject to disallowance, and requests from Great Britain for legislation had not been unknown. As one author has stated,

Although the Southern Rhodesian Government was not obliged to comply, from time to time the United Kingdom Government made requests for the introduction of legislation on particular topics and such requests were usually followed by Southern Rhodesian legislation. Indeed in the first year of operation of the responsible government Constitution the Legislative Assembly amended the Native Labour Regulations and the Pass Laws as a direct result of a request by the Secretary of State and the High Commissioner's intervention

36. See Wilson, "International Law and Some Recent Developments," p. 65n., on the claimed "humiliating rebuff" in that the prime minister of Rhodesia had been excluded from the 1964 Commonwealth Prime Ministers' Conference.

37. The argument adduced in the Rhodesian courts that the Smith regime comprised a de facto authority, if not one that was de jure, tended to raise questions whether Rhodesia was not in as favorable a position, from a legal point of view, as such a dominion as Canada in 1926. In a reply published in the British press it was noted that Canada was already recognized as having full international personality, including power to conclude in its own right political treaties with foreign countries, a power explicitly denied Rhodesia; there was the further point that the United Kingdom Parliament could not legislate for Canada except at Canada's request and consent. *Guardian,* Oct. 12, 1965.

requiring that the operation of the pre-existing law be investigated and abuses eliminated.[38]

In the course of his individual opinion when the Judicial Committee made its ruling in the *Madzimbamuto* Case on June 23, 1968, which provided occasion for inquiry into the precise relationship between the United Kingdom and Rhodesia, Lord Reid said,

> With regard to the question whether the usurping Government can now be regarded as a lawful Government much was said about *de facto* and *de jure* Governments. . . . As was explained in *Carl Zeiss Stiftung* v. *Rayner & Keeler Ltd.* [1967] 1 AC 853 when a question arises as to the status of a new régime in a foreign country the Court must ascertain the view of Her Majesty's Government and act on it as correct. In practice the Government have regard to certain rules, but those are not rules of law. And it happens not infrequently that the Government recognise a usurper as the *de facto* Government of a territory while continuing to recognise the ousted Sovereign as the *de jure* Government. But the position is quite different where a Court sitting in a particular territory has to determine the status of a new régime which has usurped power and acquired control of that territory. It must decide. And it is not possible to decide that there are two lawful Governments at the same time while each is seeking to prevail over the other.
>
> It is a historical fact that in many countries—and indeed in many countries which are or have been under British sovereignty—there are now régimes which are universally recognised as lawful but which derive their origins from revolutions or *coups d'état*. The law must take account of that fact. So there may be a question how or at what stage the new régime became lawful.[39]

In the period of deadlock which had developed between Great Britain and the Rhodesian leadership, there had been some suggestion of Commonwealth intervention for the purpose of bringing about an accommodation of views. When the prime minister of Nigeria proposed a conference of Commonwealth

---

38. Claire Palley, *The Constitutional History and Law of Southern Rhodesia* (1966), p. 225.
39. *Madzimbamuto* v. *Lardner-Burke*. P.C. App. no. 13 of 1968. There followed in the opinion of the court references to cases decided by the United States Supreme Court after the American Civil War.

representatives early in 1966, however, there was no unanimity as to the desirability or role of such a conference. On January 6, 1966, Prime Minister Menzies issued a statement to the effect that Australia would not attend as a participant but would be represented by its high commissioner to Nigeria. This statement was, in part, as follows:

1. Our prime duty is to Australia.
2. If the modern Commonwealth, on the initiative of some or many of its members, begins to claim the right to intervene in and give orders in relation to matters which are the proper concern of some individual member of the Commonwealth, good relations cannot long continue, nor can the present Commonwealth structure long endure.

As I have previously pointed out, the last Prime Ministers' Conference in 1965 unanimously declared (not for the first time) that "the authority and responsibility for leading her remaining colonies, including Southern Rhodesia, to independence must continue to rest wih Britain."

Britain having the sole authority and responsibility, is it for the rest of us to give instructions to Britain as to how she is to use her authority and discharge her responsibility?

My Government strongly believes that it is not. For if Britain can be instructed or coerced by the Commonwealth—or most of its members—in a matter which is, by concession, hers and hers alone to deal with, then Australia can some day be instructed or coerced on some matter in which the sole jurisdiction resides in Australia.[40]

40. *Current Notes on International Affairs,* XXXVII (1966), 37–38. Another part of the prime minister's statement was as follows:

> There need be no misapprehension about our attitude towards the events in Rhodesia. We have not given either orders or advice to Britain. We have supported her actions by similar actions in the fields of non-recognition, in economic and financial sanctions. We are opposed to the use of force for compelling a constitutional settlement. We wish to see, by proper degrees and with reasonable preparation, a majority of African voters in Rhodesia. We hope that Rhodesians themselves will become willing to reopen negotiations with Britain to achieve this result. . . .
>
> If, as seems painfully clear, there are Commonwealth countries which will be satisfied by nothing less than armed force directed against Rhodesia, with all its dreadful consequences for Africa and for the relationship of the races in that country, the conference could not do more than expose great differences and create much bitterness, with all the distortions and even misrepresentations which such a state of affairs would inevitably produce.

Australia was represented through its prime minister at the Conference of Commonwealth Prime Ministers held at London in September of the same year,

Dissolution of a federation within the United Kingdom and Colonies has occurred not only in Rhodesia but also in the case of the British Caribbean Federation, where dissolution took place (under the West Indies Act, 1962) not only without its being requested, but against the will of the federation government then in office. Another precedent was in the State of Western Australia's attempt to secede from the Commonwealth of Australia in 1933–1934. In that case, although secession had been favored by a two-to-one majority in a plebiscite, a United Kingdom parliamentary select committee denied the claimed right.[41]

Traditionally, refusal of a mother country to acquiesce in a declaration of independence by one of its constituent communities has not, in international law, precluded the community's ultimately attaining independence through exercise of force and having its new status recognized by outside states. In the 1960's the case against a community's attaining independence and statehood through its own declaration, even if it had the force to maintain itself, would seem to have rested upon the acceptance by the wider international community of not merely ideals but binding rules growing out of humanitarianism and the claimed entitlement of individuals qua human beings to certain political

at which nine days were devoted to discussion of Rhodesia. On Australia's position as to Rhodesia's status, see also Robert Gordon Menzies, *Afternoon Light* (1968), pp. 216–218. For text of communiqué issued at the end of the Lagos conference, see Cmnd. 2890, also reproduced in *International Legal Materials*, V (1966), 1158.

41. J. E. S. Fawcett, "Security Council Resolutions on Rhodesia," *British Year Book of International Law*, XLI (1965–1966), 103–121, at 104–105. A relevant decision by the High Court of Australia involved an action for damages by the Commonwealth of Australia against the state of New South Wales, which took the position that it was a "sovereign State" and could not be sued without its consent. The court ruled that the high commissioner was given jurisdiction by sec. 75 of the Australian Constitution and that the states of the Commonwealth of Australia were not, for purposes within the Constitution, to be regarded as "sovereign states." The court said that the Commonwealth of Australia included "the people of New South Wales as they were united with their fellow Australians." *Commonwealth of Australia v. New South Wales* (1923), 32 C.L.R. 200; *Annual Digest of International Law Cases*, II (1923–1924), 130. Aside from the matter of self-government in the Federation of Rhodesia and Nyasaland, that federation is reported to have concluded trade and customs agreements with the United Kingdom, South Africa, Australia, Canada, Bechuanaland (now Botswana), Israel, and Portugal, respectively. Fawcett, "Security Council Resolutions on Rhodesia," p. 106. On some earlier attempts (as late as 1963) to settle the "deadlock" on Rhodesia in relation to new African members of the Commonwealth, see James Barber, *Rhodesia: The Road to Rebellion* (1967), p. 180.

and economic rights. The possibility and legality of enforcing such rights through sanctions inevitably became issues for the United Nations. On November 12, 1965, the Security Council found that the Smith regime in Rhodesia was without legal authority to declare and exercise independence.[42]

In its independence proclamation of November 11, 1965, the government of Rhodesia had included the statement that "the people of Rhodesia have witnessed a process which is destructive of those very precepts upon which civilisation in a primitive country has been built" and that "they have seen the principles of Western democracy, responsible government and moral standards crumble everywhere; nevertheless they have remained steadfast." [43] Although the Rhodesian regime had moved to abolish the office of governor and to terminate appeals to the Judicial Committee of the Privy Council, there were efforts to arrive at an accommodation of views through utilization of Commonwealth mediation. On October 12, 1965, Prime Minister Harold Wilson had suggested in a message to Ian Smith that there be sent to Rhodesia a mission of senior Commonwealth prime ministers headed by former Prime Minister Robert Menzies, with a view of finding ways and means of breaking the deadlock on the question of independence. Smith reportedly rejected the suggestion on the ground that the Commonwealth had no jurisdiction so far as Rhodesia was concerned. On October 20 following, Smith suggested that the United Kingdom might grant independence and put the Rhodesian government on trust to observe and abide by a treaty to guarantee principles of the 1961 Constitution, Smith offering to abide by a treaty to guarantee those principles.[44]

The positions of individual Commonwealth countries were not uniform. Robert Menzies said that only the Parliament of Great Britain could grant independence to Rhodesia and that the unilateral declaration was illegal, the only lawful government in Rhodesia having now become the government of the United

42. S/RES/217/1965.
43. See text of the unilateral declaration as reproduced in Appendix 3, below.
44. See *Draft Report of the Special Committee on the Situation with Regard to the Implementation of the Granting of Independence to Colonial Countries and Peoples*, A/AC 109/L 327 (Sept. 13, 1966), p. 16.

Kingdom. He was also recorded as saying that the situation was not one of anarchy, Rhodesia being subject to direct authority of Great Britain; at prime ministers' conferences on each of two occasions, he said, it had been unanimously accepted that the authority and responsibility for leading Rhodesia to independence must rest with Great Britain.[45] He added that he had told Ian Smith that Commonwealth countries would not recognize an independent nationhood but that Australia would not either physically or financially contribute to the use of force. The idea of punishment was rejected as undiscriminating and therefore unjust, the problem being one to be resolved by negotiation. "What is needed in Rhodesia," the Prime Minister said in the Australian House of Representatives on November 16, 1965, "is a reasonable timetable, accompanied by a special educational campaign, to which all of us might well contribute something, to fit the African voters for their ultimate authority." [46]

Other Commonwealth statesmen had opportunity to express their views when the Rhodesian question was before the United Nations bodies. India was strongly for sanctions and for considering Rhodesia a non-self-governing territory within the meaning of the United Nations Charter. (The United Nations yearbook for 1963 had set forth the opinion of the United Nations Secretariat that Rhodesia was not a "state.") Sierra Leone's spokesman observed that the United Kingdom had made no attempt to map out a plan to lead the people of South Rhodesia to independence; in the current crisis, he said, the United Kingdom was proceeding with "lamentable weakness." During the proceedings in the Security Council, Nigeria and Uganda had joined Mali in advocating that South Africa take all necessary precautions to prevent supplies of oil from reaching Rhodesia.[47]

By the end of March, 1966, all major states that were purchasers of Rhodesian tobacco had announced that they would not thereafter buy tobacco from South Rhodesia while the Smith regime remained in power.[48] A Tanzanian representative men-

---

45. *Current Notes on International Affairs*, XXXVI (1965), 731.
46. Ibid., p. 734.   47. A/AC 109/L 327, p. 113.
48. Ibid., p. 176.

tioned that the United Kingdom had said that a unilateral declaration of independence would be an open act of rebellion but that when the Rhodesians actually made the declaration the British had argued that economic sanctions would bring the revolting regime down. The same spokesman drew attention to the fact that in 1910, in similar circumstances, the United Kingdom had granted independence to a minority group in South Africa, with a so-called safeguard to the South African majority.[49]

Even the very limited sampling of views of Commonwealth states here essayed concerning the developing Rhodesian situation may provide some basis for consideration of elements of international (as distinct from constitutional) law which is, or is still claimed to be, applicable to the Rhodesian secession. There has been some invocation of traditional international law and strong assertion of international organization law and of human rights. Those who adhere to the traditional view tend to urge that when a sizable, well-organized community attains independence in a physical sense and successfully withstands, without physical combat, the efforts of the state of which it was formerly a part to reduce it to submission, statehood has been acquired—just as in the case of states that have emerged after forceful action to attain independence, such as the United States of America in the eighteenth century. Although there is no generally admitted rule that there must be substantial recognition by other states before the emergent community may attain sovereignty in a legal sense as well as in a physical one, there is on the other hand no generally admitted right to be recognized by outside states, even when the physical attributes of sovereignty may seem to have been acquired.[50] According to the traditional rule, a seceding community may become a state upon its recognition by a generality of existing states, even before its independence has been recognized by the state of which it was formerly a part. This "right" to be a state has been claimed by the minority in power in Rhodesia even without its attaining recognition by outside states.

49. Ibid., p. 214.
50. Cf., however, on the "right" to be recognized, Hersch Lauterpacht, *Recognition in International Law* (1947), passim.

An opposing view is that the international community has come to observe, not merely as a moral principle but as law, the duty of according to individuals in every state, without limitation by race or color, the right to have applicable to them certain basic human and political rights, including rights of franchise. A corollary would be the claimed right of the international community to utilize means, such as economic force, to pressure the seceding community into a policy of according to all its people the human rights claimed. If this view has come to obtain, through construction of the United Nations Charter and/or through practice by a generality of states, the question arises of the nature and extent of force (as through sanctions) which outside states may legally bring to bear. The problem becomes more acute when, as in the British-Rhodesian case, the direct use of military force appears to be impracticable. The nature and extent of what can legally be done remains a proper subject of inquiry, which must take into account such matters as the principle of domestic jurisdiction, the extent to which that principle has been affected by the doctrine of international concern, and the sufficiency of evidence to justify the institution of sanctions at the authorization of the principal world organization.

The concept of domestic jursidiction—as mentioned in Article XV(8) of the League of Nations Covenant and Article II(7) of the United Nations Charter—is one with which Commonwealth states' spokesmen have been much concerned, as at the Paris Peace Conference, the San Francisco Conference, and in United Nations discussions. The practice of Commonwealth states has apparently had a considerable influence in this connection.[51] Actions taken concerning Rhodesia by the United Nations Security Council and by the General Assembly have raised anew questions of what is involved and the legal implications. The point has often been made that the "domestic jurisdiction" clause of the

---

51. See John M. Howell's chapter in Wilson, *The International Law Standard and Commonwealth Developments,* pp. 137–164, and by the same author, "The Commonwealth and the Conception of Domestic Jurisdiction," *Canadian Yearbook of International Law,* V (1967), 14–44, and "Implications of the Rhodesian and Congo Crises for the Concept of Domestic Jurisdiction," *Australian Journal of Politics and History,* XIV (1968), 358–372.

Charter—unlike the comparable clause of the Covenant, Article XV(8), which related to the League Council's action on disputes —is so placed in the Charter as to be a modifier of the Charter provisions as a whole.

The development of the concept of "international concern" has served in a measure to prevent the "domestic jurisdiction" clause from being a serious brake on actions by United Nations bodies. There is always the possibility of disagreement about what constitutes (or is claimed to constitute) a "breach of the peace" or threat of such a breach and the extent to which these may be made the grounds for authorization of sanctions. Some publicists have strongly taken the position, on actions taken by the United Nations bodies in the Rhodesian case, that these were in accordance with the Charter and that there has developed a body of international law in light of which the seceding community may rightfully be made the object of sanctionist actions.[52] Observing at the outset that there seems to be no legal answer to questions that have been raised as to the applicability of international law to the Rhodesian situation, one British scholar has submitted, on the point of whether this situation is a threat to the peace, that

52. See Charles G. Fenwick, "When Is There a Threat to the Peace?—Rhodesia," *American Journal of International Law,* LXI (1967), 753–755; Myres McDougal and W. Michael Reisman, "Rhodesia and the United Nations: The Lawfulness of International Concern," ibid., LXII (1968), 1–19. The conclusion of the last-mentioned authors was challenged by Dean Acheson in an address on "The Arrogance of International Lawyers," in *International Lawyer,* II (1967–1968), 591–600. The former Secretary of State (at p. 596) ascribed the authors' findings to "subjectivism," described as the "quality or condition of viewing things exclusively through the medium of one's own mind or individuality; the condition of being absorbed in one's personal feelings, thoughts, concerns. . . . The term also means personal bias, emotional predispositions, the substitution of perception for reality." In a reply, Professor McDougal wrote that "it would be a travesty upon the most basic notion of 'self-determination' to speak of it, in regard to a claim of 6% of a population against 94% of a population, when the goal of the claim is to gain absolute political control over the majority and to maintain them in a state of secondary and powerless citizenship. It would be contrary to the very purposes for which the contemporary right of self-determination has been created to employ it to justify the systematic suppression of the human rights of the vast majority of the population for no other reason than to maintain the social, political and economic superiority of a mere six percent of the occupants of the area." *International Lawyer,* II (1967–1968), 729–743, at 743.
On the importance of a distinction between a present threat to the peace and a potential threat as a basis for resolutions by United Nations bodies in regard to the Rhodesian crisis, see John M. Howell, "A Matter of International Concern," *American Journal of International Law,* LXIII (1969), 771–782.

this is a matter of "factual and political judgment" to which there is no "legal" answer. The same writer submits that "it was always intended that the Security Council should be left free to decide, at any given moment of time, and free from prior stipulations and prerequisites, whether there exists a threat to the peace, a breach of the peace, or act of aggression." [53] Earlier resolutions having called upon states not to recognize the Smith regime and having urged the United Kingdom to terminate the rebellion, and states having been urged to take economic measures against Rhodesia (including an embargo upon oil and petroleum products), there was occasion for the United Kingdom to act concerning the case of the imminent discharge of oil by the vessel *Johanna Vat Beira.* The resulting situation and possibilities led to the Security Council's determination that there was a threat to the peace—an action which could have been blocked, but was not blocked, by vote of any permanent member of the Security Council (an abstention not being counted as a negative vote).

Critical comment on the nature and effect of the principal actions taken by United Nations bodies in the Rhodesian case has noted a tendency in Security Council discussions subsequent to the council resolution of November 20, 1965, to regard measures recommended in the resolution as ones to be taken, apart from those to be taken by the United Kingdom, as measures *of the organization* which placed some obligation on the part of member states to comply. It is pointed out, for example, that a New Zealand representative referred to the council resolution of April 9, 1966, as "a further means of turning the screw of sanctions," while, on the other hand, spokesmen for other Commonwealth countries, such as India, Pakistan, and the United Kingdom, have referred to the resolution of November 20, 1965, as relating to economic sanctions that would be voluntary in character. The point is made that wording such as "called upon" is used in a

53. Rosalyn Higgins, "International Law, Rhodesia, and the U.N.," *World Today,* XXIII (1967), 94–106. The writer notes, *inter alia,* the position of South Africa, which state, as a member of the United Nations, is legally bound by the resolution of December 16, 1966 (U.N. Doc. SC/Res. 232) not to send oil to Rhodesia or allow its nationals to do so; while contacts may legitimately be carried on with the regime of Ian Smith, "South Africa is also required, under general international law, not to support its rebellion" (p. 105).

nonmandatory, recommendatory sense, and that while an organ such as the General Assembly may recommend, the measures that are contemplated are measures to be taken by the member states themselves.[54]

Political reactions to the Rhodesian situation in the period following the unilateral declaration of independence have been more vigorous than have appeals to international law, as action taken by states that are members of the Organization of African Unity has illustrated. The organization's Defence Committee having declared that the economic sanctions imposed by members of the United Nations would not work unless backed by force, the chairman of the Ministerial Council's Conference was reported as saying that the thirty-four conference delegates agreed "in principle" that military intervention would be needed for the overthrow of the Rhodesian government. The meeting further recommended the breaking of diplomatic relations with Great Britain by a specified date if the British did not crush the Rhodesian rebellion by that time. A committee including representatives from four Commonwealth states—Nigeria, Tanzania, Kenya, and Zambia—was to draw up plans for achieving the objective in mind; the deadline for breaking off diplomatic relations with Rhodesia was to be December 15, 1965, but by that date only eight of the OAU states (including Tanzania and Ghana) were reported to have broken off relations.[55] With the action of the

54. John Halderman, "Some Legal Aspects of Sanctions in the Rhodesian Case," *International and Comparative Law Quarterly*, XVII (1968), 672–705, at 692, 693. This writer points out that the phrasing of the council resolution of April 9, 1966, suggests that its purpose was to suppress the secession in Rhodesia rather than to deal with a threat to the peace, and the same is thought to be true of the council resolution of December 16, 1966, which also gives the impression that its purpose was to suppress the rebellion rather than to deal with a threat to the peace. General Assembly resolutions of November 11, 1965, and Security Council resolutions of November 12 and 20 in the same year unofficially categorized the Rhodesian secession as "unlawful." This assertion of judicial power, Halderman submits, is nowhere found in the Charter, and the idea of developing such an authority for the two organs he finds rather impractical. He reminds that a secession movement is not illegal under international law and points out that the United Nations has on several occasions recommended secessions, as in the cases of Indonesia, Algeria, and Angola. Ibid., pp. 698–701.

55. The *Hindu* and *African Diary* as cited by V. Maya Krishnan, "African State Practice Relating to Certain Issues of International Law," *Indian Year Book of International Affairs*, XIV (1965), 196–241, at 216, 217. The writer notes (p. 218) that under customary law as well as the Charter, states are obliged to refrain not only from fomenting civil wars and rebellions in other states but also from extending help to the rebels in other states.

African states of the Commonwealth may be contrasted the more moderate view as expressed by the Prime Minister of Australia.[56]

A sequel to resolutions passed in the United Nations bodies concerning sanctions, and to policy-making by individual Commonwealth states with reference to trade relations with Rhodesia, has been resort to some direct diplomatic efforts to reach an accommodation, such as the talks on board H.M.S. *Tiger* and some two years later those on board H.M.S. *Fearless*. A proposal —said to have been made to, and reportedly rejected by, the Rhodesian leaders—was that they give up on their unilateral claim to independence and return to British control during a transitional period (the present government to retain power through this period and to give way to a new government only if and when independence was achieved) and that the Rhodesian leadership "form a broad-based administration as soon as possible, including Africans." Also reported to have been unacceptable was a British proposal that Rhodesia accept the jurisdiction of the Judicial Committee of the Privy Council as the court of final appeal—which Ian Smith is reported to have described as an "impossible and indeed ridiculous obstacle." [57]

In October, 1968, the United Nations General Assembly, by a vote of ninety-two to two (with Portugal and South Africa voting against, and seventeen states, including Great Britain and the United States, abstaining), called upon the government of the United Kingdom to refuse recognition of Rhodesia's independence, unless Rhodesia established majority rule—in the words of the first paragraph of the resolution, "unless it is preceded by the establishment of a government based on free elections by universal adult suffrage and on majority rule."[58] In explanation of Britain's abstention it was said that Britain could not accept the pretension of the resolution to take responsibility for Rhodesia from the British Parliament. Also, the British view was that it would be precipitate to pass a resolution before the result of the continuing talks between the British and Rhodesians could

56. See n. 41 above.
57. *New York Times*, Jan. 16, 1969, p. 15.
58. A/RES/279 (XXIII). A separate paragraph of the resolution called upon "all states not to recognize any form of independence in Southern Rhodesia without the prior establishment of a government based on majority rule."

be known. The Canadian delegation, which voted for the resolution, reportedly did so on the ground that it must once more support the principle of majority rule, although it did not agree with that part of the proposal which related to barring all recognition of Rhodesia.[59]

In January of 1969, at a meeting of Commonwealth prime ministers in London, four (Barbados, Lesotho, Maritius, and Swaziland) of the twenty-eight Commonwealth states represented had become members since the last meeting. There was on the part of various African delegates a call for renewal of the British pledge not to grant independence to Rhodesia before provision had been made for eventual African rule in that country, but legal authority and responsibility for the terms on which Rhodesia would be brought to independence remained with Great Britain. Involved were principles of racial justice and equality and the right of all people to self-determination, as embodied in the United Nations Charter and the Declaration of Human Rights. If there should be an important change in the

59. Ibid. See also the requisites that were considered necessary if Prime Minister Wilson was to be able to claim that his "salvage operation" was to be in any way a success; these are set forth in the *Economist*, Oct. 12, 1968, pp. 13–14, under the title "On HMS Cheerless."

A report of discussions submitted as basic requirements for granting independence to Rhodesia: (*a*) the principle and intention of unimpeded progress to majority rule, already enshrined in the 1961 Constitution, would have to be maintained and guaranteed; (*b*) there would also have to be guarantees against retrogressive amendment of the Constitution; (*c*) there would have to be immediate improvement in the political status of the African population; (*d*) there would have to be progress toward ending racial discrimination; (*e*) the British government would need to be satisfied that any basis proposed for independence was acceptable to the people of Rhodesia as a whole; (*f*) it would be necessary to insure that, regardless of race, there was no oppression of majority by minority or of minority by majority. Cmnd. 3793, Annex A.

The report set out briefly the plan which the British government submitted for the functioning of the Constitutional Council in the event that council should report unfavorably on a measure on the ground that it derogated from the principle of the declaration of rights in the Constitution or had the effect of discriminating between the races. Should the council report unfavorably on a bill on either of these grounds, it was to refer the bill to the Judicial Committee of the Privy Council. Where a Constitutional Council had not made an adverse report, any citizen of Rhodesia might within a specified time ask for a certificate from the Constitutional Council that there was a case for consideration by the Judicial Committee. If the Judicial Committee should grant him a certificate, he might himself appeal to the Judicial Committee within a specified time, and the bill would not go into effect unless the Judicial Committee should reject the appeal. If the Constitutional Council should refuse to grant a certificate, there was to be no appeal to the Judicial Committee unless the committee should itself grant an application for special leave to appeal. Cmnd. 3793.

circumstances, it was suggested, a fresh look would be taken. The final communiqué of the meeting seemed to reflect the difference between Asian-African leaders and the British government on what should be done concerning Rhodesia.[60]

By the end of 1968 it had become even more apparent that the questions at issue related much more to political than to legal considerations, although the latter were not dismissed from consideration. In any case, it has apparently become a fact that sanctions are not working strongly enough to force any Rhodesian government to reach a settlement with Great Britain that would be genuinely in accord with the principles which Prime Minister Wilson and Sir Douglas-Home had set forth.[61]

On November 7, 1968, the United Nations General Assembly had approved the strengthening of sanctions and their extension to include measures against Portugal and South Africa; there was also demand that Great Britain use force against the Smith regime. The vote was eighty-six to nine, with nineteen states abstaining (including the United States, the United Kingdom, Australia, New Zealand, Portugal, South Africa, The Netherlands, Belgium, and Luxembourg).[62]

More recent developments would seem to emphasize further that there are but few basic, generally agreed upon rules of customary international law that are applicable to the problems that have been encountered in the post-1965 Rhodesian situation. To the extent that rules of that law have been invoked, they apparently have not availed to deter the seceding community. The international organization (multilateral treaty) law that is applicable has been the basis for United Nations action (al-

60. Cmnd. 3919.
61. *Economist,* Sept. 28, 1968, pp. 16–18. "This," the writer submitted, was "partly because of the huge breach in the sanctions dyke which allows everything vital to flow into and out of Rhodesia through South Africa, although there is some clash of interest in some of this trade so long as Rhodesia and South Africa do not have a full economic union; and partly because other countries are not following the sanctions rules anything like as conscientiously as Britain is trying to do (to the latest UN questionnaire on the subject, a significant number even of black African states significantly did not reply) . . . any settlement now will certainly leave most of the real immediate power in the hands of Rhodesia's white minority electorate."
62. Res. 2383 (XXIII) 23 GAOR, Supp. 18, p. 58 (A/7218), 1701th Plenary Meeting.

though there has been difference of opinion as to its interpretation and applicability under conditions that do not assure early success for the most recent sanctions experiment). In the meantime, a somewhat less complicated but disturbing issue for the Commonwealth developed with the secession of Biafra.

IV

A United States Department of State official has observed that boundaries in Africa "were not drawn in Africa by Africans for African regions." They were "delineated in Europe by Europeans for European reasons . . . [and] for the most part, they ignored a host of ethnic religious and economic considerations which might have resulted in more rational political units." Institutional framework was lacking, in most cases being "too European in . . . inspiration to meet the needs and aspirations of an African culture and society." A strong stand against secession is ascribed to Africans' feeling that "they must start from a premise that the various ethnic groups can reconcile their differences within the present national boundaries of Africa and build toward a national identity." The same official drew attention to the fact that at the time of writing (October, 1968) all except four of the forty members of the Organization of African Unity had refused to recognize the secession of Biafra. The British had the problem of whether to divide Nigeria into three parts before independence; thereafter, although Nigeria was in appearance a democracy, the actual government has been described as a tribal alliance of the North and East, and opposition based on the tribes of the West, and some tribal elements reportedly resented efforts of regionally based parties to dominate other regions. A large section of the country was said to be excluded from participation in the national government. The assassination, on January 15, 1966, of the prime minister of Nigeria and of the prime ministers of Northern and Western Nigeria, ascribed to rebel dissatisfaction with the pace of modernization, was regarded as having destroyed the instrument for achieving a national consensus. Thereafter, the Ibos moved "to reassert legality and to try to redress the damage that had been done to the national fabric." The new government, however, was too weak to punish the leaders of the coup or "to extinguish the long fuse of revenge which led to the tragic communal outbreaks in the North and resulted in the slaughter of thousands of civilian Ibo citizens who lived in that region." [63]

The final decision to secede, which came on May 30, 1967, was apparently felt very strongly by other parts of Nigeria, and there was a considerable feeling that concessions to the Ibos would splinter the entire nation. The Consultative Committee of the Organization of African Unity tried without success to end the strife, and the Commonwealth Secretariat in London sought to bring about a negotiated settlement. The federal government of Nigeria was reportedly ready to make any concessions to the Ibos (in such matters as the granting of amnesty and the provision of a police force) if Biafra would renounce secession, but the Biafran reply was that its sovereignty was not negotiable. The federal government invited the United Nations, the Organization of African Unity, and other bodies to provide an international group of observers "to satisfy themselves that Federal forces behave with discipline and restraint." [64]

Nigeria has been described as a "colonial creation," and Biafra as a country which would be "viable on its own." [65] However, there is said to be "apprehension which appears to be widespread, that secession, once admitted to be legitimate, would be destructive of all the states now existing"; kaleidoscopic changes have been envisaged if the principle of secession is unilaterally proclaimed and successfully asserted. [66] Political and military considerations have reportedly received more consideration than have the more pressing needs of the people. [67]

63. "Magnitude and Complexity of the Nigerian Problems," a statement by Joseph Palmer, second assistant secretary for African affairs, Department of State, in *Department of State Bulletin*, LIX (1968), 357–362.
64. Ibid., pp. 359, 360, 361.
65. K. W. J. Post, "Is There a Case for Biafra?" *International Affairs*, XLIV (1968), 26–39, at 37.
66. S. K. Panter-Brick, "The Right to Self-Determination: Its Application to Nigeria," *International Affairs*, XLIV (1968), 254–263.
67. "If an idea like self determination is applied down to the end, it can often raise more problems than it solves. Within Biafra were not only some 8 million Ibos but 4 to 5 million members of other tribes most of whom did not agree with the Ibos. We counseled against secession.
"The problem is that those who are in charge of the situation specifically on the

Biafra declared its independence on May 30, 1967. It was announced that all political ties with Nigeria were dissolved, that contractual obligations would devolve, that subsisting treaties and agreements would be "honored and respected," and that Biafra would adhere faithfully to the Charter of the Organization of African Unity and to the United Nations. Several African states, such as Tanzania, were reported as having expressly denounced Biafra's move, but Tanzania in the following year recognized Biafra as an "independent sovereign entity." The Nigerian high commissioner was then instructed to leave Dar-es-Salaam, and a Nigerian spokesman was reported as saying that any diplomats sent to Biafra would be treated as rebels.[68] In 1967 there was a peace movement by the Organization of African Unity, and a mission to Laos headed by Emperor Haile Selassie. The peace initiative started by the Commonwealth was reported to have involved the organization of a Commonwealth force to occupy and police the Nigerian battle zone. The Commonwealth Secretariat's move was apparently undertaken on the initiative of the Commonwealth secretary-general. In the House of Commons on January 30, 1968, George Thomson, the commonwealth secretary, said that no request for help in settling differences had been received from the Nigerians themselves but that Britain would help in any way it could to bring peace nearer.[69] On June 12 of the same year Sir Alec Douglas-Home said in the House of Commons:

. . . we cannot intervene in the affairs of an independent . . . country. If we tried to do that the Commonwealth would very quickly

---

spot in the immediate neighborhood concerned have not as yet given enough high priority to their own people and their own needs, over against political and military considerations, to permit the international community to do the job which the international community is there to do." Dean Rusk, "Some Myths and Misconceptions about United States Policy," *Department of State Bulletin*, LIX (1968), 350–356, at 353–354.

68. *Keesing's Contemporary Archives*, XVI (1967), 22089, and XVII (1968), 22672. African states which up to that time had recognized Biafra were Gabon, Ivory Coast, and Zambia. Ibid., XVII (1968), 22880. The president of Mali is reported to have said on April 23, 1968, that support for Biafran secession would create a serious precedent for the political security of every African country. Ibid., 22672. Cf. Colin Legane, "New Hope for Nigeria: The Search for National Unity," *Round Table*, no. 230 (1968), pp. 127–136, at p. 132.

69. Parl. Deb (C) 5th ser. vol. 757 (1967–1968), c. 1065.

disintegrate. . . . I hope that the Foreign Secretary will increase his efforts, with an even greater sense of urgency . . . to create a Commonwealth force which would be ready to go to Nigeria to take advantage of a political truce, to police that truce, and keep the peace in that area.[70]

Relief agencies, in a situation where there had developed a serious danger of starvation in Africa, encountered obstacles to the provision of relief. Late in 1968 a State Department spokesman was reported as considering "incomprehensible" the refusal by Nigerian authorities to allow chartered aircraft carrying food and medicines to fly by night into Uli, the major Biafran airstrip.[71] In February, 1969, there was announcement of the State Department's plan to send a representative to the administrative center of Biafra to act as coordinator of aid shipments. It was emphasized that this would not imply United States recognition of Biafra; previously the reported position of the State Department had been that the United States must honor the objections of the Nigerian federal military government, which regarded Biafra as a "rebellious" province, and that any dealings with it (even humanitarian dealings) were in the nature of support to treason.[72] There would appear to have been little, if any, advocacy by political leaders in the United States of recognizing Biafra; there was, rather, greatly increasing concern that there be a reconciliation between federal Nigeria and Biafra.[73] The United States was reported to have sold, at a nominal fee, to the International Committee of the Red Cross and to church groups in the United States, cargo planes for the carriage of nightly supplies into Biafra.

Renewed peace efforts under the initiative of the Commonwealth Secretariat and assistance of the British government appeared to have accomplished but little. Preliminary conversations at London, where the representatives of Nigeria included the chief justice of Nigeria and the representatives of Biafra included

70. Ibid., vol. 766 (1967–1968), cc. 287–288.
71. *New York Times,* Dec. 6, 1968, p. 16. A month earlier the Nigerian government had agreed to such flights by the International Committee of the Red Cross.
72. Ibid., Feb. 20, 1969, pp. 1, 4.   73. Ibid.

the chief justice of that country, led to further discussions at Kampala, but these did not lead to a composition of differences; there was still a difference as to the prerequisites for peace negotiations. There was also effort through the Consultative Committee of the Organization of African Unity.[74] In March, 1969, in the course of a seven-hour debate in the House of Commons concerning the situation in Nigeria, there was announcement by Foreign Secretary Stewart that Prime Minister Wilson was to meet with Nigerian Major General Yakubu Gowon regarding alleged bombings of civilians. Sir Alec Douglas-Home suggested that the government put the Nigerian war before the United Nations, with a view of calling for an international ban on the sale of arms to Nigeria. The Foreign Secretary indicated that to stop the arms sale would be tantamount to supporting the rebellion; he reportedly said, "We never claimed we were neutral." [75]

V

The island of Anguilla comprises some thirty-two square miles and has a population of approximately six thousand. It was a British colony for more than a century before it became, early in 1967, a part of the Associated State of St. Kitts–Nevis–Anguilla. Early in 1968 Anthony Lee, a British Commonwealth Office official, went to Anguilla to serve as administrator for one year. Ronald Webster, as chief executive of Anguilla, had carried on talks with Robert Bradshaw, prime minister of St. Kitts–Nevis–Anguilla, looking to agreements on the status of Anguilla's government. Late in 1968, after Webster had announced that Anguilla would become a republic on January 8, 1969, he also informed Michael Webster, British secretary for foreign and Commonwealth affairs, that Lee's appointment would expire

74. *Keesing's Contemporary Archives*, XVII (1968), 22893. Six member states of the Organization of African Unity (including none that had recognized Biafra) had representation on the consultative committee on Nigeria. As late as April, 1969, this committee had failed in its effort to find a formula that would be acceptable as a basis for mediation in a situation which had reportedly cost a million lives. *Economist*, April 26, 1969, p. 31.

75. *New York Times*, March 14, 1969, p. 10.

when Anguilla became independent. Meeting in February, 1969, the heads of government of Caribbean states requested that Great Britain, in collaboration with the government of St. Kitts–Nevis–Anguilla, take all necessary steps to confirm the territorial integrity of St. Kitts–Nevis–Anguilla.

Subsequent events on the island of Anguilla have been well publicized. They included the occupation of the island by some three hundred British paratroopers. Leaflets dropped from helicopters assured the Anguillans that Britain would not force them to live under a regime which they did not want and also informed them that Anthony Lee had been appointed commissioner for the island.

In the British House of Commons on March 19, Michael Stewart said that in this part of the associated state there was "a danger that somewhat disreputable characters from outside the State and possessing arms were exercising influence upon those who purported to be its Government." He touched upon responsibility under international law when he said that "if, as a result of the absence of any lawful government or good order in the island, any injury were done to the personal property of a national of any other country, we, by virtue of our responsibility for external relations, would have been held responsible." There was also reference to section 7(2) of the West Indies Act, which relates to external relations, and to the fact that what had been done was done with the full agreement of the St. Kitts Government.[76]

An opposition speaker, Bernard Braine, said that there was no power to intervene in the domestic affairs of an associated state. He also asked, in reference to Foreign Secretary Stewart's statement that what had been done was legal because it was done with the approval of the government of St. Kitts, how this would square with the assurance given the people of Anguilla that it was no part of the British government's purpose to force on the Anguillans an administration under which they did not wish to live.[77]

At the United Nations the Committee on Colonialism decided

76. *Parl. Deb.* (C), 5th ser., vol. 780, c. 497, March 19, 1969.
77. Ibid.

as a matter of urgency to consider the sending of British troops to Anguilla, and heard Jeremiah Gumbs, self-styled representative of Anguilla at the United Nations, who told the committee that the previous February Anguilla had voted to become an independent republic separate from St. Kitts–Nevis. On March 21 the committee by consensus thought it necessary to send a visiting commission to the island and decided to keep Anguilla developments under review. The United States delegation did not associate itself with the consensus, being of the opinion that the associated states of the Caribbean exercised self-determination and that, having attained self-government, they did not fall within the purview of the Committee on Colonialism.[78]

———————

That secession of one part of a Commonwealth member state from another part of that state is a possibility has been clearly illustrated in Commonwealth history. In the process the question of a legal right on the part of other Commonwealth states to intervene has been raised. In some instances there have been appeals to this right, and in still others the denial of the existence of such a legal right to intervene. Such denial has not precluded strong effort (on the part of states not parties to the disputes and on the part of the Commonwealth Secretariat) to mediate and seek bases for peace talks. That incitement to secession in itself is not a matter of breaching public international law is suggested by the fact that the principal world organization has itself in several instances recommended secessions.[79]

Without denouncing secession as law-breaking, and without (in the case of some member states) abstaining from the step of recognizing the seceding community as a new sovereign state, the Commonwealth states have in the federal Nigeria-Biafra case looked to a mediatory role for the Commonwealth and the removal of obstacles to the relief of suffering by the people of the community attempting to secede. In contrast, the most striking feature of the Rhodesian secession has been the bringing of the secession matter before the United Nations bodies, where denunciation of the de facto regime in Salisbury has rested upon a claim

78. GAOR, March 19, 1969.   79. See n. 54 above.

of racism and the denial of human rights by reason of which the international community may institute economic sanctions. The "domestic jurisdiction" clause of the United Nations Charter has not precluded action by the General Assembly and the Security Council to approve sanctions against a self-proclaimed republic. As noted above, there is nothing in the Commonwealth relationship which precludes withdrawal from that relationship, as the action of Eire demonstrated—whatever disagreement there may have been as to the constitutional aspects of Eire's withdrawal. Several Commonwealth states have threatened to withdraw from Commonwealth membership as a means of applying pressure upon Great Britain for more drastic action against Rhodesia. An eminent historian of the Commonwealth has said that "some African attempts to force the hand of the British Government by threatened secession have recoiled unfavourably upon the concept of Commonwealth." [80] In the case of Biafra there has been less emphasis upon what international law permits and requires than upon compassion and humanitarianism—through international rather than national agencies alone. The brief separatist surge in Anguilla in 1969 was not a secessionist attempt comparable with what had taken place in Rhodesia or Biafra but a move toward dissociation from a union arrangement with two other Caribbean communities within the Commonwealth. British action was defensible partly on the legal ground that the United Kingdom would be responsible internationally for injury to aliens during the disturbed situation.

80. P. N. S. Mansergh, "The Commonwealth and the Future," *International Studies,* IX (1967), 1–12, at 11. Professor Mansergh reminds, as to colonialism in Rhodesia, that this was not colonialism but "settler rule." As to "more Rhodesias" he says that there can be none, and "with the close of that episode will come, therefore, the final ending of the colonial-racial question in Commonwealth relations" (pp. 7–12).

5

Migration

A distinctive fact concerning the present-day Commonwealth has come to be its multiracial character. Implications drawn from this development have touched public law, some of these having been drawn when the association of states was still the "British" Commonwealth. The period of the existence of the dominions was not without problems growing out of claimed discrimination on an ethnic basis, and there was occasion for sociologists and demographers, as well as legalists, to analyze and consider possible solutions for such problems.[1] Subsequently, with the emergence of many new states and their becoming members of the Commonwealth, there have been many occasions, in international as well as in national forums, for invoking the principle of nondiscrimination and basic human rights. The response of some Commonwealth states has been to invoke the concept of domestic jurisdiction as it came to be recognized in both the League of Nations Covenant and the United Nations Charter, although in somewhat different contexts—"domestic jurisdiction" having been specifically mentioned in the Covenant only in connection with the Council's action on disputes, whereas in the Charter it is so placed as to be a possible limiter upon any action by the principal United Nations bodies.

Since the withdrawal of South Africa from the Commonwealth, the United Kingdom has come to face a central politico-

1. An illustrative work is that of W. D. Borrie, *Population Trends and Politics: A Study in Australian and World Demography* (1948); chap. 14 is on "Population Trends and International Relations." An earlier study of the division of functions (as between the Imperial, colonial, and dominion governments) with respect to immigration was that by Lionel Curtis, *The Problem of the Commonwealth* (1916), chap. 5, "Immigration."

legal issue in connection with migration from other Commonwealth member states, and particularly from Kenya. For the purpose of weighing this issue from the point of view of public international law, it is proposed to consider the development in relation to (*a*) the background of alleged discrimination on the part of certain dominions, (*b*) the nature and scope of legislation recently enacted in the United Kingdom pertaining to migration to Great Britain of persons who are citizens of the United Kingdom and Colonies, (*c*) recent and current practice of Great Britain and of the United States (as a nonmember of the Commonwealth) concerning the use of travel documents by migrant nationals, and (*d*) the extent to which international law is applicable to the current issue concerning migration from other Commonwealth states to the United Kingdom.

I

In the period of the Imperial Conferences, 1911 to 1937, there were at various times discussions concerning immigration and emigration within the communities over which the British authority extended. Thus, to the 1911 conference the Hindu Friend Society of Victoria sent a petition which set forth, *inter alia,* that "the present Dominion Immigration Laws are humiliating to the people of India when the aliens, such as the Japanese and Chinese, by their treaty rights, can come to Canada whereas our fellow British subjects are not allowed to enjoy the birth-right of travelling from one part of the British Empire to another." [2] The 1911 conference adopted a resolution concerning naturalization, but included therein the statement that "nothing now proposed . . . would affect the validity and effectiveness of local law regulating immigration and the like or differentiating between classes of British subjects." The Earl of Crewe, secretary of state for India, spoke at some length on the question of Indian emigration

2. Cd. 5746–1, p. 279.

and immigration, pleading for more freedom of movement and equality in the Empire.[3]

At the Imperial War Conference of 1918 Sir S. P. Sinha of India, who introduced a resolution on "Reciprocity of Treatment between India and the Dominions," noted that the position of Indian migrants in the colonies had been the cause of great difficulties (the matter having been brought up at the 1897 conference by Joseph Chamberlain and at the 1907 conference by Mr. Asquith, as well as at the 1911 conference). The general subject (with special reference to Indians) was again considered at the 1921 Conference of Prime Ministers, which adopted the following resolution:

The Conference, while reaffirming the Resolution of the Imperial War Conference of 1918, that each community of the British Commonwealth should enjoy complete control of its own population by means of restriction of immigration from any of the other communities, recognizes that there is an incongruity between the position of India as an equal member of the British Empire and the disabilities upon British Indians lawfully domiciled in some other parts of the Empire. The Conference accordingly is of the opinion that in the interests of the solidarity of the British Commonwealth, it is desirable that the rights of such Indians should be recognized.[4]

In the period between the two world wars there continued to be alleged discrimination by some Commonwealth states on the basis of race. The rule on "domestic jurisdiction," as incorporated in Article XV(8) of the League of Nations Covenant, although in terms applicable only in situations (disputes) before the League Council, seemed to some to be broadly applicable to such a matter as immigration control. South Africa was not the only Commonwealth state affirming the right to make its own policy on immigration. The first treaty made by one dominion with another was that between Australia and New Zealand, signed in 1944. Article 32 of that treaty reads, "In the peace settlement or other negotiations the two Governments will accord one another

3. Cd. 5745, p. 394. At this conference New Zealand had introduced a resolution to the effect that colored races should be encouraged to remain domiciled in their own zone. This was withdrawn before the speech by the Earl of Crewe (p. 279).
4. Cmd. 1474, p. 8.

full support in maintaining the accepted principle that every Government has the right to control immigration and emigration in regard to all territories within its jurisdiction." [5]

The inclusion and the placing of the "domestic jurisdiction" clause of the United Nations Charter did not preclude the offsetting principle of "international concern" as it developed after the coming into effect of Charter Article II(7). Yet two decades after the inclusion of this provision of the Charter, a meeting of the prime ministers of the Commonwealth was the occasion for that body's assertion that the extent of immigration into Great Britain was, as Prime Minister Menzies of Australia put it, "entirely a matter for the British government to determine." Concerning immigration to Great Britain, the Australian spokesman further said that "every country's immigration policy is its own business and this is not open to debate at a Prime Ministers' conference. . . . An association of free, independent, autonomous nations are not going to have their internal business tossed around in conference and the immigration policy is, of course, a perfect example." [6] Later the same political leader referred to the full freedom of individual member states of the Commonwealth in their recognition policies when he said that "some of us don't recognize Communist China and are not to be told at a Commonwealth meeting that we should." [7]

5. *New Zealand Treaty Series,* 1944, no. 1, 18 UNTS 357. In the article of the treaty immediately following the one quoted, the two parties referred to collaboration, exchange of information, and assistance in these matters. On the treaty generally, see Trevor Reese, "The Australian–New Zealand Arrangement, 1944, and the United States," *Journal of Commonwealth Political Studies,* IV (1966), 3–15.

6. *Current Notes on International Affairs,* XXXVI (1965), 350.

7. Ibid., p. 354. Cf. statement by an Australian scholar who, referring to a United Nations General Assembly debate between the Union of South Africa and India in 1946, noted that the representatives of colored peoples showed surprising solidarity, and that for Australia to have supported South Africa could have provided ground for an attack upon Australia's immigration policy; Australia abstained from voting. Borrie, *Population Trends and Politics,* p. 243. On the factors which affected policy in Australia at a much earlier period, including British interest in restriction, see N. B. Nairn, "A Survey of the White Australia Policy in the Nineteenth Century," *Australian Quarterly,* XXVIII (1956), 16–31. See also K. Ryan, "Immigration, Aliens and Naturalization in Australian Law," in D. P. O'Connell, ed., *International Law in Australia* (1965), chap. 18, pp. 465–499. The author submits that "it falls completely within the discretion of a State to admit to its territory the nationals of another State." He regarded as "minimal" the requirements of international law on the subject at the time of his writing.

While Australia has frequently been referred to as exemplifying a "white immigrant" policy, it has not been alone in the Commonwealth in its assertion of a right under international law to choose its own immigrants. The Canadian Privy Council, for example, in a cable communication to Sir Robert Borden at the time the Covenant of the League of Nations was in preparation, asked that signatories to the Covenant recognize that "the right of each nation to regulate and control the character of its own population by restriction of immigration is unimpaired, and . . . such control is recognized as a matter of purely domestic concern." [8] A recent study has summarized practice in the "old" Commonwealth:

The "old" Commonwealth had long carried out a white immigration policy which excluded migrants from Africa, Asia and the West Indies. Canada softened this policy in 1956 and 1958 by arrangements with India, Pakistan and Ceylon, respectively, which permitted a yearly token quota of citizens from these states to enter as migrants. Ceylon has greatly restricted immigration in an attempt to stem the tide of Indian migrants. Pakistan and India have tightened immigration controls in order to prevent the migration of Hindus and Moslems across their respective frontiers. Malaysia has also adopted restrictive policies to maintain the balance between people of Malay, Indian and Chinese origin within its borders. Cyprus has likewise attempted to restrict migration to maintain the Turkish-Greek population ratio at a constant level.[9]

Arrangements within the Commonwealth do not preclude dual citizenship, and at times migrants from the United Kingdom to such a Commonwealth state as Australia have found themselves subject to compulsory voting laws, while migrants to England

8. George P. deT. Glazebrook, *Canada at the Paris Peace Conference* (1942), pp. 69–70.
9. Robert E. Clute, "Nationality and Citizenship," in Robert R. Wilson, ed., *The International Law Standard and Commonwealth Developments* (1966), p. 107. Documentation there provided includes references both to statutes and to judicial decisions. The Judicial Committee of the Privy Council in the case of *Thornton* v. *Police*, [1963] A. C. 336, upheld a Fiji Immigraion Ordinance of 1947 which required any person entering the Islands to leave within four months, as applied to Thornton, a British subject. Clute also notes (p. 284n.) the case of *Re Munshi Singh*, 20 B.C. 243 (1914), in which a British Columbia court upheld the exclusion of a British subject from Canada, and a comparable case from South Africa while that state was still a member of the Commonwealth. See also *Rex* v. *Padsha* [1923], So. Afr. L.R. (A.D.), 281.

from such a state as Pakistan have sometimes found themselves liable to compulsory military service in England. Matters of nationality and residence (i.e., the determination by a state of who shall be its nationals and who shall be permitted to migrate to its territory) might normally be thought to be within domestic jurisdiction, although the determination by a state of who shall be its nationals or citizens is not unlimited. A recent investigation has led to the conclusion that, by and large, Commonwealth members in the period between the two world wars interpreted the "domestic jurisdiction" concept from a legal point of view which stressed the "international obligations" approach, while since World War II the new Asiatic and African states have tended to argue that matters are domestic only if they concern but one state or if they have no international repercussions—and thus has developed the so-called doctrine of international concern.[10] It is obvious that restrictive immigration policies of one Commonwealth state, if challenged on the ground of their being directed particularly against another Commonwealth state or group of states, might tend to provide occasion for the challenged state's right under traditional international law. In situations where the ruling elite continue to be Europeans the retention by them of ruling power has been an obvious factor through the period of early settlement and in later policy on the restriction of immigration. It would seem to be clear that in the case of United Kingdom settlers economic policy also figured in the making of policy with respect to immigration.

A distinct phase of related policy in the United Kingdom began when the Parliament enacted the Commonwealth Immigrants Act, 1962.[11] This was legislation for controlling the immi-

---

10. John M. Howell, "Domestic Jurisdiction," in Wilson, *The International Law Standard and Commonwealth Developments*, pp. 163–164. Howell submits (p. 164) that experience before the political and judicial organs of the United Nations "suggests that a 'new' Commonwealth member may abandon 'international concern' for the 'international obligations' approach when its own actions and policies are called into question," while "the record indicates that 'old' Commonwealth countries will at times embrace the 'international concern' doctrine." See also Howell, "A Matter of International Concern," *American Journal of International Law*, LX (1969), 771–782.
11. 10 and 11 Eliz. 2, Act of 1962, *Public General Acts and Measures of 1962*, p. 112.

gration into the United Kingdom of certain categories of persons holding United Kingdom passports and being citizens of the United Kingdom and Colonies (along with persons who were included in the passports of such persons). The law provided for the deportation of certain Commonwealth citizens who had been convicted of offenses that were punishable by imprisonment and whose deportation had been recommended by the court. By its terms the law did not apply to a person born in the United Kingdom, or to one whose father was born in the United Kingdom, or to one whose parents (or either of them) had been ordinarily resident in the United Kingdom at the time of the person's birth. Excepted also were persons who had come to be citizens of the United Kingdom and Colonies by virtue of naturalization in the United Kingdom, or who were citizens by virtue of their being adopted in the United Kingdom, persons registered under the British Nationality Act of 1948,[12] or wives of persons within the foregoing descriptions. The part of the act relating to deportation applied to British-protected persons and citizens of the Republic of Ireland as it applied to Commonwealth citizens. Should the question arise whether a person was a Commonwealth citizen to whom section 6(4) applied, it should "lie on him to prove that he is not such a citizen." The secretary of state might revoke a deportation order at any time. Exceptions were made for members of the amed forces, and the secretary of state could extend the classes of persons set out under this category. Separate provisions related to searching authority, detention of immigrants pending their removal, and stowaways.

Following the passage of the 1962 Commonwealth Immigrants Act, when the Conservatives were in power, there was apparently a period of strict enforcement. In August, 1965, the Labour government announced additional measures to restrict immigration

12. 11 and 12 Geo. 6, c. 56. By the provisions (sec. 1), "(1) Every person who under this Act is a citizen of the United Kingdom and Colonies or who under any enactment for the time being in force in any country mentioned in subsection (3) of this section is a citizen of that country shall by virtue of that citizenship have the status of a British subject. . . . (3) The following are the countries hereinbefore referred to, that is to say, Canada, Australia, New Zealand, the Union of South Africa, Newfoundland, India, Pakistan, Southern Rhodesia and Ceylon." Since passage of the act there have been amendments to subsection 3 for the purpose of including other countries.

from Commonwealth countries. Instead of allowing 20,000 permits a year to be issued, it was announced that 8,500 would be issued in each year to those having needed skills or those having jobs awaiting them. In announcing to the House of Commons the policy the government proposed to follow, Herbert Brown, leader of the Commons, said that Britain realized the valuable contribution made by workers from other parts of the Commonwealth, but that nearly everyone appreciated that there was a limit to the number the "small and overcrowded country" could absorb. A curb on work permits, as announced in a White Paper, was said to be legal recognition of a restriction that had actually been in effect for nearly a year; no such permits for unskilled workers without jobs, it was pointed out, had been issued by the Ministry of Labour since 1962. Most of the applicants from Commonwealth countries, the government statement indicated, were Indians, Pakistanis, and Jamaicans. In the previous year some 23,500 Commonwealth citizens had come to Britain to work, accompanied by 51,500 dependents, and there had come to be nearly one million immigrants in Britain, most of them being classified as "colored" (this classification including Indians and Pakistanis as well as Negroes). The main resulting problems related to housing, education, employment, and health.[13]

Not merely in the United Kingdom, but in the Commonwealth generally, such discrimination as there has been in states where the common law provides a principal background has been based upon statutory provisions rather than the common law. Since the common law developed in England when racial differences were not of great moment, differences of race and color were not serious factors in policy. When the Commonwealth Immigrants Act, 1962, was under debate there was criticism of it as "a plain anti-Commonwealth measure in theory, and a plain anti-colour measure in practice." [14] The *Times* said editorially that the legis-

13. *New York Times,* Aug. 3, 1965, p. 6. The issuance of the government statement came after the report of a mission by Admiral Mountbatten of Burma, who had visited Malta, India, Pakistan, Nigeria, Canada, Jamaica, Trinidad and Tobago, and Cyprus, with a view of examining the question of immigration from these Commonwealth countries to Britain. It was reported that Lord Mountbatten had recommended that there be a quota of 10,000 immigrants a year.
14. *Times* (London), Nov. 17, 1961, p. 11.

lation struck "at the very roots of British tradition and Commonwealth links." [15] The United Kingdom had adopted a policy which, while not in terms based upon race or color, was widely regarded as discriminatory from one or both of these points of view.

That an alien in a Commonwealth state might sometimes actually be in a more favorable position than is a British subject—by reason of treaty rights which the Commonwealth state in question has granted to the country of which the alien is a national—was brought out in a decision of a Canadian court in 1908. [16]

There was apparently strict enforcement of the 1962 act. The race issue was touched upon in a government spokesman's statement that "it is recognized that the presence in this country of a number of immigrants with differing social backgrounds, and in particular their concentration in a few areas where there is already a housing shortage and pressure on the social services, has given rise to a number of difficulties." [17]

As is well known, the United Kingdom is not the only state in the Commonwealth to be accused of discrimination, in its legislative policy, on racial or color lines. The centrality of Britain's position in the Commonwealth, however, has tended to keep it in the spotlight in recent years concerning this matter, especially since 1962, as the Commonwealth has become increasingly multiracial and multilingual. It is against this background that United Kingdom policy of the 1960's, and particularly the relevant legislation of 1968, may be considered from the point of view of international law.

II

Toward the end of the year 1967 several thousand East African and Asian holders of British passports arrived in the British Isles.

15. Ibid. For a fuller summary of the background of the legislation, see Robert R. Wilson and Robert E. Clute, "Commonwealth Citizenship and Common Status," *American Journal of International Law*, LVII (1963), 566–587.

16. *In re Nakake Nocazake*, 13 Brit. Col. Rep. 370 (1908). Nakake Nocazake appealed from the application (to Japanese nationals in British Columbia) of certain restrictions upon entry, basing the appeal upon a treaty with Japan according rights of entry and sojourn.

17. White Paper referred to in n. 13 above.

Their coming at that time was ascribed to legislation in Kenya which had come into force on December 1, 1967. By its terms, residents of European and Asian origin who had not become Kenya citizens but who desired to continue working there were required to apply to Kenyan immigration authorities for work permits. These permits were obtainable at considerable cost and were renewable annually (on payment of an additional fee) for a maximum period of five years; they would be granted only if, in the opinion of the Kenyanization Bureau of the Ministry of Labour, no suitably qualified Kenyan citizens were available for the employment in question. Other legislation, passed in the summer of 1967 to become operative April 1, 1968, required all traders to be licensed and restricted (to Nairobi and other main localities in Kenya) the area in which persons who were not citizens of Kenya could carry on business activities.[18]

When, in the British House of Commons, on November 15, 1967, there was question as to what the British government proposed to do about persons whom this Kenya legislation would affect, the home secretary pointed out that the Asians affected were citizens of the United Kingdom and colonies (a citizenship created by the British Nationality Act of 1948). Such persons, he said, as were affected by the Kenyan Act (mostly Indians and Pakistanis) in coming as migrants to Great Britain were exercising a right which they acquired when their respective countries became independent. They could opt, he pointed out, for retention of this status if they were unwilling to acquire new citizenship, i.e., the citizenship of the country of their domicile. Except for the opting arrangement, many of these Asians would have become stateless. Duncan Sandys, who had been Commonwealth secretary at the time three East African communities attained independence, said that citizenship arrangements were never intended to provide a "privileged back-door entry into the United Kingdom."[19]

On February 12, 1968, five Conservative Privy Councilors sponsored a motion for immediate curtailment of the influx of immigrants into Britain, and an amendment submitted by a group of

18. *Keesing's Contemporary Archives*, XVI (1968), 22575.
19. *Parl. Deb.* (C), 5th ser., vol. 754 (1967–1968), c. 506.

Conservatives and some fifteen Labour members referred to the necessity of passing such legislation in order to avoid grave problems. It was submitted that when the rate of migration exceeded ability to assimilate the newcomers action was necessary; it was also thought necessary to avoid any situation which would increase racial disharmony and prejudice the position of immigrants who were already resident in the United Kingdom. Sandys denied that Asians had been given assurance that they could come to Britain if the Kenya government discriminated against them; he called upon the government to put "these people" into the same position regarding citizenship and right of entry into the United Kingdom as they had been in immediately before their respective countries had attained independence.[20]

Two days later there was a report that the Commonwealth Office had issued a statement (on the previous day) to the effect that, since Kenya was a colony before it became independent, all Kenya citizens before the date of independence had had the same right of entry into Great Britain as any other British citizens; 100,000 Asians, not Kenya citizens, were still in the same position. The Commonwealth Immigrants Act, the statement submitted, had no reference to Kenya until after Kenya's independence.[21] The high commissioner of Kenya in London issued a statement that the crisis was not one in his country, but rather a "British national crisis." [22]

The Commonwealth Immigrants Act, 1968, as finally passed,[23] drew strong criticism from the National Committee for Commonwealth Immigrants. The latter "grievously regretted" the claimed absence of consultation concerning the possible effects of the legislation upon that committee's work. The Archbishop of Canterbury, in his capacity as chairman of the National Committee, noted that there were four features of the legislation that were "thoroughly wrong":

(1) A racial discrimination was for the first time embodied into law of the United Kingdom;

20. Ibid., vol. 759 (1967–1968), cc. 1271–1279.
21. *Times* (London), Feb. 19, 1968.
22. *Keesing's Contemporary Archives*, XVI (1968), 22576.
23. Reproduced in Appendix 4. See R. Boston, "How the Immigrants Act Was Passed," *New Society*, no. 287 (1968), pp. 448–452.

(2) The Bill failed to include recommendations of the Wilson Committee for a system of appeals and the provision of a comprehensive welfare service;

(3) The number of Asian immigrants to be permitted entry was . . . unjust for persons classed as United Kingdom citizens.

(4) The Bill created a class of virtually stateless persons.[24]

An Indian-born Nairobi lawyer, Shivabhai Amin, announced on February 23 that lawyers in London and Nairobi had been instructed to prepare test cases designed to challenge the validity

24. The report of the Wilson Committee on Immigration Appeals (Cmnd. 3387, at p. 63) included in its recommendations, concerning rights of appeal, the following:

(1) Any Commonwealth citizen or alien (including one who is coming or has come as a member of the crew of a ship or aircraft) should have a right of appeal against (*a*) exclusion at a sea or airport (paragraphs 83 and 89); (*b*) refusal of an entry certificate or visa (paragraphs 90 and 91); (*c*) refusal to withdraw a standing instruction for his exclusion (paragraph 92); (*d*) refusal to vary a condition of entry in a manner favourable to him (paragraph 96); (*e*) variation of a condition of entry in a manner unfavourable to him (paragraph 97); (*f*) a proposal to deport him or to remove him under certain other procedures applicable to persons who have gained entry to the country (paragraphs 93 and 98); (*g*) refusal to revoke a deportation order (paragraph 99). In any case of exclusion or deportation an appeal should lie not only on the question whether the person concerned is to be allowed to enter or remain in the country, but also on the question to what country he should be sent if excluded or deported (paragraphs 88 and 95).

(2) We would not think it wrong in principle, or destructive of the general value of the appeal system, to withdraw from its scope cases in which exclusion, deportation or other restrictive action appears to the Home Secretary to be justified on grounds which are primarily of a political character (paragraph 143).

Among other recommendations, the committee submitted (p. 67) that up-to-date information about the rules governing entry to the United Kingdom should be available from the Home Office and from British posts overseas, and should be disseminated as far as possible through passport offices of other governments, shipping companies and airlines, reputable travel agents, and other channels through which it is likely to reach those whom it concerns (paragraphs 179 to 181).

We would like to see established an organization, recognisably independent of Government control, the functions of which would include that of advising Commonwealth citizens and aliens who are in difficulties with immigration control and, where necessary, assisting them in presenting their cases to the Home Office and the appellate authorities. Such an organisation might be set up jointly by appropriate existing voluntary bodies concerned with the welfare of immigrants. It should receive such financial support as is necessary from public funds. The Home Office should take the initiative in promoting cooperation among voluntary bodies for this purpose and should provide facilities for workers employed by the organisation to be stationed at the main ports of entry (paragraphs 182 to 190).

At p. 17n. of the Wilson Committee's report is a listing of judicial decisions to support propositions in the report relative to the jurisdiction of courts with respect to deportation orders.

of the bill before the International Court of Justice. In his view, "to restrict a citizen from entering a country is to deprive him of his fundamental rights." [25] A prominent Nairobi businessman, formerly a member of Kenya's Legislative Council, was reported as saying, "Britain will now be termed worse than South Africa. South Africa is at least not a hypocrite. But Britain, who always claimed to be fighting for justice and fair play and against racialism, is now proved to be hypocrite no. 1 in the world." [26]

A telegram to the Queen from certain Asian leaders on February 25 asked that the royal assent be withheld from the Commonwealth Immigrants Act, which was described as "contrary to fair play and centuries-old British standards of justice and fair play, and also contrary to fundamental human rights enunciated by the United Nations Charter" and as "a breach of the solemn undertaking given to the Asian community at the time of independence of Kenya in 1963." There arrived in London on February 26 a delegation whose leader described the bill to reporters as "unnecessary, wrong, immoral, unjustified, and inhuman." He was reported as saying that out of about one hundred thousand Asians eligible to come to Europe probably not more than forty to fifty thousand intended to do so; some twenty thousand to thirty thousand were reported to have left Kenya already, some of them going to India and Canada.[27]

The home secretary, when moving the second reading of the bill before its passage by the House of Commons, told the members that the issue before the House was one of the great issues of the time, one which could unite the members or "tear them apart." All parties, he observed, were committed to the development of a multiracial society; the proposed legislation had not had its origin in panic or prejudice. There were at least one million people living in the various parts of the Commonwealth overseas who were able either actually or potentially to enter

25. *Keesing's Contemporary Archives*, XVI (1968), 22677.
26. Ibid. (remarks of Kantilal Punchanchand Shah).
27. Ibid., p. 22678. As of April, 1969, there was reported to be a "steady" flow to Canada of immigrants from Pakistan, the West Indies, and North Africa, this being ascribed to the easing of Canada's immigration laws, which had formerly restricted the entry of non-Europeans. *New York Times*, April 3, 1969, p. 78M.

Great Britain free of immigration controls, most of them possessing local citizenship in addition to being citizens of the United Kingdom and Colonies. There resulted, therefore, for Great Britain the liability of taking well over one million of them "without any kind of control," and there had been an increase in the number coming to Great Britain since the passage of the Kenya Immigration and Trade Licensing Acts. It was pointed out that *ad hoc* machinery looked to the creation of machinery to hear appeals on the basis of the law laid down by the Wilson Committee. The home secretary also explained the voucher system it was proposed to have; the number to be issued every year, it was thought, would be between six thousand and seven thousand, and the vouchers would be issued not by the minister of labor but by the United Kingdom high commissioners in the countries concerned.[28] The same speaker, while viewing "with abhorrence" the idea of devaluing a British passport, directed attention to the fact that the bill covered "equally with Asians" many people in Asia of "pure White origin." The bill was not thought to be a racist measure in any offensive sense of the word, since control would still have had to be applied if Great Britain had been faced with the prospect of a comparable influx of people from Scandinavia, Italy, or France; furthermore, it was proposed to have a court of appeal.[29]

One of the sharpest criticisms was that of Sir Dingle Foot (Labour), who inquired whether it was proposed to tear up the obligations deliberately assumed in 1962. He also referred to international legalism, describing the bill as a "most retrograde step in . . . international law." The aims of the British government over the past twenty-five years, he said, had been to make private rights a matter of international obligations; but in 1968, the human rights year, the bill would have the effect of taking away human rights of British citizens and was such that it would be racialist in effect. He described the proposed legislation as "shameful, shabby, miserable." [30]

In support of the bill, Duncan Sandys said there was nothing

28. Parl. Deb. (c) 5th ser., v. 759 (1967–1968), cc. 1241–1258.
29. Ibid. 30. Ibid., cc. 1267–1271.

new about restricting the right of United Kingdom citizens to enter Great Britain. The Kenya Independence Act merely assured individuals that United Kingdom citizenship which they possessed would not be taken away unless they acquired Kenyan citizenship. Persons affected, he said, might return to India or Pakistan, which "certainly would not refuse them admission." The fact had to be faced that once Great Britain had granted independence to a colony, it was "no longer in position to look after its inhabitants as we did before." The influx into Britain had created considerable tensions.[31] Another speaker for the government observed that in the past ten to fifteen years Great Britain had absorbed about one million immigrants from the Commonwealth.[32]

In the House of Lords there was reference to the assertion that the bill was in conflict with the Declaration of Human Rights. Statistics on the probable effect of the legislation were offered by Lord Gardner, who suggested, as estimates of the number of United Kingdom citizens to whom the bill would apply, 167,000 from Kenya, 100,000 from Malaysia, 55,000 from Singapore, 49,000 from Trinidad and Tobago, 10,000 from Sabah and Sarawak, 6,000 from Malawi, 4,000 from Cyprus, 3,000 from Jamaica, 30,000 from Uganda, 20,000 from Tanzania, 1,000,000 Chinese from Maylasia, 600,000 Tamils from Ceylon, and 10,000 Somalis from South Yemen.[33]

The 1962 Immigration Act was the object of further criticism, and it was claimed that the new legislation proposed was "racist," Lord Brockway saying that no one could doubt that it was such. The bill would never have been introduced, he said, if people pouring in from Kenya had been British and white.[34] Upon passage of the measure, Lord Beaumont said, "we have ruined our relationship with the Commonwealth, with the United Nations and with the Human Rights Movement. We are disgraced."[35]

The 1968 bill came into force at midnight on March 1. Shortly afterward lawyers who had been appointed by the Lord Chancel-

---

31. Ibid., cc. 1277–1279.   32. Ibid., c. 1354.
33. Parl. Deb. (L) 5th ser., v. 289 (1968), cc. 924–925.
34. Ibid., cc. 955–956.   35. Ibid., c. 1215.

lor to hear appeals from Asians in East Africa arrived in Nairobi. As noted above, prior to the introduction of this legislation, there had been an extensive report by the Committee on Immigration Appeals (generally referred to as the Wilson Committee). This report had pointed out that the prior-existing legislation left rules governing entry and deportation of aliens largely to be determined by the home secretary at his discretion. It noted that the number of Commonwealth citizens admitted to Britain in 1966 was 442,742, while admission had been refused at the port of entry to 1,339. Deportations, except for crime or breach of landing conditions, were described as rare, the home secretary having discretion in the matter. The committee expressed disappointment in its finding that only one Commonwealth citizen in five coming to the United Kingdom had an entry certificate, which, if properly obtained, would be normally a guarantee of admission. Noting that such states as Australia and New Zealand had no system of appeals against refusal of entry, the report set forth the "firm conclusion" that appeals should lie, and there was suggestion of a two-tier system. There was also suggestion that the addition of a judicial element in appeals would become important if the United Kingdom should join the European Economic Community, in which there would be freedom of movement. The committee proposed that, should there be an appeals tribunal in England, no fees should be paid by Commonwealth citizens in such appeals cases.[36]

The Commonwealth Immigrants Act, 1968, drew further criticism because of its conferring new discretionary powers upon immigration officers without subjecting decisions of these officers to such a system of appeals as that proposed by the Wilson Committee, whereas under the Commonwealth Immigrants Act, 1962, any citizen of the United Kingdom and Colonies holding or included in a passport currently in force and issued by the United Kingdom government was exempt from the restrictions the 1962

36. Cmnd. 3387, pp. 4, 22, 28, 29, 32, 52, 54. The report noted (p. 42) that there were precedents in Continental administrative law for the kind of procedure it recommended. In Appendixes IV and V of the report (pp. 76–83) are summary descriptions of the practice of the United States and of Canada with respect to immigration appeals.

act imposed, so that he had an automatic right—unless he or at least one of his parents or grandparents was within named categories. These categories included persons born in the United Kingdom or naturalized therein, or persons who have become citizens of the United Kingdom and Colonies on the basis of adoption in the United Kingdom, or who have been registered as citizens under the British Nationality Acts in the United Kingdom or in a specified Commonwealth country. A critic pointed out that on one occasion prior to the passage of the 1962 Commonwealth Immigrants Act Parliament had "temporarily abandoned" the principle that a state will always receive its own subjects into its territory, the Prevention of Violence (Temporary Provisions) Act, 1939, having authorized the home secretary to issue prohibition and expulsion orders against persons not ordinarily resident in Great Britain if such persons were believed to be concerned in the preparation or instigation of acts of violence (the measure permitting action against suspected members of the Irish Republican Army).[37] At the time one publicist commented, "this illustrates . . . what havoc *ad hoc* legislation can play with the principles which the common law so cherished. . . . For this duty to admit subjects is a principle which Great Britain has carefully fostered in the past and the precedent created by its unwitting abandonment will not go unremembered abroad."[38]

Unless there is acceptance of the Blackstone doctrine that international law is a part of the common law,[39] what the common law includes would not necessarily be identical with international law on the point. Before the passage of the 1968 act there had been judicial holding that there could be a distinction between a passport issued by Her Majesty through the governor of a colony (in exercise of the power granted to the governor of such colony) and a passport issued by the United Kingdom. In the case of *Regina v. Secretary of State for Home Department and Others, Ex parte Bhurosah and Others,* decided August 11,

37. B. A. Hepple, "Commonwealth Immigrants Act, 1968," *Modern Law Review,* XXXI (1968), 424–428, at 424.
38. *Annual Survey of English Law* (1939), pp. 93–94.
39. See discussion in Robert R. Wilson, ed., *The International Law Standard and Commonwealth Developments* (1966), pp. 75–77, 85.

1967, and involving holders of passports issued in Mauritius, the holding was that

the passports were not "United Kingdom passports," for they were issued in exercise of the Royal prerogative, not by the Government of the United Kingdom but by the Government of Mauritius in the name of Her Majesty and the holders were, therefore, not exempt from the restriction on entry into the United Kingdom imposed by the Act of 1962.

Lord Denning, master of the rolls, said:

When Parliament passed this Act it intended it to apply, not only to the independent countries of the Commonwealth, but also to the colonial territories of the Queen which have not yet attained independence. If there were any doubt on this point, it can be resolved by looking at section 18 of the Act. It specifically says that the Channel Islands and the Isle of Man are to be treated as though they were part of the United Kingdom. . . . If it was intended to put Mauritius and the other colonial territories in the same position as the Channel Islands and the Isle of Man, that was the place to do it. Parliament did not do it.[40]

There continue to be differences between states of the Commonwealth with respect to laws touching dual citizenship. Acquisition of such status may be automatic, or through the voluntary act of registration. The so-called common status continues in existence, although it was changed to some extent by the United Kingdom Nationality Act of 1948,[41] which was amended by the act of 1958.[42] In substance, legislation of the individual Commonwealth states provides that a person who is a citizen of the enacting state, or who under an enactment in force in any other country of the Commonwealth is a citizen of such other country, shall by virtue of such citizenship have the status of a British subject, and, as the 1948 statute sets forth, such person "may be known either as a British subject or a Commonwealth citizen." The sequel to the enactment of the 1948 legislation, as it was later amended, has been summarized as follows:

40. *Law Reports*, [1968] Q.B. pp. 267, 284–285.
41. 11 and 12 Geo. 6, c. 56.   42. 6 and 7 Eliz. 2, c. 22.

Not every country of the Commonwealth has enacted this clause and where action has been taken there have been differences in form. Thus the legislation of Canada, Australia, and New Zealand provides that citizens of the country concerned and of all other Commonwealth countries are British subjects. The legislation of the African Commonwealth countries and of Malaysia, Jamaica, Trinidad and Tobago, and Malta provides that citizens of the country concerned and of all other Commonwealth countries are Commonwealth citizens. The Indian Act provides that citizens of other Commonwealth countries shall have the status of Commonwealth citizens, but does not confer the status of Commonwealth citizen upon Indian nationals. The Pakistan Act provides that citizens of Pakistan are Commonwealth citizens but does not provide in terms that citizens of other Commonwealth countries possess the same status, though it provides that the expression "Commonwealth citizen" in the Act means a person described as such in the British Nationality Act 1948 and that a Commonwealth citizen is not an alien for the purposes of the Pakistan Act. Ceylon has not made any provision for common status, although its Citizenship Act defines an alien as a person who is not a British subject (as defined in the British Nationality Act of 1948). Nor have Cyprus, Guyana and Barbados yet made any provision for common status. Despite these differences no citizen of any country of the Commonwealth is an alien in any other, and in all cases citizens of the country concerned still possess the status of British subjects (or Commonwealth citizens) under United Kingdom law.[43]

All of the Commonwealth members reportedly impose some restrictions on the entry of persons not possessing the citizenship of the admitting state. Such restrictions are said to be less onerous than those which may be imposed upon aliens (i.e., persons from non-Commonwealth states). In the matter of admitted Commonwealth citizens' enjoying the privilege of the franchise, there is some variance in practice.

At the meeting of Commonwealth heads of government in London from January 7 to 15, 1969 (the first conference of its kind since 1966), while the matter of immigration to Britain was not on the agenda, there was occasion for informal discussion by some of the representatives on problems of migration between their respective countries. The spokesmen for these countries

---

43. *Nationality and Citizenship Laws of Countries of the Commonwealth,* British Information Service, R. 5024/67, p. 31.

requested the secretary-general to examine, in consultation with their respective countries' representatives, "general principles relating to short and long term movement of people between their countries, and to consider the possibility of exploring ways and means of studying this subject on a continuing basis with a view to providing relevant information to those governments." There was reaffirmation of the declaration made at prior conferences of this kind (such as those held in 1964 and 1965) that for all Commonwealth countries "it should be an objective of policy to build in each country a structure of society which offers equal opportunity and non-discrimination for all its people, irrespective of race, colour or creed." There was envisaged "constructive leadership in the application of democratic principles in a manner which will enable the people of each country or different racial and cultural groups to exist and develop as free and equal citizens." [44]

Since passage of the 1968 act a still tighter control of migration to Great Britain has had some advocacy. Edward Heath, the Conservative Party leader, was reported as saying to an enthusiastic Conservative group that legislation should be introduced immediately to give the government "complete control over immigration." The desire was to know what migrants were coming, whence they were coming, and where and for how long they were going to stay. As reported in the press, Heath said that the Conservative proposal "would enable the authorities here to make sure that, before anyone is allowed in, the social conditions and community resources in the area in which he wants to work are adequate and that an immigrant worker is needed in this country on economic grounds." Advocating a rule that the immigrant's permit to stay in Britain be renewable annually and that work permits be renewable with each change of job, the Conserv-

44. *Survey of British and Commonwealth Affairs*, British Information Service, III (1969), 95. According to press report, refusal of the British Government to assure delegates from Tanzania, Kenya, Uganda, and Zambia that the Commonwealth Immigrants Act, 1968, would be changed caused the representatives of these four states to boycott the talks. *New York Times*, Jan. 15, 1969, p. 18. For the United Kingdom, there was emphasis on Britain's unfettered right to control immigration, the fact that immigration had become a major issue in Britain, and that country's right to insure that the situation would not be aggravated. *Keesing's Contemporary Archives*, XVII (1969), 23181.

ative spokesman said that, "as with aliens, a decision as to whether a Commonwealth citizen is to be granted the status of permanent residence will be taken only after five years' residence, but not as a right and only on evidence of good character." The proposal "would put an end to abuses with which the present law fails to cope: false identities, false ages, false claims to relationship, phony fiancées and other abuses of this kind." [45]

The reaction to the Conservative Party leader's speech was apparently very strong. The leader of the Indian Workers Association (said to include five thousand members) reportedly called the speech "the most vicious and dangerous" one made up to that time by a politician discussing immigration. "In India," he is said to have warned, "people, if not the Government, will seize British investment and for every Indian forced to leave Britain an Englishman will be forced to leave India." Defending his proposal, Heath, according to the press, said that his sole object was to enable race relations to improve, and that his proposal was "consistent with Conservative Party policy that immigrants from the Commonwealth should be treated like people coming, for instance, from France, Sweden, West Germany or America." [46]

As was to be expected, there have been reports of hardships in East Africa for Indian businessmen who have migrated to that region and have been the objects of measures to "purge" them. The withdrawal of licenses to do business has apparently been followed by closing of shops to avoid notification that businesses would be wound up. As of January, 1969, there were said to be in Kenya some 160,000 persons of Indian origin (out of a total population in Kenya of some ten million) who had known since Kenya's becoming independent that the Kenya government would move to loosen the Indians' grip on the country's commerce (80 percent of which was said to be controlled by Indians). Kenya was not the only country in Africa where the problem had arisen, and there were said to have been purges in Tanzania and in Zambia. The *Sunday Nation*, an English-lan-

45. Thomas A. Johnson's dispatch, "Tory's Plan Shocks British Immigrants," *New York Times*, Jan. 27, 1969, p. 7.
46. Ibid.

guage newspaper in Kenya, in defense of the Kenya government policy said editorially that "the Government is being pilloried for trying to bring about a revolution in the economic life of the country peacefully and smoothly," adding that the fact of the affected traders' being Indians reflected the "old, old problem of the general coincidence of racial and class grouping."[47]

III

Aside from the broad lines of policy relating to immigration, law and practice concerning travel documents have an important part in the carrying out of what legislative bodies have laid down. Administrative measures for the implementation of policy, and general practice that has developed in connection with the rights of individual persons, will naturally have bearing upon the effect of general policy. A general review of such practice not being practicable in a brief study of issues involved, it is instructive to consider the subject from the point of view of British and American practice,[48] noting particularly points at which this practice may relate to general international law.

One of the critics of the Commonwealth Immigrants Act, 1968, proceeded from a legal standpoint in submitting that the Act "authorizes the violation of the duty imposed on the United Kingdom by international law to admit its own citizens." Observing that there were probably not more than a hundred thousand East Africans and Asians who "through choice or inadvertence

47. Reported in *New York Times*, Jan. 14, 1969, p. 2. The dilemma of Asians in Kenya is similar to that in other East African countries. The pattern of discrimination apparently varies from country to country. In Uganda, for example, there are said to have been boycotts, intimidation, and violence even before that state became independent in 1962. Zambia's President Kaunda said that "our Asian brothers and sisters must realize that when they are in Zambia they must identify themselves with Zambia. Many of them still cling to their British passports." According to the President, his feelings were shared by President Nyerere of Tanzania, President Obote of Uganda, and President Kenyatta of Kenya. President H. Kamuzu of Malawi is said to have solved the question of anti-Asian prejudice by refusing to recognize it; not only Asians, but also white persons, have reportedly been expelled from the country for profiteering. *New York Times*, Sept. 4, 1968, p. 27.

48. As mentioned above (n. 36), the Wilson Committee noted the practice of the United States, along with that of Canada, in its report.

did not acquire citizenship of the countries in which they reside within the required period after independence and who hold U.K. citizenship and U.K. passports" and who wished to come to the United Kingdom, the critic suggested that the United Kingdom could have achieved its purpose by administrative steps to withdraw the passports issued these persons. He notes, however, that this would have been a "shameful breach of international standards" and that no right of action would have accrued to the passport losers. The effect of the legislative action which was taken was thought to "narrow down" the category of persons deemed to "belong" to the United Kingdom. Legislation expressly discriminating on racial grounds or the denationalization of certain United Kingdom citizens, the writer noted, would have been "utterly repugnant" to international law. If an Asian trader residing in Kenya and having a United Kingdom passport and United Kingdom citizenship should be expelled from Kenya, then "as a matter of international law," the critic asserted, the United Kingdom would be obliged to admit him, if no other country would have him. Illustrative situations were suggested in support of the view that the legislation in question would "become ineffective once its application would constitute a direct breach of international law." [49]

While migration in general tends to touch more upon national laws and regulations than upon international law, the legality (in the international sense) of state action may be challenged by a state other than the enacting one,[50] and of course may be the occasion for challenge in a municipal court. In the case of states that are members of the Commonwealth the practice of legislating concerning what has come to be called the "common status" has drawn attention to the retention of a residue of rights for individuals—British subjects in the new sense of the term, citizens of the Commonwealth as a whole, or British-protected persons.[51] The effect had been to create a situation in which no citizen of any country of the Commonwealth was, in the full

49. Hepple, "Commonwealth Immigrants Act, 1968," pp. 425, 426.
50. Illustrated in the *French-Morocco Nationality Decrees* case, P.C.I.J., Ser. B, no. 4, 1923, and in the *Nottebohm* case, 1955 I.C.J. Rep. 4.
51. A summary treatment of the general subject is in Wilson and Clute, "Commonwealth Citizenship and Common Status."

sense of the term, an alien in any other. At the mid-twentieth century United Kingdom legislation envisaged continuance of the common status in what has sometimes been referred to as an "attenuated" form. As a summary statement has recently pointed out,

each of the countries of the Commonwealth has accepted the principle of the "common clause" which, as generally enacted, provides that "Every person who under this Act is a citizen of the United Kingdom and Colonies [or, as the case may be, a New Zealand citizen, etc.] or who under any enactment for the time being in force [in any other country of the Commonwealth] is a citizen of that country shall by virtue of that citizenship have the status of a British subject. . . . Any person having the status aforesaid may be known either as a British subject or as a Commonwealth citizen.[52]

The question whether the policy of the United Kingdom concerning migrants from other countries who are not only citizens of those countries (such as India and Pakistan) but also citizens of the United Kingdom and Colonies touches international law may be considered in the light of more than concepts concerning passports and other travel documents. A preliminary question relates to the distinction between nationality in the municipal law sense and in the international law sense. As one writer has noted,

the meaning of the term nationality in international law . . . may be both wider and narrower than its meaning as defined by municipal law. Persons may be regarded as nationals in the usage of international law who, for some reason or other, are not deemed to be nationals under the municipal law of the State concerned—as is the case with British Protected Persons—as long as that State is under a duty of international law to grant them a right of sojourn on a territory under its sovereignty and to admit them to such territory, and as long as its right of protection is recognised by international custom. On the other hand, persons may be considered not to be nationals of a certain State according to international law, although for certain reasons they may be deemed to be nationals under the municipal law of that State.[53]

52. *Nationality and Citizenship Laws of the Commonwealth*, British Information Service, R. 5024/67, p. 31. See also quotation from the same publication at p. 150 above.
53. Paul Weis, *Nationality and Statelessness in International Law* (1956), pp. 61–62.

As a matter of terminology, the term "nationality" is necessarily based on municipal law, but has come to have a distinctive meaning in international law, and is distinguishable from the term "citizenship." It is possible to have noncitizen nationals, as was formerly the case with American Indians living in the United States, and such a classification does not preclude the state's protecting their interests internationally.[54] In an international forum evidence of the nationality of an individual, as submitted by an applicant or respondent state, would have to be consistent with international law in order to be accepted by the international tribunal. While passports comprise prima facie evidence of nationality, the international tribunal would, in the last analysis, decide.[55]

On the matter of the international legal effect of a state's conferring its nationality upon natural persons, the decision of the International Court of Justice in the *Nottebohm* case,[56] with its emphasis upon the principle of there being a "genuine link" between the naturalizing state and the individual, seems likely to influence future decisions by, or in any case must be taken into account by, international tribunals.[57] Closer, however, to the case of Indians and Pakistanis in Kenya who, while holding passports attesting their citizenship in the United Kingdom and Colonies, have been restricted in their claimed right of migration to the British Isles, are precedents relating to the withdrawal of passports. In June, 1968, in the House of Lords the following question was placed on the Order Paper: "To ask Her Majesty's Government whether the protection afforded by the possession of a valid British passport is the normal right of a British-born subject

---

54. Robert R. Wilson, "Gradations of Citizenship and International Reclamations," *American Journal of International Law*, XXXIII (1939), 146–148.

55. Weis, *Nationality and Statelessness in International Law*, pp. 245–246. See also the same author's article, "The United Nations Convention on the Reduction of Statelessness, 1961," *International and Comparative Law Quarterly*, XI (1962), 1073–1096. In "Allegiance, Diplomatic Protection and Criminal Jurisdiction over Aliens," *Cambridge Law Journal*, IX (1945–1947), 330–348, Hersch Lauterpacht dealt with the celebrated case of *Joyce v. Director of Public Prosecutions* (1 All E.R. 186), decided in 1946, in which an alien who had obtained a British passport under false pretenses was convicted and executed.

56. 1955 I.C.J. Rep. 26.

57. See Ian Brownlie, "The Relations of Nationality in Public International Law," *British Yearbook of International Law*, XXXIX (1963), 284–364.

either in the United Kingdom or the Colonies; and for what, if any reasons it can be withheld or withdrawn."

The reply of the joint parliamentary under secretary of state for foreign affairs was as follows:

. . . the protection of a British-born subject does not derive from the possession of a passport but is the exercise of one of the normal functions of a sovereign State. No British subject has a legal right to a passport. The grant of a United Kingdom passport is a Royal prerogative exercised through Her Majesty's Ministers and, in particular, the Foreign Secretary.

The Foreign Secretary has the power to withhold or withdraw a passport at his discretion, although in practice such power is exercised only very rarely and in very exceptional cases. First, in the case of minors suspected of being taken illegally out of the jurisdiction; secondly, persons believed on good evidence to be fleeing the country in order to avoid prosecution for a criminal offence; thirdly, persons whose activities are so notoriously undesirable or dangerous that Parliament would be expected to support the action of the Foreign Secretary in refusing them a passport or withdrawing a passport already issued in order to prevent their leaving the United Kingdom; and fourthly, persons who have been repatriated to the United Kingdom at public expense and have not repaid the expenditure incurred on their behalf.[58]

There appears to be no general rule of international law that would preclude a state's restricting, through executive officers as well as through legislative enactments, the use of passports for purposes (such as travel to particular areas) upon the basis of evidence that such travel would not be in the public interest. Practice and judicial holdings in the United States support this view. On May 24, 1952, for example, the Department of State issued a press release which stated that "the Secretary of State has discretionary authority in the issuance of passports, both as a power inherent in the exercise of the Presidential authority to conduct foreign relations and as a matter of statutory law." There followed the statement that the Department of State had refused passports for many reasons; noted particularly were policy and practice relating to applicants who were believed to be Commu-

58. *Parl. Deb.* (L), 5th ser., vol. 209 (1958), c. 86.

nists and subversives.[59] That action with respect to refusal of passports is not, however, unlimited, finds illustration in the case of *Bauer* v. *Acheson,* in which the court concluded that revocation of the plaintiff's passport without notice and hearing before revocation, as also refusal to renew the passport without an opportunity for the holder to be heard, was without authority of law. The secretary of state, the court said, "should be directed to renew or revalidate the plaintiff's passport without the amendment making it valid only for return to the United States, unless a hearing is accorded her within a reasonable time." [60]

Further evidence of the authority exercisable by the secretary of state in the matter of passports is indicated in a 1966 decision involving an individual whose passport was withdrawn following his unauthorized travel to North Vietnam, his previous unauthorized travel to North Vietnam, and his unwillingness to assure the secretary of state that he would not use the passport (if it were restored to him) for travel to restricted areas. The evidence was

---

59. *Department of State Bulletin,* XXVI (1952), 919–920. In press conference remarks on another occasion the secretary of state noted the then current procedure of the Department of State. He said that "(1) only the Secretary of State may grant and issue passports in the United States . . . (2) passports shall be granted only to those owing allegiance, whether citizens or not, to the United States . . . (3) the Secretary of State is authorized in his discretion to refuse to issue a passport, to restrict it for use only in certain countries, to restrict it against use in certain countries, to withdraw or cancel issued passports, and to withdraw passports for the purpose of restricting their validity or use in certain countries . . . (4) the protection of the United States may be withdrawn from a person while he continues to reside abroad if such person has knowingly used, or attempted to use, his passport in violation of its conditions or restrictions or the provisions of the rules." Whiteman, *Digest of International Law,* VIII (1967), 255.

60. 106 F. supp. 445, 452–453 (D.D.C. 1952). After decision in this case the department published regulations having for their purpose to assure a hearing consonant with due process of law. A Board of Passport Appeals was established for persons who might be tentatively denied passports, and there was a right of appeal from adverse decisions upon their applications.

In 1955 a decision in *Schactman* v. *Dulles, Individually and as Secretary of State* involved denial of a passport solely because the applicant was on the attorney general's list of subversive organizations. The court said that for the court "to hold that the restraint thus imposed upon appellant is not arbitrary would amount to judicial approval of a deprivation of liberty without a reasonable relation to the conduct of foreign affairs. Unless some additional reason is supplied for the denial, a citizen is prevented indefinitely from traveling to Europe while at the same time it is impossible for him to remove the cause, even though we must assume in the present state of the pleadings that he would be able to do so if afforded the opportunity." 225 F. 2nd 938, 943–944 (D.C. Cir. 1955). The government did not appeal the decision and did not grant Schactman a new hearing, but did grant him a passport. Whiteman, *Digest of International Law,* VIII (1967), 257.

found to be sufficient for denial of the plaintiff's motion.[61] In the *Frank* case a writer was refused validation of his American passport when he wished to go to China at the invitation of the Chinese Communist government to lecture at the University of Peking. When, in 1957, the secretary of state decided that it was in the interest of the United States to allow a specified number of American newsmen to enter Communist China, Frank sought validation of his passport on the ground that he was a representative of several Spanish-language newspapers of Latin America. The District Court and the Court of Appeals of the District of Columbia decided against Frank, Judge Burger of the Court of Appeals saying in a concurring opinion,

It is axiomatic that the conduct of foreign affairs necessarily involves flexible measures and policies which can be adjusted to meet changing conditions. . . .

In the implementation of our foreign policy . . . the State Department recently concluded that a limited number, approximately 40, news representatives would be permitted to go to the Chinese mainland, on an experimental and temporary basis, provided the forces in control of the area would receive them. . . .

Our duty is not to decide whether the Secretary of State has developed the best formula and criteria for this "experimental and temporary program, . . ." but simply whether he has exceeded his authority in acting as he has thus far.[62]

In the case of a congressman who applied for validation of his passport in order that he might travel to Communist China in search of information to be used in his legislative duties, the federal court's decision was against the congressman, the Court of Appeals saying that the issue was "merely between a claim of an inherent right asserted in his individual capacity by a member of the legislative branch, and the plenary power of the executive branch asserted by it in relation to and in its conduct of the Nation's foreign affairs." [63]

61. Unreported case, Whiteman, *Digest of International Law,* VIII (1967), 276–277.

62. *Waldo Frank v. Christian A. Herter, Secretary of State,* 269 F. 2nd 245, 248, 249 (D.C. Cir. 1959); certiorari denied, 361 U.S. 918 (1959).

63. *Charles O. Porter v. Christian A. Herter, Individually and as Secretary of State,* 278 F. 2nd 280, 282 (D.C. Cir. 1960); certiorari denied 361 U.S. 918 (1959), 3–4; 364 U.S. 837 (1960).

American courts have also had occasion to decide whether action by the secretary of state in a matter involving a passport application may be based upon the use of confidential information in the files of the Department of State. In the *Boudin* case a district court ruled that the right of a quasi-judicial hearing must mean more than the right to permit an applicant to testify and present evidence, that it must "include the right to know that the decision will be based upon evidence of which he is aware and can refute directly," and that all "evidence upon which the [Passport] Office may rely for its decision under Section 51.135 must appear on record so that the applicant may have the opportunity to meet it and the court to review it." The Court of Appeals returned the case for more specific findings of fact by the secretary of state, saying,

We do not reach . . . the contention made by Boudin that the Secretary [of State] cannot rely on confidential information in reaching his decision. But since that question may arise at a subsequent stage, we think the Secretary should—if he refuses a passport to Boudin after the further consideration we have ordered—state whether his findings are based on the evidence openly produced, or (in whole or in material part) on secret information not disclosed to the applicant. If the latter, the Secretary should explain with such particularity as in his judgment the circumstances permit the nature of the reasons why such information may not be disclosed.[64]

---

64. *Boudin* v. *Dulles, Secretary of State*, 235 F. 2nd 532, 536 (D.C. Cir. 1956). Subsequent developments with respect to the principal questions are summarized in Whiteman, *Digest of International Law*, VIII (1967), 312–317. Testifying in 1959 before the House Committee on Foreign Affairs, the administrator for security and consular affairs, Department of State, said that the court of appeals in the *Boudin* case and in three other cases had held that confidential information "is something upon which the Secretary [of state] can rely." *Hearings before the Comm. on For. Affairs, H.R., 86th Cong., 1st Sess., on HR. 9069 and other Bills Relating to the Issuance of Passports*, as partially reproduced in Whiteman, p. 313.

On Canadian passport practice, see reply from the Canadian Department of External Affairs to a recent enquiry from a high commission in Ottawa, which reply stated in part:

> There are no Canadian restrictions on travel. In peace-time a Canadian citizen is normally free, so far as Canadian law is concerned, to leave Canada [and is readmissible as of right] . . . .
> There is no statute governing the issuance of Canadian passports and no person has a legal entitlement to one. In Canada the legal position is that the Secretary of State [for External Affairs] has discretionary power to issue or withhold a passport.

Canadian Yearbook of International Law, VI (1968), 278.

In the wider (international) community the necessity for and the utility of travel documents have been under discussion at various times, particularly over the past two decades. The First International Conference of National Travel Organizations, held in 1947, recommended that the United Nations convene an official conference on the simplification of frontier formalities. Later the secretary-general of the United Nations called a meeting at Geneva in 1947 of experts on passports, visas, and frontier formalities. One of the subjects the experts considered was the possible return to the system that had existed before 1914, with the abolition of passports and the substitution, in lieu thereof, of identity documents such as those already in the possession of most countries. The committee concluded that abolition of passports was not feasible at that time. At a United Nations Conference on International Trade and Tourism held at Rome in 1963 the conclusion reached was that, while some countries had abolished passports on a regional basis, abolition on a worldwide basis was still not feasible.[65]

The current British position, which is relevant to action that might be taken with respect to holders of passports of the United Kingdom and Colonies, is presumably not basically different from that of the 1950's when there were fewer independent states that were members of the Commonwealth. When asked in 1954 whether the British secretary of state for home affairs would consider raising in proper channels the matter of the possible abolition of passports, the joint under secretary of state for foreign affairs said in the House of Commons,

Any British subject can leave this country without a passport, but I know of no country where he is likely to be received if he arrives without a passport. . . . [T]he Geneva Convention on Passport and Frontier Formalities recommended that the general abolition of the passport for purposes of foreign travel is not feasible at present.[66]

Nearly five years later, in a written answer to a question concerning the abolition of passports, the joint under secretary of state for foreign affairs said:

65. U.N. Conf. on Int. Trade and Tourism, Recommendations, Rome, 21 Aug.–3 Sept., 1963, U.N. Doc. E/CONF.47/18, pp. 6, 7; ECOSOC Res. 995 (XXXVI).
66. *Parl. Deb.* (C), 5th ser., vol. 525 (1954), c. 816.

It is still the position that British subjects traveling abroad need to be able to establish readily their identity and nationality both to facilitate their passage through the various frontier controls and in the event of their requiring the assistance and protection of their own Government. It is the view of Her Majesty's Government that the passport is the most satisfactory document for these purposes.

Every effort has been made to simplify both the passport and the arrangements for its issue, but some safeguards are essential in order to assure that passports are granted only to people entitled to hold them.[67]

IV

The general practice followed in Anglo-American applications of national law with respect to nationality and to travel documents attesting the status of persons is but indirectly connected with the contemporary issue involving restraint upon Indian and Pakistani persons in Kenya who desire to migrate to Great Britain. The broad statement that every state has an obligation under international law to admit its own citizens might be difficult to establish, although there would appear to have been considerable support for such a proposition. Protocol number 4 to the European Convention for the Protection of Human Rights and Fundamental Freedoms—to which, as of April, 1969, the United Kingdom had not become a party—provides that "no one shall be deprived of the right to enter the territory of the state of which he is a national." [68] It is possible to envisage a situation in which further admission of persons, even its own nationals, to a state might mean some deprivation for persons already resident in the state. A comparable right might be that of asylum, as to which recent research has supported the view that the state in which asylum is sought has the right, but not the duty, to admit the person seeking asylum, rather than the fugitive's having the right to enter the state in which he seeks asylum.[69] Established (cus-

67. Ibid., vol. 598 (1959), cc. 30–31 (written answers).
68. Art. 3, para. 2.
69. Hamid H. Kizilbash, "United Nations Discussions on Asylum as an International Human Right," *Journal of Research* (*Humanities*), University of Punjab, II (1967), 123–154.

tomary) international law has traditionally emphasized the right of a state to protect its nationals rather than the *duty* to protect them, or duty to receive them into a particular part of its territory if they, or their parents, have not previously resided therein.

The International Covenant on Economic, Cultural, and Social Rights asserts in its article 24(3) that every child has the right to acquire a nationality, and the following article looks to every citizen's right and opportunity to take part in the conduct of public affairs, to vote and be eligible for election at genuine, periodic elections, and to have access (on general terms of equality) to public service in his country. Article 26 seeks to protect against discrimination on the grounds, among others, of race, color, national or social origin, birth, or other status. The current issue in Great Britain concerning migration from East Africa is relatable to Britain's traditional inclusion in its citizenry of persons of various ethnic origin within the territory of the United Kingdom and Colonies. The very right to enter the country has now been denied to many persons on the basis of the claimed need for protecting the economic welfare of the country. The potential migrants are no longer "subjects" in the traditional nineteenth-century meaning of the term, but citizens of the United Kingdom and Colonies, with the moral (if not the enforceable legal) right to be accorded treatment that is reasonable in light of the situation of the totality of other citizens now resident in Great Britain. If the administration of the legislation recently coming into force concerning migrants is carried out so as to avoid unnecessary hardship to individuals—as, for example, through having reasonable quotas and allowing a right of appeal to courts in cases where grave hardships may result from exclusion—there would seem to be little possibility of securing more favorable treatment, such as the termination of substantially all restrictions upon all potential citizen-migrants.

Traditionally, the regulation of immigration has been a matter for each state to determine for itself, customary international law not limiting a state's right to decide who shall be admitted to its territory. In this area the concept of "domestic jurisdiction" has continued to be invoked, however limited it has been or may come to be by the doctrine of "international concern." In the past, considerations of race have affected policies of some Commonwealth states, although they have not been the only communities to limit admission on this basis. Since international law finds application mostly in terms of "nationals" rather than citizens, it has been possible under that law for states to have gradations and even to have some noncitizen nationals. While the power of a state to confer its citizenship is not unlimited, the transition from Empire to Commonwealth has been marked by the inclusion of many persons of the newly independent states in the category of citizens of the United Kingdom and Colonies. The limitation of the rights of such persons in the matter of migration to the British Isles has placed great strain upon the principle that every person has the right to enter "his own country." Recent legislation in Great Britain having limited such right of Asian persons who are citizens of their respective countries (such as India or Pakistan) but who also are citizens of the United Kingdom and Colonies, accusations that racial bias has affected policy-making have been answered by arguments based upon claimed economic necessity. There has also been acknowledgment by national courts that in its general interest a state may, through withdrawal of ordinary passports or other travel documents, exercise the right of protecting its own interests.

The matter of basic human rights has come into discussion, although there has not yet been acceptance, by the principal state involved in the issue with respect to migration to Great Britain, of international covenants that might have bearing upon the extent of authority which a state may exercise over its own nationals. The Universal Declaration of Human Rights asserts (article 13[2]) that "everyone has the right to leave any country, including his own." Such rights, however, are not unqualified. By the following paragraph of the covenant (article 13[3]), "The above-mentioned rights shall not be subject to any restriction except those which are provided by law, are necessary to protect national security, public order (*ordre public*), public health or morals or the health or morals of others, and are consistent with other rights recognized in the present Covenant." There follows the statement (article 13[4]) that "no one shall be *arbitrarily* deprived of the right to enter his own country." [70] Pending the more universal acceptance of the covenant provisions, as also of protocol 4 to the European Convention for the Protection of Human Rights and Fundamental Freedoms, reasonable regulation of the type of migration to Great Britain which present United Kingdom legislation applies would seem to be justifiable without doing violence to presently accepted international law. From the point of view of humanitarianism as well as legalism, such reasonableness would seem to be evidenced through a system of appeals (by potential migrants) from administrative rulings to judicial agencies, as provided for in the Immigration Appeals Act, 1969. [71]

70. Emphasis added. On the point that the British Parliament's creation of a citizenship of the United Kingdom and Colonies did not of itself confer on them a right of free movement between British territories see J. E. S. Fawcett, *The Application of the European Convention on Human Rights* (1969), p. 60.

71. Eliz. 2, c. 21. This act provides for a two-tiered appellate authority comprising an immigration tribunal and adjudicators. There are rights of appeal to this authority against action taken under the Commonwealth Immigrants Act, 1962. Clause 13 permits appeals to be taken in connection with the admission and removal of aliens by order in council under the Aliens Restriction Acts. An exception is made as to appeals against deportation following conviction of a criminal offense; such a convicted person may, however, appeal against a decision to deport him to a particular country. The bill provides for the home secretary to make grants toward expenditures incurred by voluntary organizations concerned with the welfare of immigrants to provide welfare advisory services for persons appealing under the immigration appeals bill. The legislation is the subject of comment in *Survey of British and Commonwealth Affairs*, III (1969), 153.

6

Defense

The evolution of communities from colonies through self-governing status to full statehood as independent members of the Commonwealth has involved considerable alteration of the United Kingdom's responsibilities. There has been, however, a continuing assumption of the need for protective armed forces in wide geographical areas. At the same time the issue of defense, and particularly the relation to it of rights and duties of states in general, has come to have new significance with the development of public international organization and the general acceptance of new rights and duties concerning threats to the peace, breaches of the peace, or acts of aggression. Invocation or application of public international law becomes relevant not only in relation to traditional responsibilities of Great Britain but also from the point of view of United Nations Charter provisions. To be considered in this context are (a) the general background of British responsibility for arrangements looking to the protection of the Empire and later Commonwealth, and the attempted adaptation of policy to new conditions following World War II; (b) regional defense agreements, particularly as illustrated in British commitments to Malaysia and Singapore; and (c) in connection with the development of newer kinds of forces (such as that in Cyprus) the evolution of rules of international law relating to the authority, status as regards immunities, and functions of such forces.

I

Viscount Castlereagh is credited with having observed that Britain's policy was to secure the Empire against future attack and that to do this there had been acquisition of " 'the keys of every great military position' in the world." [1] This would seem to presuppose that such positions were well known, and that there could be adaptation to changing techniques in warfare. There was also the possibility that concepts of the *duty* of defending might not remain the same. In the nineteenth century a change in the conception of the obligation of imperial defense was developing, one view being that the grant of representative institutions to the outlying communities carried with it the idea of their defending themselves, such conception as there was of strategy and imperial defense in the nineteenth century being "only to strengthen the effects of this purely political approach." [2] By the early years of the twentieth century there had come into existence a Committee of Imperial Defence—a prime minister's committee, which is said to have provided a model for the American Joint Chiefs of Staff and for the Allied Combined Chiefs of Staff in World War II.[3] After the conclusion of that war the United Kingdom moved to provide for future defense in the light of experience, and the matter became an important subject of discussion at the meeting of Commonwealth prime ministers in 1946. At that time the question arose whether, if regional defense was to be the accepted plan, the Committee of Imperial Defence would cease to exist or would have its own branches in the several regions involved. There was also a question whether, if

1. N. H. Gibbs, "The Origins of Imperial Defence," an inaugural lecture at Oxford, 1955, p. 4. On the late nineteenth- and early twentieth-century developments relating to the general subject, see Donald C. Gordon, *The Dominion Partnership in Imperial Defense* (1965), especially chaps. 2, 3, and 5.
2. Gibbs, "The Origins of Imperial Defence," pp. 6–7. One naval officer is reported as saying late in the Victorian period, "We looked on the Navy more as a World Police Force than as a warlike institution. We considered that our job was to safeguard law and order throughout the world—safeguard civilization." Vice Admiral Humphrey H. Smith, *A Yellow Admiral Remembers* (1932), p. 54; quoted after Gordon, *The Dominion Partnership in Imperial Defense*, p. 47.
3. Gibbs, "The Origins of Imperial Defence," p. 24.

defense was to be under treaty arrangements, the respective parties thereto would have to approve the actual machinery that would need to be created.[4] A White Paper of October, 1946, set forth the basis for the new regional defense idea. Among the commitments were those for "the maintenance of internal security and settled conditions throughout the Empire" and "the safeguarding of . . . communications and the upkeep of . . . bases." During World War II, it was asserted, collaboration with the dominions and India had been "comprehensive, continuous and effective"; and there was mention of the "long accepted principle" whereby His Majesty's forces throughout the Empire had been "trained, organised, and equipped on the same basis," this principle having "proved its value in . . . all theatres of war."[5]

The need for cooperative action within the Commonwealth had been demonstrated, and there developed the idea of individual states' determining their own policies. As one observer has said, with respect to Canada, "The first Dominion at the outset had established a principle that was to be basic for the Commonwealth of the future—that the constituent nations must have full and unquestioned control of their military affairs and of their own forces." He points out, however, that Canada was not yet prepared to defend itself or to contribute sufficiently to the common defense, and that military autonomy "long rested uncomfortably upon the shoulders of the young Dominion."[6] In a statement made shortly after World War I there had been official assertion that

---

4. W. C. B. Tunstall, *The Commonwealth and Regional Defence* (1959), p. 17.

5. Cmd. 6743. There was acknowledgment of the "tremendous efforts put forward in the common cause by the whole Commonwealth and Empire." Early in 1944 Australia and New Zealand had set forth in an agreement that "within the framework of a general system of world security, a regional zone of defence comprising the South West and South Pacific areas" should be established. *New Zealand Treaty Series,* 1944, no. 1, 18 UNTS 537. In a presentation of a "Central Organisation of Defence" in October, 1946, para. 36 related to cooperation for defense, which was to be developed by continuous consultation of all defense matters of mutual interest, the organizing, training, and exercising of the armed forces under a common doctrine, joint planning, interchange of staffs, and coordination of policy. Cmd. 6923.

6. Richard A. Preston, *Canada and "Imperial Defense"* (1967), p. 82.

whatever may be the decision of Canada at the present juncture, Great Britain will not in any circumstances fail in her duty to the Oversea Dominions of the Crown.

She has before now successfully made head alone and unaided against the most formidable combinations [of the greatest military powers] and she has not lost her capacity [even if left wholly unsupported, of being able] by a wise policy and strenuous exertions to watch over and preserve the vital interests of the Empire.[7]

A *Statement on Defence* (1952) reflected the broadened basis of the cooperation envisaged in the common interest. Its section 6, on cooperation with the Commonwealth and other countries, affirmed that the defense policy of the United Kingdom continued to be based on the closest possible cooperation with other Commonwealth countries and with those of the North Atlantic Treaty Organization. It also stated that a conference of ministers from Australia, New Zealand, South Africa, and Southern Rhodesia had been held to consider defense problems in "regions of common concern," including the Middle East. The defense problems of this area and the related problems of Southeast Asian defense had been examined in the light of the defense contributions each of the governments participating in the conference could make. The governments of Australia, New Zealand, and South Africa had accepted invitations of the United Kingdom, the United States, and France to join with them and other interested governments in setting up an Allied Command Organization in the Middle East. Units from the United Kingdom, Canada, Australia, and New Zealand, it was pointed out, were serving with the United Nations forces in Korea, and forces from

7. Cd. 6513. On Imperial defense between the two world wars, see Lord Hankey, *Government Control in War* (1945), pp. 66–67. W. C. B. Tunstall observed, of the Committee of Imperial Defence between the two world wars, that it was a device for advising the United Kingdom and no more. *The Commonwealth and Regional Defence*, p. 9.

Soon after the ending of hostilities in World War II there was occasion for discussion between the United States and certain Commonwealth countries concerning jurisdictional rights over areas in the Pacific. See generally, *Foreign Relations*, V (1946), 1–49. In this connection the Department of State said, in Annex A of a memorandum to the Australian Legation: "The United States possesses rights . . . to have exclusive jurisdiction over United States military personnel present in the Admiralty Islands in the exercise of the rights accorded." Ibid., p. 19. In the United States view, this point would be covered by United States rights under international law, but the inclusion of this specific provision might be desirable.

Australia, New Zealand, and Southern Rhodesia had cooperated with the United Kindgom and colonial troops in Malaya.[8]

In line with the new policy outlook, there was some withdrawal of British forces from bases which had in the past assumed relatively large importance from the standpoint of Imperial and Commonwealth planning. Withdrawals from Ceylon provide illustration. On the eve of Ceylon's assuming fully responsible government within the Commonwealth, the drafting of a defense agreement, to take effect when Ceylon's new constitutional status was attained, looked to this new state's granting all the necessary facilities to the British, while the United Kingdom was to help in the training and development of forces.[9] The British were, in particular, to have the use of the naval base at Trincomalee and the air station at Katunayake. Less than a decade later, however, the government in power at Colombo took the position that British retention of these bases was not consistent with Ceylon's sovereignty. Agreement was reached through an exchange of letters in 1956 whereby Britain was to hand over the bases but might retain facilities for communication and storage; the training of troops by the British was to continue. Limited use of facilities might also continue until 1962, but the Ceylonese retained the right to withhold use from the British if any situation should arise in which, in pursuance of its general international policy, the Ceylonese government should find it necessary to do this.[10]

An authoritative observer has expressed the opinion that if warships of one Commonwealth state cannot make full use of the ports and anchorage of another Commonwealth state on a cobelligerency basis, the exercise of British sea power will be greatly and perilously restricted.[11] The loss of the use of particular naval

8. Cmd. 8475, Sec. VI, paras. 59, 60, 61.
9. Cmd. 7257.
10. Cmnd. 197. There was further understanding to the effect that if any difficulties in this connection should arise the two governments would consult together in order to arrive at a satisfactory conclusion. In connection with the carrying out of the agreement, there was reference to a "rundown" period, which could be extended by mutual agreement of the parties.
11. Tunstall, p. 66. Tunstall suggested (pp. 64–65) that at the time of his writing the notion of Commonwealth defense was only understandable in terms of the regional alliances of the individual members.

or air bases, such as had been available in Ceylon, could not always be offset by acquisition of bases elsewhere in the same general region, as was apparently shown by the British experience with an air post in the Maldive Islands, where conditions were said to make the establishment of a base unsuitable.[12] Furthermore, the achievement of complete independence by the states associated in the Commonwealth has apparently underlined the factor of explicit commitment as a base for legal obligation. While such a Commonwealth state as India has seemed to avoid such commitments, the same has not been true of Malaya (and later Malaysia), concerning which part of the Commonwealth the issue of defense, and the commitment of Great Britain with reference thereto, would seem to invite analysis by legalists as well as by politicians and news commentators.

II

Simultaneously with Malayan independence, the British-Malayan Agreement on External Defence and Mutual Assistance (selected as an illustration here in preference to the later short-lived defense pact that Great Britain made with Nigeria, which lasted only a year, being abrogated in 1962, only fifteen months after Nigeria's attainment of independence) came into effect in September, 1957.[13] By its Article I the United Kingdom was to

12. Cmnd. 662. While South Africa was still a member of the Commonwealth there had been (in 1955) an exchange of letters on defense between South Africa and the United Kingdom, together with a memorandum on the need for international discussions with regard to regional defense, which included a statement that the defense of Southern Africa against external aggression lay not only in Africa but in the gateways to Africa, including Southern Africa and the Middle East. In an annex there was reference to the transfer of the naval base at Simonstown and to arrangements for its future use; agreement on this was to "remain in force until such time as the two Governments decide otherwise by mutual agreement." Cmd. 9520.

13. Cmd. 263. The relevant parts of the agreement are:
Art. VI. In the event of a threat of an armed attack against any of the territories or forces of the Federation of Malaya or any of the territories or protectorates of the United Kingdom in the Far East or any of the forces of the United Kingdom within those territories or protectorates or within the Federation of Malaya, or other threat to the preservation of peace in the Far East, the Governments of the Federation of Malaya and of the United Kingdom will consult together on the measures to be taken jointly or separately to ensure the fullest co-

assist Malaya in the external defense of its territory. Britain was also to assist with the training and development of the armed forces of the newborn federation. Malaya, in turn, agreed to Britain's maintaining in the federation such naval, land, and air forces (including a Commonwealth Strategic Reserve) as should be agreed upon by the two governments as necessary to the carrying out of Commonwealth and international obligations. There was preambular mention of the fact that Australia and New Zealand proposed to associate themselves with the British-Malayan agreement. There was what would appear to be a clear indication of the United Kingdom's right to withdraw British forces from the territory of the federation, but also stated is the obligation of Great Britain to consult with Malaya in the event of Britain's decision to withdraw the forces. Neither party, however, made any explicit commitment to come to the assistance of the other except as indicated in the terms of the agreement itself.

At the time the 1957 British-Malayan agreement was concluded, Singapore was still under the control of the Colonial Office and was therefore not directly involved, in a legal sense, by the agreement. Singapore as a Crown Colony, however, was inevitably affected by what Malaya and the United Kingdom would do in the matter of defense in the general region. At the time of

---

operation between them for the purpose of meeting the situation effectively.

Art. VII. In the event of an armed attack against any of the territories or forces of the Federation of Malaya or any of the territories or protectorates of the United Kingdom in the Far East or any of the forces of the United Kingdom within any of those territories or protectorates or within the Federation of Malaya, the Governments of the Federation of Malaya and of the United Kingdom undertake to cooperate with each other and will take such action as each considers necessary for the purpose of meeting the situation effectively.

Art. VIII. In the event of a threat to the preservation of peace or the outbreak of hostilities elsewhere than in the area covered by Articles VI and VII the Government of the United Kingdom shall obtain the prior agreement of the Government of the Federation of Malaya before committing United Kingdom forces to active operations involving the use of bases in the Federation of Malaya; but this shall not affect the right of the Government of the United Kingdom to withdraw forces from the Federation of Malaya.

With this may be compared the reported agreement between the United Kingdom and Mauritius signed in March, 1968, concerning the existing rights and facilities in Mauritius, the agreement to run for six years. *Guardian,* Jan. 28, 1968.

the creation of the state of Malaysia, of which Singapore became a part, there was wording in the federation agreement whereby the prior agreement between Great Britain and Malaya was to apply to Malaysia, with a proviso that the government of Malaysia would allow the British government the right to continue to use "the bases and other facilities at present occupied by their Service authorities within the State of Singapore" and "would permit the Government of the United Kingdom to make such use of these and other facilities as that Government may consider necessary for the purpose of assisting in the defence of Malaysia, and for Commonwealth defence and for the preservation of the peace in South-East Asia." [14]

As a sequel to the conclusion of the British-Malaya (later British-Malaysia) agreement concerning defense, probably the most publicized development has been the announcement by the British government of its plan to withdraw its forces from Malaysia and Singapore. In July, 1967, Prime Minister Wilson, speaking on this subject, reemphasized that the British government intended to withdraw from Malaysia and Singapore by the mid-1970's and said that to delay this move too long was "the very way of provoking instability in the area." [15] The government motion was approved in the Commons by a vote of 297 to 230. On the following January 16 the Prime Minister announced that British forces would be withdrawn from the Far East (except Hong Kong) by the end of 1971 instead of by the mid-1970's and would also be withdrawn from the Persian Gulf by that date. The number of aircraft based on Cyprus, he also said, would be reduced. The Prime Minister continued:

We have . . . decided to accelerate the withdrawal of our forces from their stations in the Far East which was announced in the Supplementary State of Defence Policy of July 1967 (Cmnd. 3357) and

14. Cmnd. 2094 (1963), art. 6. Professor L. C. Green, former dean of the Law School at the University of Singapore, has expressed the opinion, concerning the effect of the last-quoted language, that it "would appear to be an amendment of the original agreement, giving the United Kingdom sole discretion as to when and how the Singapore bases . . . could be activated." Article entitled "Malaya/Singapore/Malaysia," in *Canadian Yearbook of International Law*, IV (1966), 3–42, at 33.
15. *Parl. Deb.* (C), 5th ser., vol. 750 (1966–1967), cc. 2472–2474.

to withdraw them by the end of 1971. We have also decided to withdraw our forces from the Persian Gulf by the same date. The broad effect is that, apart from our remaining Dependencies and certain other necessary exceptions, we shall by that date not be maintaining military bases outside Europe and the Mediterranean.

Again, by that date, we shall have withdrawn our forces from Malaysia and Singapore: We have told both Governments that we do not thereafter plan to retain a special military capability for use in the area. But we have assured them both, and our other Commonwealth partners and allies concerned, that we shall retain a general capability based in Europe—including the United Kingdom—which can be deployed overseas as, in our judgment, circumstances demand, including support for United Nations operations.[16]

The Prime Minister also drew attention to the fact that during a recent visit to Kuala Lumpur Commonwealth Secretary George Thomson had told the government of Malaysia that the British wished to reach a new understanding with them concerning the Anglo-Malaysian Agreement and to make it fit changed conditions. The Prime Minister pointed out that the agreement itself contained provisions for a review of this nature; other governments had been assured of Britain's continued interest in the maintenance of security in Southeast Asia with the forces that would be available in Great Britain. "Meanwhile," the Prime Minister noted,

if our Commonwealth partners so desire and mutually satisfactory arrangements can be made, we would be prepared to assist them in establishing a future joint air defence system for Malaysia and Singapore and in training personnel to operate it. We have informed the Governments of Malaysia and Singapore that we will discuss with them the aid implications of our accelerated withdrawal. We shall amend our force declarations to S.E.A.T.O. as our forces in the area are run down.

Great Britain's decisions, the Prime Minister added, had been made in the knowledge of her allies that were directly concerned.[17]

There followed, at a five-state meeting held in Kuala Lumpur on June 10 and 11, 1968, discussion of defense problems arising

16. Ibid., vol. 756 (1967–1968), cc. 1580–1581.
17. Ibid., cc. 1581, 1582.

out of the British government's decision. At this meeting the representatives of Malaysia and Singapore, respectively, made it clear that they regarded the defense of their two countries as indivisible. Participants in the talks apparently felt that there should be a new understanding concerning the Anglo-Malaysian Defence Agreement and that consultations would be necessary to that end. British Secretary for Defence Healy in a statement on June 17 reiterated that the British decision to leave Southeast Asia by 1971 did not mean that the British were turning their backs on an area in which Britain had "deep historic ties." He explained that while the British would not maintain a "special capacity" for use outside Europe, British forces based in Europe would be rapidly deployed in the Southeast Asia area if Britain should judge it necessary.[18] Mrs. Ghandi, India's prime minister, had been reported as saying in a press conference at Canberra on May 22 that the security of Southeast Asia was the responsibility of states in that area; she had predicted that nations in the area would become strong, as had India.[19]

The extent of the legal commitments of Great Britain to Malaysia and Singapore with respect to the defense of these states became the subject of considerable speculation in the press during 1968 and 1969. Some of this was directed to the possible connection between British obligations under the SEATO treaty and those under arrangements with Malaysia and Singapore. A correspondent in Bonn, asserting that Britain had virtually ended its military commitments to SEATO as a result of cuts in military spending, said that other SEATO members had demanded Britain's expulsion (along with that of France and Pakistan) for failure to support the war in Vietnam—Britain having from the start argued that the SEATO treaty did not commit the country to military support beyond what Britain chose to give, and article 4 of the treaty being to the effect that in the event of armed attack on the treaty area each signatory state would act to meet the common danger in accordance with its military processes.[20]

18. Ibid., vol. 766 (1967–1968), cc. 713–715.
19. *Keesing's Contemporary Archives*, XVI (1968), 22941.
20. *Japan Times*, Jan. 9, 1968.

Referring to the visit of the Commonwealth secretary to Kuala Lumpur and Singapore in January, 1968, an editorial comment from within the region said that the secretary had come to Malaysia to inform, not to negotiate.[21] The secretary himself was reported as saying that Britain did not intend to leave SEATO but that, as British forces ran down, its commitments would have to be adjusted.[22] He was elsewhere reported as saying that the treaty with Malaysia was binding on Britain and that the British "would honor it, of course."[23] With further reference to the same treaty, there was the observation that the text of the agreement said that Britain would give Malaysia such assistance as that state might require, but that elsewhere it merely said Britain would "consult" its partners over major changes in forces.[24]

Still other editorial comment noted that the British and other Commonwealth states were in Malaysia and Singapore under "a mixture of treaties, *ad hoc* agreements and informal invitations." From all this there had emerged "one simple and indispensable thing—a unified command," described as "British, acceptable and even popular"; the writer suggested that all the way from Wellington to Kuala Lumpur the question was being asked of what was to replace it.[25] There was some suggestion of possible embarrassment if the treaty objective should be made completely explicit.[26]

Apparently there came to be general agreement, in the course of 1968, on the need for reviewing the Anglo-Malaysian-Singapore arrangements concerning regional defense. In August of that year the defense minister of Malaysia, Tun Abdul Razak, was reported as saying that the defense treaty would definitely be

21. *Straits Times* (Malaysian ed.), Jan. 10, 1968.
22. *Evening Standard*, Jan. 12, 1968.
23. *Times* (London), Jan. 13, 1968.
24. *Sunday Telegraph*, Jan. 14, 1968. The reference was apparently to Article I as contrasted with Art. VII.
25. *Daily Telegraph*, Feb. 29, 1968.
26. An officer of the Institute of International Relations at the Australian National University was reported as saying that he did not expect a full-scale defense pact to emerge among Britain, Australia, New Zealand, Singapore, and Malaysia. "If they (Singapore and Malaysia) did press the case for a formal alliance between the five countries, they would be asked the embarrassing question. 'Whom is this alliance meant to be against'—and the answer would be either Indonesia or another and either of these would be more embarrassing than the question." *Straits Times* (Malaysian ed.), Feb. 16, 1968.

reviewed after 1971.[27] In the meantime, Great Britain had paid to Malaysia the first installment of an amount to offset the effects of British withdrawal. According to a British Information Services release, the payment was the first since the exchange of letters in July, 1968, which brought into force the Special Aid Agreement that had been announced in the British Parliament on the previous May thirtieth.[28] In October, 1968, a news dispatch from Australia noted the existence of a "vague feeling in Australia, which regretably has to be reported," that the British might not come back to Australia but that they might feel obliged (by treaty) to help others in the area of Australia.[29] Tengku Abdul Rahman of Malaysia was reported as saying to the Imperial Defence College that Commonwealth defense partnership was not only very important for the security of his country and of Singapore but that it was also necessary for the protection of trade routes that were vital to the free world and "in a very real sense" for the safety of Australia and New Zealand as well.[30] There were to be further talks in February, 1969, in which Great Britain and the Commonwealth states most directly concerned would participate, concerning the safety of the region after 1971.[31]

From the point of view of positive legal commitments, it appears that the Anglo-Malaysian agreement, while clearly envisag-

27. *Straits Times* (Malaysian ed.), Aug. 21, 1968.
28. Ibid., Aug. 29, 1968.
29. Stuart Harris's dispatch from Rockhampton, Queensland, as reported in the *Times* (London), Oct. 8, 1968.
30. Ibid., Jan. 24, 1969. Shortly afterward the Malaysian leader was reported as saying that, as to the defense agreement, there would be no abrogation of it, but that its terms must be modified to suit defense arrangements due to the accelerated pull-out of British troops, and that when Malaysia and Singapore parted, one of the conditions had been that Singapore would work closely with Malaysia in matters of defense and economy. He envisaged a nonaggression pact, such as he said could be included in any treaty of friendship between the two countries, and favored a neutrality pact under which the two states would agree to make the region neutral in the event of war or trouble of that sort. *Straits Times* (Malaysian ed.), Feb. 1, 1968.
31. *Daily Telegraph*, Dec. 20, 1968. A later press comment noted what was described as the "sheer uncertainty" about what status the Anglo-Malaysian defense agreement would have after the British withdrawal. Australia and New Zealand, it was noted, had attached themselves to the general principles by an exchange of letters with the governments concerned. Any attempt to spell out the full range of contingencies was regarded as more difficult for the ANZAC countries than for Great Britain. *Straits Times* (Malaysian ed.), March 1, 1969.

ing retention by the United Kingdom of the *right* to send or withhold forces for the defense of the two Commonwealth states of South Asia that are most directly concerned as parties to the agreement, stopped short of committing the United Kingdom to continue forces there for an indefinite period or to accept the *duty* of defending the two states. As has been seen,[32] there is also a question of the possible effect upon the obligations under the 1957 agreement with Malaya of the wording in the 1963 agreement with Malaysia. In the absence of evidence to the contrary in the preparatory work relating to the wording of the agreements, there would seem to be little more in the United Kingdom's legal obligations than the commitment to consult with the state of Malaysia and the state of Singapore, and presumably also with the two other Commonwealth states closely in interest (Australia and New Zealand) that would be affected in their planning by the withdrawal of British forces from Malaysia and Singapore. In the totality of international legal arrangements for defense in areas once controlled by Great Britain, the commitments accepted in relation to SEATO and NATO, as also in the Baghdad Pact,[33] and the more recently reported agreement projected with Mauritius (by which Britain would use the island as a naval, army, and air base),[34] would need to be taken into account. Possible new arrangements which the United Kingdom may make with Malaysia and Singapore would presumably require to be undertaken in the light of United Nations membership and operations within the terms and spirit of the Charter.

Law and practice as to collective security in general touch matters in which the principal Commonwealth member state has naturally been concerned. This finds illustration in the case of Cyprus, a former British colony.[35] A matter of policy as well as legality is suggested by a question and answer in the Australian Senate on August 19, 1964. A member of the Labour Party asked whether the Malaysian government would have the right to call

32. N. 14 above.   33. 233 UNTS 199.
34. *Guardian*, March 13, 1968, and *Daily Telegraph* of the same date.
35. See exchange of letters between the United Nations and Cyprus concerning the status of the UNFICYP, March 31, 1964, 492 UNTS 57.

on Australian troops without reference to the Australian government in *any* situation affecting Malaysia. Replying in the negative, the minister for defense added:

I think it has been stated on a number of occasions that Australia
stands for territorial integrity and for the political independence of
Malaysia. Australian forces are stationed in Malaysia as part of the
strategic reserve and have already undertaken various tasks in the
maintenance of the territorial integrity of Malaysia. In the present
circumstances, our forces would be available by the consent of the
Australian government if requested by the Malaysian government to
take part in assisting to deal with armed infiltration. It appears . . .
that at the present time the Malaysian forces have the situation well
in hand and that stage has not yet arisen. I want to make it perfectly
clear . . . that should such a request be made by the Malaysian government, then the Australian government would acquiesce in that
request.[36]

Effort to discern the international legal significance of the defense issue within the Commonwealth without reference to regional arrangements (to which some Commonwealth states, but
also some non-Commonwealth states are parties) would perhaps
be unrealistic.

The ANZUS Pact was reportedly considered at first by Australian leaders as affording assurance of some protection against a
revived Japanese imperialism, but later the anti-Communist
objectives of the treaty seem to have assumed greater importance
for Australia.[37] In the case of SEATO the parties became committed jointly and separately, through self-help and mutual aid, to
maintain and develop their individual and collective capacity to
resist armed attack. The parties agreed to assist each other in
preventing and countering "subversive activities directed from
without against their territorial integrity and political stability."

36. *Current Notes on International Affairs*, XXXIV (1964), 36. In reply to an
earlier question the minister for defense had stated that the situation in Malaysia had not assumed the proportions of a full-scale invasion. Thirty or forty
infiltrators had landed on the Malaysian coast at various points, but the Malaysian authorities had not yet called on the British Commonwealth forces stationed in Malaysia to take direct military action.

37. N. C. H. Dunbar, "Australia and Collective Security," in D. P. O'Connell,
ed., *International Law in Australia* (1965), pp. 401–402.

This wording has been said to present the issue of possible antipathy on the part of at least one of the signatories to joining in actions against peoples engaged in truly revolutionary movements seeking to carry out the will of the people in one of the countries to which the commitment applies.[38]

Attention has been drawn to the legality of the implication that the purpose of the treaties is to enable the party states "to coordinate their efforts for collective defence for the preservation of peace and security." Attention has likewise been directed to the rider in the ANZUS Pact reading, "pending the development of a more comprehensive system of regional security in the Pacific Area." In this connection may be noted Kelsen's reported view that "collective self-defense" is objectionable in the treaty context because, in defending another, one cannot be said to defend oneself. That aggression against one of the parties to the defense treaties constitutes aggression against all of the parties is considered to be the understanding, but there is still some question whether, in legal contemplation, parties to the treaties have an *inherent* right of self-defense if and when attacks are made upon states that are not parties to the treaties.[39] The operative part of

38. Ibid., pp. 403–409. The same author draws attention to the reluctant acceptance by Australia of a United States reservation to the treaty stating that "its recognition of the effect of aggression and armed attack and its agreement with reference thereto in Article IV, paragraph 1 apply only to communist aggression but affirms that in the event of other aggression or armed attack it will consult under the provisions of Article IV, paragraph 2."

Cf. statement from a correspondent in Bonn that Britain had virtually ended its military commitments to SEATO as a result of cuts in military spending, and that in the previous year other SEATO members had demanded Britain's expulsion, along with that of France and Pakistan, for failure to support the war in Vietnam. It was noted that the British had argued that the SEATO treaty did not commit the country to military support beyond what it chose to give. *Japan Times*, Jan. 9, 1968.

39. Dunbar, "Australia and Collective Security," pp. 414–419. Dunbar also notes (p. 415) that hearings before the United States Senate on the NATO treaty revealed some uncertainty that the treaty was designed to establish a full-scale regional organization in accordance with arts. 51–54 of the United Nations Charter or a more limited collective-defense arrangement. D. W. Bowett, *Self-Defence in International Law* (1958), observes (p. 200) that art. 51 of the United Nations Charter did not introduce a novel concept into international law but was declaratory of existing custom, while A. L. Goodhart, "The North Atlantic Treaty of 1949," *Recueil des cours*, LXXIX (1951) part 2, 187–236, takes the position that if a regional arrangement does not fit within the terms of Charter art. 52, this does not mean that its validity is necessarily impaired. The ANZUS Treaty has a restricted list of parties, but an Australian publicist has pointed out that a favorable feature of the treaty derives from the fact that

article 51 of the United Nations Charter provides that "nothing in the present Charter shall impair the inherent right of individual or collective self-defense if an armed attack occurs against a Member of the United Nations, until the Security Council has taken the measures necessary to maintain international peace and security." A British publicist, commenting on the general subject, has observed that

in the Charter, unlike the Covenant, the right of self-defence is not a right which is left altogether outside the collective system for maintaining peace. Self-defence is recognised to be a necessary exception to the fundamental principle in Article 2(4) that resort to force by an individual State is illegal without the prior authority of the United Nations. But the exercise of the right of self-defence is made subject to the subsequent judgment and control of the international community. The individual State necessarily decides whether or not to use force in self-defence but the propriety of its decision is a matter for the United Nations.

On the other hand, the fact that resort to force in self-defence is lawful without the prior authority of the Security Council is of vital importance from the point of view of the veto. Action may be begun in self-defence without a prior recourse to the Council and therefore a single Permanent Member is not in a position to negative action being initiated by a State in self-defence. Moreover, once action in self-defence is in motion, it requires an affirmative decision of the Council, including the concurring votes of the Permanent Members, to order the cessation of the defensive action. Thus, action in self-defence under Article 51 cannot be barred by the veto and cannot be terminated except by the unanimous vote of the Permanent Members. Hence comes the great importance which is now attached to the right of collective self-defence under Article 51 as a means of avoiding the frustration of the Council caused by the Soviet Union's veto. There is, of course, another side to the picture. The veto can be used to protect a State which has illegitimately resorted to force in pretended self-defence by preventing the Council from making any pronouncement concerning the illegality of the resort to force. That is a very serious drawback because acts of aggression are commonly represented to be

---

there is no definition of the quarter from which a threat of an attack might come. R. G. Casey, *Friends and Neighbors: Australia and the World* (1955), p. 81.

As to the application of both the ANZUS and SEATO commitments if there should be an armed attack in the region, see also Julius Stone, "Problems of Australian Foreign Policy, January–June, 1955," *Australian Journal of Politics and History*, I (1956), 1–26.

acts of self-defence. If the right of self-defence is not to prove simply a cloak for aggression, it is essential that it should always be subject to international investigation and control. The difficulty has been met by the secondary security machinery established in the Uniting for Peace Resolution.[40]

Given a measurement of agreement on the part of Common-wealth states as to the aims and principles of the United Nations Organization, there remains the question of the legal (as well as the political and military) bases for action that may be taken for the purpose of defending individual states, and in a broader sense the international community in general, from attack. That the prevention of strife between communal groups, as well as mediatory efforts looking to political and material progress, may be the objective (through the agency of elements from outside the state or states in which there has been disunity and strife) is illustrated in the history of independent Cyprus in the seventh decade of the twentieth century.[41]

A complete inquiry into the international legal aspects of defense commitments would involve much more than one part of a single volume. This need not preclude, however, a summary examination of some of the legal problems which the issues have presented. While Commonwealth states' experience in this general field may not have been unique, there would seem to have been, at least in the past, a natural propensity for defense commitments by states having between themselves the ties, even if changing ones, which Commonwealth states acknowledge.

III

The contemporary issue of defense is far from being limited to Commonwealth states. They have, however, had occasion to consider the relevant law as well as the practice, whether as individual members of their peculiar association, as members of the

---

40. C. H. M. Waldock, "The Regulation of the Use of Force by Individual States in International Law," *Recueil des cours*, II (1952), 455–517, at 495–496. The author refers, in this context, to Hans Kelsen, *Recent Trends in the Law of the United Nations* (1951), chap. 4.

41. See chap. 3 above, pp. 82–90.

United Nations, or, as in the case of Cyprus, as "host" states to military contingents from other states (whether Commonwealth or non-Commonwealth). One observer has pointed to the fact that failure of the move to create permanent forces available to the Security Council under article 43 of the Charter was not regarded with great dismay, while the difficulties of carrying out what was necessary for effectuating plans for an international force began to be realistically understood.[42] The same observer has emphasized that "the only form in which it has in fact proved possible to mobilize United Nations forces, of limited dimensions and capabilities, has been through voluntary contributions by member-states to meet particular situations on an *ad hoc* basis."[43] Other writers have suggested, concerning the United Nations, that "Insofar as it works to any effect, it does so by virtue of . . . the right that some of the world public thinks it has to represent mankind's conscience and respect for law."[44] A legal scholar who had part in the UNCIO deliberations at San Francisco has subsequently submitted that

when the framers decided that the Charter should not specify particular kinds of measures to meet particular situations, they were, of course, placing the responsibility for such decisions upon the competent United Nations organs. Certainly they did not intend it to be exercised on the basis of pure political discretion, or even upon a basis of strictly legal considerations. If, for example, the principle of non-intervention did not seem to be legally applicable to a given situation, it might still have demands to make as a basic principle of the Charter having a bearing upon the equities of the case, and there would be a clear responsibility upon the competent authorities to take such considerations into account. Generally speaking, there can be no question that the framers intended the discretion conferred upon the United Nations in such matters to be exercised with all responsibility and concern for the potential consequences of applying tangible pressures to international situations.[45]

42. Evan Luard, *Peace and Opinion* (1962) p. 113.
43. Ibid., p. 114.
44. Arthur Lee Burns and Nina Heathcote, *Peace-Keeping by U.N. Forces* (1963), p. 4.
45. John W. Halderman, "Legal Basis for United Nations Armed Forces," *American Journal of International Law*, LVI (1962), 996. See also his volume, *The United Nations and the Rule of Law* (1966), chap. 8.

A prominent Canadian internationalist has questioned "whether we may not be in danger of letting the UN become a mere service agency hiring out policemen to maintain agreements in which it plays no part." He goes on to note that

in West Irian and Yemen the UN had no real say at all in the truces or settlements agreed on by the parties with the good offices or pressure of great powers; and yet it has organized the supervision. A similar role for the UN has been designed in Cyprus . . . one must not under present circumstances reject reasonable settlements reached off the UN premises. . . . While avoiding the pretensions to settle old disputes by captious majorities, the UN must at the same time avoid the humiliation of being used by powers, great or small, for their private purposes.[46]

An Australian scholar has expressed the opinion that the hard questions about the UN forces are not the legal ones but, rather, questions of "power alignment, of will to advance commitment, of foresight, of situations as relevant to present commitment, of discrimination between situations deemed to require intervention, and the interplay of all these." Preferring to exclude from consideration any "merely legal" possibility of designing a United Nations Security Force capable of meeting directly threats to the security of mankind, he has also counseled avoidance of "loose" use of such terms as "International Forces" or "U.N. Forces," preferring to substitute such a term as "forces performing U.N. functions." He has distinguished merely symbolic presence or interposition from other functions [47] and has referred to "legally licensed powers" of the General Assembly.[48]

Among the legal matters considered at the same Oslo conference were those related to the *extent* of the obligations of United Nations members, authorizations of self-defense, the possibility of "reactivating" article 43 of the United Nations Charter, legal responsibility of the United Nations for acts committed by United

46. John W. Holmes, "The Political and Philosophical Aspects of U.N. Security Forces," in Bjorn Egge, Per Frydenberg, and John C. Sanness, eds., *Peace-Keeping Experience and Evaluation: The Oslo Papers* (1964), p. 89.
47. Julius Stone, "Legal Bases for the Establishment of Forces Performing United Nations Security Functions," in Egge et al., *Peace-Keeping Experience and Evaluation*, pp. 277–300, at pp. 277, 279, 280.
48. Ibid., pp. 290–291.

Nations forces, the continued application of the laws and customs of war and of the Geneva Conventions of 1949 for the protection of war victims, and possible commitments of the United Nations with respect to the "right of revolution." On the first of these points there was apparently agreement that in this subject matter the United Nations Charter touched only upon the *minimal* obligations of United Nations members—and that there might be agreement on such further obligations as would assist in fulfilling the purpose set forth in the Charter. As to self-defense, it was emphasized that when centralized actions should fail, the right of individual members to defend might be of great importance; such defensive acts should be reported to the Security Council.[49] There was reference to the fact that when the United States extended aid to Greece and Turkey under the Truman Doctrine the agreements for this provided that assistance should be withdrawn if the Security Council or the General Assembly should find that action taken (or assistance furnished) by the United Nations made the assistance by the United States unnecessary or undesirable. As to Charter article 43, there was apparently some optimism, particularly in view of attitudes following the Cuban missile crisis and Sino-Soviet divergence. Concerning legal responsibility of the United Nations for acts of forces performing United Nations functions, it was said that the world organization had in the past assumed some responsibilities, although not penal ones. War being a factual situation, its prosecution would entail some legal consequences—a matter on which there has apparently been some confusion when operations in the Congo were under consideration. However, the United Nations position regarding the laws and customs of war, the conference summary

49. Professor Stone expressed the view that "the State against which individual members may join in the exercise of their alleged rights of self-defense under the Uniting for Peace Resolution has no legal obligation to submit to such hostile action, even though that hostile action may be provisionally deemed to be legally licensed. Military 'sanctions,' in this situation, can only mean measures voluntarily undertaken by the cooperating members of the United Nations under a claim of individual and collective self-defense, to which the object of the measure is also not legally obliged to submit. Moreover, since the General Assembly has no power to determine authoritatively the claim of self-defense, even this provisional licensed power may be subject to nullification if the claim is subsequently rejected by a competent forum, such as the Security Council." Ibid., pp. 291–292.

submitted, had not been clearly defined. It was thought that there might be clarification through conventions that might regulate United Nations actions.[50]

A subject which was reported as presenting some problems at the Oslo conference from the point of view of United Nations operations relative to internal conflicts was that of the so-called right of revolution. One view was that the United Nations should, in the case of a revolution, take no position concerning the *substance* of the conflict and should not enforce such a position by employing a United Nations force but should limit itself to preventing foreign intervention and support and to preventing "international" violence. The relevance to the Commonwealth, in which civil strife has not been unknown, is apparent. There was suggestion, however, that there were already in the United Nations voting procedures some guarantees against imprudent violations of the "right of revolution." There was reference in this connection to the "five permanent members rule" in the Security Council and the two-thirds majority rule in the General Assembly.

The foregoing brief discussion of some of the problems of defense has left for separate attention a less controversial subject, but one in which some Commonwealth countries have been and are in some measure currently concerned, namely the matter of legal relations between friendly foreign armed forces and the country which may with some measure of accuracy be described as the "host" country. The issue of defense may be involved.

Even before the Commonwealth came to include so many independent states there had been a problem of the status of such forces.[51] The latter—whether they are present in another state

50. Ibid., pp. 308–311.
51. In the mid-1950's an American scholar referred to the matter of criminal jurisdiction over friendly armed forces in a state not their own as the "most radical innovation of our era." A. G. Freeman, "Responsibility of States for Unlawful Acts of Their Armed Forces," *Recueil des cours* (1956), pp. 267, 271.
American coauthors of a volume based on field study of the subject have said in their introduction that "for the first time in the modern era, the sometimes radically different systems of law of two sovereign nations are operating within the same territory and in respect to the same individuals. Such a situation is not contemplated by the municipal law of either sovereign, thus creating the necessity of a mutual accommodation of the two systems within the somewhat meager framework provided by the Agreement. In the day by day solution of the prob-

under collective security arrangements, regional pacts, or *ad hoc* commitments between friendly states for contingents to be stationed in (or to carry out maneuvers within) a country other than their respective flag states—have legal rights and are subject to certain legal restrictions.

The relation of this matter to development with respect to the defense of other Commonwealth countries was and is of concern to the United Kingdom. Writing in 1964, a well-known authority on Commonwealth military relations observed that

ten years ago, the reorientation of Commonwealth defense arrangements on the basis of regional alliances which had been foreshadowed in the British White Paper of 1946, when the ghost of the Committee on Imperial Defence was laid to rest, had been completed. Britain and Canada had for six years been members of NATO. Australia and New Zealand had since 1951 been allied to the United States in the ANZUS Security Pact. In the previous year, 1954, Britain and Pakistan had become linked by treaty, as well as by the unspecified obligations of the Commonwealth, to Australia and New Zealand (and to the

---

lems thus presented, a new body of law is rapidly being developed which cuts across many of the traditional branches of legal science, for which the new name of conjurisdictional law may not be inappropriate." Joseph M. Snee and A. Kenneth Pye, *Status of Forces Agreements and Criminal Jurisdiction* (1957), p. 10. The authors note that the phrase "conjurisdictional law" owes its inspiration to a remark by Professor Julius Stone.

A part of the Commonwealth, the Federation of the West Indies, became party to the Agreement with the United States concerning United States Defence Areas in the Federation. Article IX of this agreement, which became effective on February 10, 1961, provided in the first two sections (related to criminal jurisdiction):

(1) Subject to the provisions of this Article, (a) The military authorities of the United States shall have the right to exercise within the Territory all criminal and disciplinary jurisdiction conferred on them by United States law over all persons subject to the military law of the United States; (b) the authorities of the Territory shall have jurisdiction over members of United States forces with respect to offences committed within that Territory and punishable by the law in force there.

(2) (a) The military authorities of the United States shall have the right to exercise exclusive jurisdiction over persons subject to the military law of the United States with respect to offences, including offences relating to security, punishable by the law of the United States but not by the law in force in the Territory. (b) The authorities of the Territory shall have the right to exercise exclusive jurisdiction over members of the United States Forces with respect to offences, including offences relating to security, punishable by the law in force in the Territory but not by the law of the United States.

There was also provision as to the primary right to exercise jurisdiction and provision for waivers of such right under certain circumstances. 12 UST 409, p. 415.

United States, France, Thailand and the Philippines) by the Manila Treaty which created for the South East Asia Treaty Organization.[52]

The same author has pointed out that in 1963 there were over eight hundred British officers and noncommissioned officers serving in the countries of the new Commonwealth, some on secondment and within the national command system, some acting as training teams outside the national system of command. It was noted that not all arrangements were bilateral ones with the United Kingdom. Canada had at the time of his writing a thirty-man training mission in Ghana, the Ghana air force had been established with the help of Indian (and Israeli) officers, and the Malaysian navy had been trained partly by Australia and commanded by an Australian.

It has become increasingly apparent that there is need for better understanding of the status of friendly armed forces, a subject which has received attention particularly since World War II.[53] The principle of broad jurisdictional immunity for public ships visiting foreign states has been frequently traced back to the decision of John Marshall in the well-known case of *Schooner Exchange* v. *McFaddon*,[54] in which was set forth the rule, attributed to customary international law, that there was complete immunity from the courts of the territorial states when a friendly foreign armed force was in the territory of that state. This view now seems to have become considerably modified. When, in the *Foreign Forces* case the Supreme Court of Canada was asked for an advisory opinion concerning the existence and the extent of immunities (from criminal prosecution) of United States military and naval forces that were in Canada for the purpose of prosecuting the war in which Canada and the United

52. Alastair Buchan, "Commonwealth Military Relations," in W. B. Hamilton, Kenneth Robinson, and C. D. W. Goodwin, eds., *A Decade of the Commonwealth, 1955–1964* (1966), pp. 195–196.

53. The two general points of view were set forth in the writing of Archibald King, "Jurisdiction over Friendly Foreign Armed Forces," *American Journal of International Law*, XL (1946), 257–279, and G. P. Barton, "Foreign Armed Forces: Immunity from Supervisory Jurisdiction," *British Year Book of International Law*, XXVI (1949), 380–413.

54. 7 Cranch 163 (1812).

States were engaged as allies, an argument for immunity was rejected by a majority of the judges.[55] The subsequent development has been toward a reasonable scope of jurisdiction for the host state over visiting armed forces on a basis of reciprocity. Perhaps the most generally known treaty provisions are those in the NATO Status of Forces Agreement.[56] One commentator has discerned a trend on the part of receiving states toward according immunity or priority of jurisdiction in the sending state with respect to offenses of the visiting personnel inter se and has further noted that

receiving states have also shown a perhaps less well marked willingness to recognize the on-base concept, either as alone justifying according exclusive or prior jurisdiction to the sending state, or at least as an added factor supporting according such jurisdiction to the sending state over *inter se* offenses committed on a base. These attitudes are in marked contrast to the reluctance of receiving states to recognize such jurisdiction in the sending state over duty-connected offenses. Much of the reluctance arises from a state's interest in protecting its citizens from the criminal acts of the visiting forces, even though the acts were done in the performance of duty. A part of the reluctance stems, however, from difficulties encountered in defining the concept, determining which acts fall within it, and deciding who is empowered to make the decision on whether a particular act was or was not duty-connected. Many misunderstandings could be avoided if these matters could be clarified.[57]

55. Supreme Court of Canada, S.C.R. 483 [1943]; 4 D.L.R. 11; J.-G. Castel, *International Law Chiefly as Interpreted and Applied in Canada* (1965), p. 665.
56. TIAS 2846.
57. Roland J. Stanger, "Criminal Jurisdiction over Visiting Armed Forces," United States Naval War College, *International Law Studies, 1957–1958*, LII (1965), 264–265.
On the essential nature of forces, Julius Stone has written: "If we do not stick in the bark of the question whether a Force is 'truly' international or 'truly' U.N. (as the late Secretary-General tended to do with UNEF), we can quickly admit that a Force for performance of U.N. functions may be based on voluntary action by Members in fields where international law leaves them at liberty to act or not to act. I here exemplify this by reference to the liberty of individual and collective self-defense reserved under Article 51 of the Charter, as well as under customary international law to the extent that this is not restrained by provisions of the Charter." "Legal Bases," in Egge et al., *Peace-Keeping Experience and Evaluation*, p. 297.
On the question of immunities from jurisdiction which members of visiting forces enjoy, compare statements in *Peace Research Reviews*, II (1968), 35ff., where, after reference to studies by Bowett, by Seyersted, and by Attia, the opinion is expressed that "in the present state of international law no satis-

Inquiry into why particular visiting forces have not been able to accomplish more than they have accomplished is apt to proceed upon the basis of the relative strength of the forces and upon *ad hoc* arrangements rather than upon developing rules of customary international law,[58] and there is continuing need for clarification of the authority involved. Defense, not only in the traditional sense but in a broader community sense, has marked a changing and not entirely peaceful world. As affecting the Commonwealth member states in particular, the issue of defense has related to national and regional policy, has involved the interpretation of treaty commitments for extending aid to Commonwealth states that would seem to be particularly vulnerable, and has at the same time occasioned the reexamination and testing of some still-remaining ties between member states of the Commonwealth.

With respect to defense in general, the traditional position of Great Britain in the Empire and later Commonwealth is in contrast to the recently announced change of British policy. Reduced

---

factory solution has been found, although neither suggestions nor constructive proposals are lacking."

Other research has led to the conclusion that the NATO Status of Forces Agreement, 1951 (285 UNTS 105), was a conventional statement of principles and practices that had previously emerged in customary international law, and that when states send such forces abroad under the United Nations flag they have no real reason to expect that these forces have rights in addition to those to which they would be entitled under such (customary) law. The same author points out that United Kingdom legislation has provisions whereby matters of discipline and international administration may proceed as under the laws of the state to which the forces belong. See D. S. Wijewardane, "Criminal Jurisdiction over Visiting Forces with Special Reference to International Forces," *British Year Book of International Law*, XLI (1965–1966), 122–197, at 130, 146, 196.

58. Compare the statement by Lt. Gen. E. L. M. Burns, formerly UNEF chief of command, on the inability of UNFICYP to prevent the Greek-Cypriot assault on the Turks in the Kokkina area, which inability, he submits, resulted in the Turkish air attack on Greek-Cypriot troops and villages: "Because it had not liberty of movement, because the Greek-Cypriot irregular forces had been reinforced by 'volunteers' from the Greek mainland, and by very heavy shipments of armaments, so that if UNFICYP had tried to use force to prevent the assault it would have been faced by superior military force." Section on problems and prospects, in Ivan L. Head, ed., *This Fire-Proof House* (1967), p. 71.

For a list of United States Supreme Court decisions limiting the power of military authorities to try by court-martial civilian employees or civilians who are members of United States forces, see Wolfgang Friedmann, Oliver Lissitzyn, and Richard Pugh, *International Law Cases and Materials on International Law* (1969), p. 525.

commitments, such as Britain has come to have, raise primary questions for national decision. International law of course applies to the interpretation of agreements of the United Kingdom that are still in force concerning the defense of some states that are now independent members of the Commonwealth.

Along with undertakings between Commonwealth states, there has been some trend toward utilization of wider (regional) arrangements to which some Commonwealth member states and some non-Commonwealth states are parties. Increasingly, attention has been directed to the force and effect of bilateral defensive commitments in the light of broader multilateral ones. As to what may be done within a Commonwealth state in order to preclude possible action by nearby states that are closely in interest, there has been instructive experience with Cyprus, even if authorizations for the retention of elements comprising the UNFICYP within that Commonwealth state have been repeatedly continued for only a few months at a time.

In the course of the general development, international legal questions arising have included that of the precise meaning of such a term as "self-defense," [59] and the possible impropriety of using such descriptive wording as "United Nations forces" rather than referring to national forces on United Nations missions. One field of international law in which there has been considerable progress and wide agreement is that concerning the jurisdictional immunities of friendly foreign forces while these are in the territory of a state other than their own.

59. Cf. *Defence in A New Setting*, Fabian Tract 386 (1968), p. 27. As one publicist has expressed it, "While the new members, like the old, are all opposed to a Commonwealth defense policy, all continue to co-operate with the old in matters of defense." M. S. Ragan, "Relations between the Old and the New Members," in Hamilton et al., *A Decade of the Commonwealth*, p. 164.

7

Measure of Relevance

International law has supplanted an earlier system of rules which Commonwealth states observed inter se. This fact does not necessarily preclude some element of interdependence. It does perhaps explain why, until rather recently at least, international law has probably not been the principal point of view from which Commonwealth states' relations with each other have been studied. With the complete independence of member states, appraisal of their policies and actions concerning external affairs in the light of contemporary international law would seem to be in order. As in the case of states generally, the relative attention given to this law may vary from state to state, although it is not necessarily true that there will be more emphasis upon it in long-established foreign offices than in relatively new ones. Extension of the law to new subject areas, and particularly the inclusion within it of principles and rules touching rights of individual human beings, has had bearing upon its relevance to policy in the multiracial Commonwealth.

Separation of international legal aspects from other aspects of state policy and practice may not be easily achieved in all situations, particularly if interest is in the contemporary rather than in past events. Yet the element of international law is frequently discernible in situations where primary attention is directed to state policy and interests.[1] Practice in the Commonwealth in

1. Cf. Lord McNair's observation in his preface to volumes of opinions by law officers of Great Britain: "It is a delusion affecting the minds of many laymen and not a few lawyers that governments in the conduct of their foreign affairs act independently and capriciously and without reference to legal principles." *International Law Opinions* (1956), p. xvii. With this may be compared a statement in the records of the International Law Association: "Undoubtedly the line of demarcation between the strictly juridical and the political is often difficult

general has been such as to invite attention from the particular perspective of public international law and to essay the distinction of law from policy.

Issues given attention in the foregoing chapters are ones which have confronted and still confront not only the United Kingdom but also, to a lesser extent, other Commonwealth states. There has been no attempt to weigh issues from the point of view of their comparative seriousness. Invocation of or apparent acknowledgment of international law in parliamentary debates, and in decision-making, provides some bases for estimation of the law's admitted relevance and of its utility in various contexts. As in the larger international community, there is in the states now comprising the Commonwealth great diversity in size, natural resources, and population. For all of them, however, whether through constitutional provisions or through policy, there is the practical question of the relationship of international law to elements of national policy. The nature and significance of that relationship is discernible not so much through broad generalizations or acknowledgment as through positions taken on specific issues. Criteria for the selection of issues have included the degree of publicity accorded to them in parliamentary debates, in diplomacy, and in public international forums, as well as attention given to them in Commonwealth prime ministers' meetings and in national courts. Since the issues here selected are contemporary ones, some press comments on the selected subjects have seemed to merit attention, in addition to government records of discussion and action.

The broad issue (or group of issues) relating to state succession has been a very central one for the newer Commonwealth states, since these states' inheritances depend in large measure upon preindependence arrangement of boundaries, disposition of public and private property, determination of the nationality of

---

to determine since the rules of the Law of Nations may be regarded as a curb imposed on the possible excesses of national policies, with the consequence that any violation of the rules of public international law will always have political implications." International Law Association, *Report of the Fifty-Third Conference*, Buenos Aires, Aug. 25–31, 1968, p. 5. See also Ralph Braibanti, "The Role of Law in Political Development," in Robert R. Wilson, ed., *International and Comparative Law of the Commonwealth* (1968), pp. 1–26.

persons, arrangements for continuity of internal legal order, and the continuance in force of presuccession treaties. On the last-mentioned topic, there had been prior to the emergence of many of the new Commonwealth states two general theories of the effect of succession upon preexisting treaties—one of them that the successor state has a "clean slate" as to which of the treaties made by its predecessor state it will accept; the other that, in general, treaty commitments made by the predecessor state devolve upon the successor. Apparently neither of these two theories has come to be accepted in its entirety. Earlier doctrinal rigidity has in recent Commonwealth experience yielded to the developing practice of utilizing "inheritance" or "devolution" agreements. The nature of these may vary with the degree of maturity of the particular states. Developing custom—as reflected in formulations by such bodies as the International Law Commission, the Asian-African Legal Consultative Committee, and the International Law Association—seems to have influenced in some measure Commonwealth state practice in this general area. Legal scholars in Commonwealth states have had an important part in clarifying, and presumably also in influencing, the development of practice relating to state succession.

The effect of such succession upon preexisting private rights of aliens in the successor state is relatable to the background of international law concerning responsibility of states with respect to foreign-owned property.[2] Diplomacy may avail to avert arbitrary rulings, and bilateral commitments between the predecessor and the successor state will presumably be preferred by the former. Relevant to one phase of the subject matter likely to be involved is the Resolution on Permanent Sovereignty over Natural Resources, as passed by the United Nations General Assembly in 1962.[3] There continues to be challenge of the proposition that, even without treaty provisions imposing upon a successor state the obligation to respect private property rights of nationals of a predecessor state, customary international law proscribes

2. The general subject of property protection in relation to treaties of friendship, commerce, and navigation, is considered in Robert R. Wilson, *United States Commercial Treaties and International Law* (1960), pp. 95–104.
3. General Assembly Resolution 1803, GAOR 17th sess., supp. 17 (A/5217).

uncompensated expropriation. While sound reasoning can be adduced against the legality of such expropriations, Commonwealth state practice in the recent past tends to look to the new states' rightful insistence upon inquiry into the nature of private property rights that are claimed and into the effect of a general rule of the sanctity of such rights without consideration of social effects. Despite the inclusion in the Universal Declaration of Human Rights (Article XVII) of an individual's rights to own property, commitments in bilateral or multilateral form would still seem to be the most practicable means of spelling out the legal liability of a successor state to resident aliens (including nationals of the predecessor state) who continue to own property in the successor state.[4]

Questions concerning succession in the case of public rights to property would appear to be more easily settled on the basis of customary law and practice, and recognition of the principle that each state may determine who shall be its nationals. International commitments may supplement the force of custom as to inhabitants' right to retain their presuccession status rather than to become citizens of the successor state, although discontinuance of residence may be a condition of this. The concept of "common status"—once widely recognized in the Commonwealth, and not at variance with principles of international law, is not so prevalent as it formerly was, although it is still possible to have dual or multiple citizenship in the Commonwealth, and there is no rule of customary international law which proscribes such citizenship. As to nationality and citizenship in general, the "genuine link" principle, enunciated by the International Court of Justice in the *Nottebohm* ruling,[5] might have applicability in the exceptional case.

4. For a critical consideration of several possible positions which may be taken on international law pertaining to private foreign investments, see A. A. Fatouras, "International Law in the Third World," *Virginia Law Review,* L (1964), 783–823. The suggestion is offered in the article that the emergence of the "third world" following the second decade after World War II, while not eliminating the East-West conflict, has changed its character by providing "powerful new elements of diversity" and thereby improving "the stability of the international legal order."

5. 1955 I.C.J. Rep. 4. For a critical analysis of the decision, see Josef L. Kunz, *The Changing Law of Nations* (1968), chap. 24.

The existence within certain Commonwealth states of ethnic divisions so strong that they not only have effect upon public policies within these states but also have led to pressures and even to forceful action by other states presents situations for which international law seems to provide no directly applicable norms except as to the proscription of forceful intervention and, on the other hand, retention of customary rules as to protection of nationals abroad. There is also, however, a strong trend toward appeal to humanitarian principles. That communalism may have effect upon international policy is illustrated in the three states taken as examples, although these are not the only Commonwealth states in which communalism is to be found.

To the communal situation in Malaysia can apparently be ascribed the partial breakup of a federation, and bloody rioting such as that in Kuala Lumpur in May and June of 1969. Constitutional arrangements favoring Malays had been considered as necessary for internal peace. Between the now separate states of Malaysia and Singapore there continues to be official cooperation and formal adherence to customary international law. Commonwealth ties have apparently assisted toward these ends.

In the case of Ceylon, where a major problem developed as a sequel to the movement to that country in the nineteenth century of needed Tamil workers, an already existing communal situation growing out of Sinhalese-Tamil relations has been further complicated. The international agreement concluded in 1964 for the return to India of over half a million Indian Tamils was consistent with international legalism. Questions have arisen concerning the status, with respect to nationality and citizenship, of the retained persons (i.e., those not to be repatriated to India) as also of those who will return to India. In this context, invocation of basic human rights seems more likely to avail than would reliance upon customary international law, although the traditional law concerning responsibility for protection of admitted nationals of another state would presumably apply. Established rules on the interpretation of treaties would, of course, also apply to construction of the 1964 Indo-Ceylonese agreement.

In Cyprus there has been cessation of open strife between opposing communal elements, and possibly some progress toward peaceful unity, achieved largely through the mediatorial role of the United Nations. There has been, consistent with international law, an emphasis upon the principle of nonintervention by the outside states most directly in interest, from an ethnic point of view, and a continuance (on a basis of renewal at the end of each six-months period) of the UNFICYP. In the case of Cyprus there has perhaps been more invocation of United Nations law than of the general principles of customary international law, except insofar as the latter provides against forceful intervention by outside states. There has been occasion to look to rules of developing international law concerning the jurisdictional status of visiting contingents of friendly foreign states that are in Cyprus with the consent of the Cypriot government and as agents of the United Nations.

The issue of secession in the Commonwealth has recently come under discussion throughout the world, perhaps to a greater extent than has any other single issue in Commonwealth history, with the possible exception of South Africa's withdrawal. Secession in the Commonwealth may presumably occur in some situations without giving rise to controversial questions of international law (as the separation of Eire from Great Britain would seem to have illustrated). In contrast, the purported secession of Rhodesia, which as a Commonwealth entity has had less than full dominion status, has raised not only constitutional questions as to the entity's status within the United Kingdom but also international legal questions touching nonrecognition and resort to sanctions by United Nations members. The holding of the Judicial Committee of the Privy Council concerning certain trials in Rhodesia looked initially to constitutional rather than international legal commitments, but questions raised by Rhodesian judges concerning de facto and de jure status of the government in Rhodesia clearly touched upon international law. Neither refusal to recognize,[6] nor resort to sanctions by Britain and other Commonwealth

6. On the point that, as President Nyerere of Tanzania is reported to have said, on only two occasions in the past has the United Kingdom relinquished control of a colony to a government that was not based on the clear will of the majority in the colony (one of these being South Africa and the other Zanzibar), see David R. Smock, "The Forgotten Rhodesians," *Foreign Affairs*, XLVII (1969), 532–544, at 543, 544.

states, nor the decision by Rhodesians (i.e., those enfranchised in June, 1969) would seem to have changed the international legal situation. Invocation of relevant multilateral conventions has attended the Commonwealth states' announced withholding of recognition from Rhodesia and their refusal to have formal relations with the Smith regime. In this situation the mere carrying on of informal conversations between the British government and the regime in control of Rhodesia (talks such as those on board H.M.S. *Tiger* and H.M.S. *Fearless*) would not seem to present serious questions of rights and duties under international law. For the time being at least, sanctions more forceful than those already imposed, even though more forceful moves have been demanded by leaders of some Commonwealth states, have apparently not seemed to the principal Commonwealth state to be practicable, even if they would be legally justifiable.

The attempted secession of Biafra from Nigeria has provided occasion for some invocation of multilateral treaty law, such as the Geneva Conventions. The claimed right of humanitarian agencies to send in food for the civilian population, along with requested permission for neutral observers to inspect, has given rise to much discussion. Mediatory efforts by the Organization of African Unity, which efforts were apparently unsuccessful, are to be considered in the same light, so far as customary international law is concerned, as mediation by any friendly state or states.

As of January, 1969, when the independence movement came to an end, only two Commonwealth states (Tanzania and Zambia) had recognized Biafra. In Commonwealth relations, aside from Nigeria's position with respect to Biafra, the so-called right of revolution has not been formally denied except in the case of Rhodesia. Against Rhodesia there has been invocation of international organization law, along with insistence upon human rights in the spirit of neonationalism and antiracism so vigorously emphasized in the contemporary Commonwealth.[7]

7. As to human rights, one proposal which the Human Rights Commission endorsed and which has been brought before the United Nations General Assembly, is for the establishment of an international ombudsman or high commissioner for human rights. See note by Aaron Etra on the proposal for establishing such a high commissioner and the observation that the proposal has importance from a legal as well as a humanitarian point of view. *Columbia Journal of International Law*, V (1966), 150–155.

As a matter of policy rather than international law, the course of action which the United Kingdom followed for several months in 1969 with respect to complainant groups in Anguilla would seem to indicate a reasonable respect for the principle of self-determination, with adherence to existing constitutional arrangements.

The issue of migration within the Commonwealth has recently occasioned the invocation of some rights under international law, although the principal political controversy has involved United Kingdom policy. The "Kenyanization" move in East Africa and official British action to prevent the worsening (through immigration) of the economic and social situation in the British Isles would normally appear to be exercises of rightful authority under municipal law. There have, however, been some claims (in behalf of potential migrants to Great Britain and by their sympathizers) of international legal rights. In the process there has been suggestion looking toward universal (or, in any case, wider multilateral) adoption of the principle that each individual has a human right to a nationality and a right to enter a country of which he is a national. The Universal Declaration of Human Rights, which is influential, includes the statement that everyone has the right to a nationality, and that everyone has the right to leave any country, including his own, and to return to his country,[8] but the declaration is not a treaty in the international law sense.[9] The

8. Arts. 13(2) and 15.
9. The International Covenant on Civil and Political Rights, in addition to providing that every child has a right to acquire a nationality (art. 24 [3]) sets forth that no one shall be arbitrarily deprived of the right to enter his own country (art. 12 [4]). GAOR, 21st sess., supp. 12 (A/6316). On the background of the general development, see S. A. de Smith, "Fundamental Rights in the New Commonwealth," *International and Comparative Law Quarterly*, X (1961), 83–102, 215–237; referring to the European Convention on Human Rights, which the United Kingdom ratified in 1951, and to the extension of its obligations to forty-two dependent territories in 1953, the writer noted that these obligations were binding upon the United Kingdom in international law but that in the matter of remedies the United Kingdom had not at the time of his writing accepted the obligatory jurisdiction of the European Court of Human Rights.
Another writer suggests that there is no evidence that at the time of the drafting of the European Convention the United Kingdom foresaw "any occasion when it might be called upon to implement the terms of the Convention in its domestic law." There was reference in this connection to the tradition that it was for governments and governments alone to take decisions concerning international obligations. Ralph Beddard, "The Status of the European Convention on Human Rights," *International and Comparative Law Quarterly*, XVI (1967), 206–217,

United Kingdom is a party to the European Convention for the Protection of Human Rights and Fundamental Freedoms, but it does not appear that this convention would in turn be directly applicable to the questions raised in connection with the British Immigration Act of 1968.

The history of immigration in what was formerly the "British" Commonwealth does not support the claim that citizens of one Commonwealth state have an unlimited legal right to migrate to another such state. As to the United Kingdom itself, there has heretofore been a liberal policy of allowing potential immigrants from such countries as India and Pakistan to have the status of "citizens of the United Kingdom and Colonies" and as such to migrate to the British Isles. The recent (1968) denial of the right of such persons to make their homes in Great Britain (except as to a relatively small quota each year) has encountered criticism primarily on humanitarian grounds but in part also on legal grounds. Both considerations may have influenced the inclusion in British legislation passed in 1968 of the right of appeal for individuals affected against arbitrary administrative rulings, but humanitarianism would seem to have been the most potent factor in dealing with the problem.

Recent developments concerning migration to Great Britain have also provided occasion for renewed discussion of the legal rights of passport holders. A commonly claimed right has been that of leaving, and returning to, a country of one's own nationality. That states may impose limitations in these matters, not precluded by international law, would appear from state practice. Decisions by United States courts, for example, have upheld the legality of a considerable degree of state control over the movement of its own passport holders when such control has been found by the courts to be necessary for the protection of the country. International agreements with respect to passports and

at 210. Described as a "better view" is the claim that there is an obligation on states that are parties to the convention to ensure that their municipal systems of law measure up to standards laid down in the European Convention and to amend their municipal law where necessary. Ibid., p. 216. See also *The United Nations and Human Rights: Eighteenth Report of the Commission to Study the Organization of Peace* (1968), 1–29.

other travel documents necessarily leave much to individual state policy. While traditional international law does not preclude a very considerable state control, in practice some Commonwealth states have adhered to a rather liberal policy. Contemporary British practice, although marking definite departure from that of the past, does not appear to give to any other Commonwealth state a sound basis for protesting on more than moral and policy grounds. Here, again, appeal to human rights, rather than to international legal rights in any traditional sense, would appear to be evident. There is little likelihood that states, Commonwealth members or others, will relinquish passport control systems or the regulation of migration to their respective territories. It is conceivable, however, that an effect of this particular issue's arising in the Commonwealth may be the further clarification of migrants' and passport holders' rights as they affect Commonwealth relations, and possibly some further understanding through more universal international agreements.

The present-day issue of defense touches international law, particularly in the case of the United Kingdom, with respect to the British government's contractual arrangements with such other Commonwealth states as Malaysia and Singapore. Great Britain's scaling down of its once far-reaching commitments in Southeast Asia and certain other areas has given rise to questions concerning the interpretation of bilateral agreements which must still be read in the context of commitments to NATO, ANZUS, and SEATO. As to the "right" to be defended, no general customary norms of international law, but new continuing international obligations in conventional form, are relevant. These may involve action in support of decisions by United Nations bodies. In connection with rights and duties in this area there continue to be questions concerning the legal force and effect of such a term as "self-defense." Also relevant are questions of the jurisdictional status of such a force as that which has been utilized in the Commonwealth state of Cyprus. Still other international legal questions have to do with armed forces not necessarily "of the United Nations" but engaged in United Nations service. Post-World-War-II development of conventional law in this general field is reflected in such instruments as the Agreement between the Parties to the NATO Treaty Regarding the Status of Their Forces.[10] In this subject area there continue to be questions as to the legal force and effect of such terms as "self-defense." Jurisdictional immunities of visiting forces while they are in a "defended" state, as well as the legal bases for their presence in such a state, have come to be determinable on the basis of considerable practice, in the course of which some Commonwealth states have been involved. Elements of international law that are relevant have been the subject of judicial rulings, as, for example, in the courts of Canada.

Experience with peace-keeping in Cyprus has been incident to another of the issues examined (communalism) and has continued to be under United Nations auspices. The cooperating states have renewed their commitments for but a short period of months at a time. The UNFICYP operates with the consent of the state wherein action has been taken against possible danger from certain outside stakes, as well as against the danger of open communal strife.

Issues of the kinds that have been examined in preceding chapters have developed in varying circumstances and have differed considerably in the extent to which they have given rise to application of already established rules of the law of nations. That the issues examined do in some measure have bearing not only upon some prior-made agreements and traditional international law but also upon some relatively new rules envisaged for application in the wider international community is indicated in this brief examination of some developments in the recent history of the Commonwealth. Experience incident to efforts to meet the selected issues would seem to have bearing not only upon the tasks of political strategists but also upon progress (however slow) toward the international rule of law in general, and incorporation within it of rights not only of states as such but also of

10. 199 UNTS 67. Perhaps more illustrative, for the present purpose, is the agreement between the United Nations and Cyprus concerning the status of the UNFICYP, 492 UNTS 57 (1964).

individuals qua human beings, as distinguished from nationals of particular states.[11] As an element in this context, consideration of international law may have had effect in designing national policy that is less provincial, more cosmopolitan, and more regardful of the needs of humanity in general.[12] Progress toward clarification of new and more generally applicable principles of international law may conceivably be assisted through Commonwealth prime ministers' conferences, as well as through judicial construction and legislative bodies' discussions, such as have figured in recent Commonwealth experience.

One effect of the invocation of international law that is applicable in dealing with particular issues such as those examined in the preceding chapters may be to underline the limitations of the traditional law of nations and to encourage progress toward more universally applicable norms. The current tendency in Commonwealth relations seems to be toward invocation of a widening community base for such law. A distinguished international judge has, in the course of his dissent in a case before the International Court of Justice, referred to a "permanent community international standard" and has sharply questioned the view that the law is too rudimentary to be applied.[13]

The multiracial Commonwealth has provided examples of possibilities, and problems, in a collective approach to issues that concern all (or groups) of its members. The still-existing ties between these associated states, however tenuous in some subject areas, have facilitated a considerable measure of understanding

11. Legal scholars have pointed out, with respect to the limited jurisprudence of the Court of Human Rights (under the European Convention for the Protection of Human Rights and Fundamental Freedoms, which convention the United Kingdom, Cyprus, and Malta, among other states, had ratified by 1967), that even the prospect of an adverse decision by the court has in some instances led to the respondent government's altering its policies or amending its legislation. Wolfgang G. Friedman, Oliver Lissitzyn, and Richard Pugh, eds., *Cases and Materials on International Law* (1969), p. 230.

12. Cf. n. 1 above. As to the distinct types of interest that may be asserted in an international claim, see J. E. S. Fawcett, *Application of the European Convention on Human Rights* (1969), p. 293.

13. Dissenting opinion by Judge Philip C. Jessup in the *South West African* case, Second Phase, 1966 I.C.J. Rep. 441. See also comment by Milton Katz, *The Relevance of International Communication* (1968), pp. 132–142.

and cooperation. The member states can clearly assist still further toward the clarification and more effective development of law within the wider international community.[14]

14. Cf. extract from the text of a statement and commitment made on December 12, 1966, in the Third Committee of the United Nations General Assembly by the Canadian representative in explanation of Canada's vote on the item concerning human rights. This was in part as follows: "Our position is well known. . . . We have sought wherever possible to widen as well as to deepen the involvement and commitment of the world community in the human rights area; and in our collaborative search for modern measures of implementation, my delegation has attempted to steer a middle course that would avoid, on the one hand, the rather routine conservatism of pro forma reporting and conciliation, and, on the other hand, the overly optimistic systems of compulsion that are beyond our reach at this stage of international relations." GAOR, 21st sess., 3rd comm., A/C.3/SR 1456, as reproduced in *Canadian Yearbook of International Law*, VI (1968), 277.

· Appendix 1 ·

Commonwealth Office Note *

Note on the Question of Treaty Succession on the Attainment of Independence by Territories Formerly Dependent Internationally on the United Kingdom

1. Under customary international law certain treaty rights and obligations of an existing State are inherited automatically by a new State formerly part of the territories for which the existing State was internationally responsible. Such rights and obligations are generally described as those which relate directly to territory within the new State (for example those relating to frontiers and navigation on rivers); but international law on the subject is not well settled and it is impossible to state with precision which rights and obligations would be inherited automatically and which would not be.

2. Most of the Territories attaining independence within the Commonwealth in recent years have wished to bring about the continuance of the application to them of the rights and obligations of the United Kingdom Government applicable to them under existing international agreements immediately before independence. With this end in view an agreement has been made with the United Kingdom Government, usually effected in the form of an exchange of letters between the High Commissioner for the United Kingdom to the country concerned and the Prime Minister or other Minister of that country at the time of inde-

* Reprinted with permission from International Law Association, *Report of the Fifty-Third Conference*, Buenos Aires, 1968 (1969), pp. 619–624.

pendence. Such exchanges have taken place with Ghana, the Federation of Malaya, Nigeria, Sierra Leone, Jamaica, Trinidad and Tobago, Malta and The Gambia. The letters are registered and published by the United Nations. Such an agreement is not, of course, directly binding on third States but gives those States which are members of the United Nations notice of the new State's intentions and it is reasonable to assume that any State which raises no objection within a reasonable time accepts the arrangements embodied in it. The reasons in favour of the conclusions of such an exchange of letters from the point of view of the new State are as follows:

(i) third States will be more ready to grant recognition of the new State, and to grant it the benefits under international agreements, if there is a binding undertaking by the new State to accept responsibilities under such agreements;

(ii) the position between the new State and the U.K. is clarified;

(iii) States or international organisations which are compiling lists of parties to treaties, or which act as the depositaries of multilateral treaties, will accept these agreements as evidence of succession;

(iv) it is possible that if third states do not protest at a devolution agreement, a novation of treaty relations occurs between these third states and the new state.

So far as is known, third States have in practice accepted the new State as a party to existing agreement where an agreement of the kind described has been made between the new State and the United Kingdom. It must, however, be recorded that the legal effect of such agreements is not certain, and the inability to append to them a definitive list of the treaties covered is a further drawback. The British Government would be reluctant to enter into an exchange of letters which specifically excluded treaties with certain countries from the scope of the exchange, since it is intended that the agreements should cover all classes of treaties except those under which the rights and obligations are not capable of being transferred (see paragraph 7 below).

3. An alternative procedure adopted by Tanganyika, Uganda, Kenya and Malawi was for notice of the new State's intention concerning treaties applicable in respect of its territory immediately before independence to be given by means of a unilateral declaration by the Government of the new State. This declaration was sent to the Secretary-General of the United Nations and circulated to Members by him, followed by a disclaimer of responsibility by the United Kingdom. Indeed, if for any reason the new State does not wish to assume the existing rights and obligations without qualification but desires (so far as customary international law may allow) to disclaim some of them or to accept some of them for a limited period only pending the negotiation of new arrangements with the third State concerned, this alternative may be more convenient. Before deciding to pursue such a course, the Government of the new State should take account of the magnitude and complexity of the task of renegotiating a large number of treaties. The effectiveness of this alternative procedure is just as dependent on acceptance by other States as is the devolution agreement procedure. The possibility should be borne in mind that third States may accept an arrangement whereby existing treaty rights and obligations are assumed generally by the new State, but may not be willing for the new State to pick and choose. Once it is apparent that the new State proposes to review existing treaties and negotiate new arrangements or to accept some existing treaties and reject others, other States may themselves decide to review the position and the result may be in effect that the retention of valuable existing rights by the new State becomes a matter of some difficulty. On the other hand, as has been said, the procedure by declaration does allow the new State to disclaim some obligations which it may not desire to continue.

Zambia has adopted the declaration procedure, but in a form differing substantially from all previous declarations. While the Zambian form, like the other declarations, entails a review of existing treaty commitments and consequently may be accompanied by the same unwillingness on the part of other States to accept such an arrangement, it does eliminate the necessity of negotiating for the continuance of variation of treaties with those States. (See paragraph 5 below.)

4. *Form of agreements*

Inheritance agreements concluded in the form of exchanges of letters in the cases mentioned in paragraph 2 above have been in substantially similar form in each case. The standard form of British letter now reads as follows:

> "I have the honour to refer to the . . . . Independence Act
> . . . and to state that it is the understanding of the Government of the United Kingdom that the Government of . . . are in agreement with the following provisions:
>
> (i) All obligations and responsibilities of the Government of the United Kingdom which arise from any valid international instrument shall as from (the date of independence) be assumed by the Government of . . . insofar as such instrument may be held to have application to . . . . ;
>
> (ii) The rights and benefits heretofore enjoyed by the Government of the United Kingdom in virtue of the application of any international instrument to . . . . shall, as from (the date of independence) be enjoyed by the Government of . . . . .
>
> "I shall be grateful for your confirmation that the government of . . . . are in agreement with the provisions aforesaid and that this letter and your reply shall constitute an agreement between the two Governments."

In the case of Cyprus, the matter was dealt with in article 8 of the Treaty of Establishment. Although substantially to the same effect, the wording varies slightly from that usually employed in the exchanges of letters.

Article 8 reads thus:

> "(1) All international obligations and responsibilities of the Government of the United Kingdom shall henceforth, insofar as they may be held to have application to the Republic of Cyprus, be assumed by the Republic of Cyprus.

(2) The international rights and benefits heretofore enjoyed by the Government of the United Kingdom in virtue of their application to the territory of the Republic of Cyprus shall henceforth be enjoyed by the Government of the Republic of Cyprus."

Special considerations applied in the case of The Gambia where the standard form was modified to take account of the lapse of time (some fifteen months) occurring between the date of independence and the date of the exchange of letters.

5. *Unilateral declarations*

In the case of Tanganyika, the Tanganyika Government made a declaration, deposited with the United Nations Secretariat, that they would regard bilateral treaties as remaining in force for a period of two years from the date of independence, during which period they would negotiate with regard to the continuance or variation of such treaties. In addition the Tanganyika Prime Minister said his Government would deal with each multilateral treaty previously applicable in Tanganyika by specific arrangements as soon as possible and that the Government would, on the basis of reciprocity, consider them as still in force in Tanganyika. The United Kingdom Government deposited its own declaration to the effect that they were no longer responsible for the observance of the existing treaties in relation to Tanganyika.

The Uganda Government followed the example of Tanganyika and in a note to the United Nations declared that they would continue on a basis of reciprocity to apply the terms of bilateral and multilateral treaties from the time of independence, *i.e.*, 9 October 1962, until 31 December 1963, or such later date as might be notified, unless they were abrogated or modified by agreement with the other contracting parties before that date. At the expiry of the period the treaties would be regarded as terminated unless surviving under customary international law. The Uganda Government further stated that in the case of multilateral treaties they intended before the expiry of the period of review to indicate to the depositary in each case the steps they wished to take in regard to each instrument. This is considered an improvement on the Tanganyika declaration in that the Uganda note gives scope for expanding the period under which treaty obligations are automatically recognised by Uganda. Kenya and Malawi followed Uganda's example—in each case the United Kingdom Government deposited its own declaration disclaiming responsibility for the observance of existing treaties as in the case of Tanganyika.

The Zambian note acknowledged that Zambia succeeded to many rights and obligations upon independence by virtue of customary international law, but, since it was likely that certain treaties had lapsed, it was proposed that each treaty be submitted to legal examination. Thereafter the Zambia Government would indicate which, if any, of the treaties which might have so lapsed it wished to treat as having lapsed. Until such a decision was taken it was desired that it be presumed that each treaty had been legally succeeded to by Zambia and that action be based on this presumption. Where the Government was of the opinion that it had legally succeeded to a treaty the operation of which it wished to terminate, it would in due course give notice of the termination in the terms thereof. This form has the advantage of affording the opportunity of terminating the operation of particular treaties while placing no time limit upon the period in which treaty obligations are recognised and also of eliminating the need for extensive renegotiation. As in the case of the previous declarations, the United Kingdom deposited its own declaration disclaiming responsibility for the observance of existing treaties.

6. The British Government has provided the government of territories approaching independence with a list of the treaties considered to apply to those territories. It is not, however, possible to guarantee that such a list will be fully comprehensive or accurate though every effort is made to render it so. The number of treaties involved is enormous and the position concerning the re-application to dependent Territories often obscure. Such lists cannot therefore be regarded as definitive, and they have not been appended to any of the inheritance agreements or otherwise published.

7. Finally it is necessary to mention that there are some international rights of the United Kingdom Government which are not capable of being included in the general acceptance by a newly independent country of existing rights and obligations of the United Kingdom applicable in respect of that country whether evidenced by a devolution agreement or by a declaration. The clearest example of such rights and obligations is, of course, the case of those applicable only to dependent territories, *e.g.*, under I.L.O. conventions on labour standards in non-metropolitan countries. In this case a declaration is required by the organisation from the new State that international obligations relating to I.L.O. previously in force in the territory will continue to be respected. Another example is where rights and obligations arise from membership of an international organisation. Normally the constitution of the organisation or the agreement establishing it lays down a specific procedure for the acquisition of full membership of the organisation which has to be followed by any new State desiring such membership. As final examples of agreements which are not transferable mention may be made of personal treaties in which the continuing international personality of the contracting State is essential to the treaty. This class includes political and most financial treaties.

Commonwealth Office   October, 1966

• Appendix 2 •

India-Ceylon Agreement Regarding the Status and Future of Persons of Indian Origin in Ceylon *

Joint Communiqué

At the invitation of the Prime Minister of India, Shri Lal Bahadur Shastri, the Prime Minister of Ceylon, Her Excellency Mrs. Sirimavo Bandaranaike, visited Delhi from the 22nd to the 29th October, 1964. The Prime Minister of Ceylon was accompanied by His Excellency Mr. T. B. Ilangaratne, Minister of Internal & External Trade & Supply, His Excellency Mr. Felix Dias Bandaranaike, Minister of Agriculture, Food & Fisheries and Parliamentary Secretary to the Minister of Defence and External Affairs, Mr. N. Q. Dias, Permanent Secretary to the Ministry of Defence and External Affairs, and other officials of the Government of Ceylon.

The Prime Minister of Ceylon assisted by His Excellency Mr. T. B. Ilangaratne, His Excellency Mr. Felix Dias Bandaranaike, the High Commissioner for Ceylon in India, His Excellency Mr. H. S. Amerasinghe, and Mr. N. Q. Dias and other officials of the Government of Ceylon, and the Prime Minister of India assisted by the Minister of External Affairs, Sardar Swaran Singh, the Minister of Works in the Government of Madras, Shri V. Ramaiah, the Commonwealth Secretary, Shri C. S. Jha, the High Commissioner for India in Ceylon, His Excellency Shri B. K. Kapur, and other officials, held discussions on the outstanding issues relating to the problem of persons of Indian origin in Ceylon.

* Reprinted with permission from the *Indian Journal of International Law*, IV (1964), 637–640.

The talks were frank and friendly and were held in an atmosphere of mutual understanding. The discussions were characterised by a sincere desire on the part of both Prime Ministers to arrive at a mutually satisfactory equitable and honourable settlement of the problem, without prejudice to their respective earlier positions.

In their search for a solution to the problem the two Prime Ministers agreed to a fresh approach to the problem. They reached agreement to the effect that out of 975,000 persons Ceylon will accept as Ceylon citizens 300,000 and India 525,000 persons. The status of the remaining 150,000 persons of Indian origin in Ceylon was left for determination at a subsequent meeting of the Prime Ministers in Ceylon at an early date. It was agreed that the admission to Ceylon citizenship of the 300,000 persons and the repatriation of the 525,000 persons should be spread over a period of 15 years and that the two processes should keep pace with each other. The text of the Agreement in the form of exchange of letters between the two Prime Ministers is being released separately.

During the visit, opportunity was taken by the two Prime Ministers to make a general survey of the international situation in the light of recent developments and their possible consequences on the situation in Asia and on the problems of peace and disarmament.

The Prime Minister of Ceylon conveyed to the Prime Minister of India her warm appreciation of the friendly welcome and hospitality extended to her and members of her delegation. The Prime Minister of India expressed the great pleasure of the people and the Government of India at the Prime Minister of Ceylon's visit to India.

Sd/–Lal Bahadur   Sd/–Sirimavo R. D. Bandaranaike
Prime Minister of India.   Prime Minister of Ceylon.
New Delhi, October 30, 1964.

Letter I

PRIME MINISTER
CEYLON

No. CIT/ICP/62

New Delhi,
30th October 1964.

Your Excellency,

I have the honour to refer to the discussions which we have had from the 24th to the 30th October 1964 regarding the status and future of persons of Indian origin in Ceylon and to refer to the main heads of agreement between us which are as follows:

(1) The declared objective of this agreement is that all persons of Indian origin in Ceylon who have not been recognised either as citizens of Ceylon or as citizens of India should become citizens either of Ceylon or of India.

(2) The number of such persons is approximately 975,000 as of date. This figure does not include illicit immigrants and Indian passport holders.

(3) 300,000 of these persons together with the natural increase in that number will be granted Ceylon citizenship by the Government of Ceylon; the Government of India will accept repatriation to India of 525,000 of these persons together with the natural increase in that number. The Government of India will confer citizenship on these persons.

(4) The status and future of the remaining 150,000 of these persons will be the subject matter of a separate agreement between the two governments.

(5) The Government of India will accept repatriation of the persons to be repatriated within a period of 15 years from the date of this agreement according to a programme as evenly phased as possible.

(6) The grant of Ceylon citizenship under paragraph 3 and the process of repatriation under paragraph 5 shall both

be phased over the period of 15 years and shall, as far as possible, keep pace with each other in proportion to the relative numbers to be granted citizenship and to be repatriated respectively.

(7) The Government of Ceylon will grant to the persons to be repatriated to India during the period of their residence in Ceylon the same facilities as are enjoyed by citizens of other states (except facilities for remittances) and normal facilities for their continued residence, including free visas. The Government of Ceylon agrees that such of these persons as are gainfully employed on the date of this agreement shall continue in their employment until the date of their repatriation in accordance with the requirements of the phased programme or until they attain the age of 55 years, whichever is earlier.

(8) Subject to the Exchange Control Regulations for the time being in force which will not be discriminatory against the persons to be repatriated to India, the Government of Ceylon agrees to permit these persons to repatriate, at the time of their final departure for India, all their assets including their Provident Fund and gratuity amounts. The Government of Ceylon agrees that the maximum amount of assets which any family shall be permitted to repatriate shall not be reduced to less than Rs. 4,000/–.

(9) Two registers will be prepared as early as possible, one containing the names of persons who will be granted Ceylon citizenship, the other containing the names of persons to be repatriated to India. The completion of these registers, however, is not a condition precedent to the commencement of the grant of Ceylon citizenship and the process of repatriation.

(10) This Agreement shall come into force with effect from the date hereof and the two Governments shall proceed with all despatch to implement this Agreement and, to that end, the officials of the two Governments shall meet as soon as possible to establish joint machinery and to

formulate the appropriate procedures for the implementation of this agreement.

I have the honour to propose that the above sets out correctly the Agreement reached between us. My letter and your reply thereto shall constitute an Agreement between the Government of India and the Government of Ceylon.

Accept, Your Excellency, the assurances of my highest consideration.

Yours sincerely,
Sirimavo R. D.
Bandaranaike
Prime Minister of Ceylon.

His Excellency
Lal Bahadur,
Prime Minister of India,
New Delhi.

Letter II

PRIME MINISTER
INDIA

No. 446/PMO/64

New Delhi,
30th October 1964.

Your Excellency,

I have the honour to acknowledge receipt of your letter No. CIT/ICP/62 of date, which reads as follows:

(Text not reproduced, see Letter I)

I have the honour to confirm that the above correctly sets out the Agreement reached between us. Your letter and my reply thereto shall constitute an Agreement between the Government of India and the Government of Ceylon.

Accept, Your Excellency, the assurances of my highest consideration.

Yours sincerely,
Lal Bahadur
Prime Minister of India.

Her Excellency
Sirimavo R. D. Bandaranaike,
Prime Minister of Ceylon,
New Delhi.

· Appendix 3 ·

Rhodesia: Proclamation of Independence *

Proclamation by Prime Minister

The following is a proclamation read over Rhodesia radio by the Prime Minister, the Hon. Ian Douglas Smith, at 1.15 P.M. today, November 11, 1965:

"Whereas in the course of human affairs history has shown that it may become necessary for a people to resolve the political affiliations which have connected them with another people and to assume amongst other nations the separate and equal status to which they are entitled:

"And whereas in such event a respect for the opinions of mankind requires them to declare to other nations the causes which impel them to assume full responsibility for their own affairs:

"Now therefore, we, the Government of Rhodesia, to hereby declare

"That it is an indisputable and accepted historic fact that since 1923 the Government of Rhodesia have exercised the powers of self-government and have been responsible for the progress, development and welfare of their people;

"That the people of Rhodesia having demonstrated their loyalty to the Crown and to their kith and kin in the United Kingdom and elsewhere through two world wars, and having been prepared to shed their blood and give of their substance in what they believed to be the mutual interests of freedom-loving peo-

* Reproduced from a press statement issued by the Rhodesian Ministry of Information as reprinted in *International Legal Materials,* V (1966), 230–231.

ple, now see all that they have cherished, about to be shattered on the rocks of expediency;

"That the people of Rhodesia have witnessed a process which is destructive of those very precepts upon which civilisation in a primitive country has been built; they have seen the principles of Western democracy, responsible government and moral standards crumble elsewhere; nevertheless they have remained steadfast;

"That the people of Rhodesia fully support the requests of their Government for sovereign independence but have witnessed the consistent refusal of the Government of the United Kingdom to accede to their entreatie

"That the Government of the United Kingdom have thus demonstrated that they are not prepared to grant sovereign independence to Rhodesia on terms acceptable to the people of Rhodesia, thereby persisting in maintaining an unwarrantable jurisdiction over Rhodesia, obstructing laws and treaties with other states and the conduct of affairs with other nations and refusing assent to laws necessary for the public good; all this to the detriment of the future peace, prosperity and good government of Rhodesia;

"That the Government of Rhodesia have for a long period patiently and in good faith negotiated with the Government of the United Kingdom for the removal of the remaining limitations placed upon them and for the grant of sovereign independence;

"That in the belief that procrastination and delay strike at and injure the very life of the nation, the Government of Rhodesia consider it essential that Rhodesia should attain, without delay, sovereign independence, the justice of which is beyond question;

"Now therefore, we, the Government of Rhodesia, in humble submission to Almighty God who controls the destinies of nations, conscious that the people of Rhodesia have alway shown unswerving loyalty and devotion to Her Majesty the Queen and earnestly praying that we and the people of Rhodesia will not be hindered in our determination to continue exercising our undoubted right to demonstrate the same loyalty and devotion, and seeking to promote the common good so that the dignity and freedom of all men may be assured, do, by this Proclamation, adopt, enact and give to the people of Rhodesia the Constitution annexed hereto.

"GOD SAVE THE QUEEN"

Ministry of Information,
P.O. Box 8232, Causeway,
Salisbury, Rhodesia.   November 11, 1965.

· Appendix 4 ·

Commonwealth Immigrants Act, 1968 *

Elizabeth II

1968 CHAPTER 9

An Act to amend sections 1 and 2 of the Commonwealth Immigrants Act 1962, and Schedule 1 to that Act, and to make further provision as to Commonwealth citizens landing in the United Kingdom, the Channel Islands or the Isle of Man; and for purposes connected with the matters aforesaid.   [1st March 1968.]

Be it enacted by the Queen's most Excellent Majesty, by and with the advice and consent of the Lords Spiritual and Temporal, and Commons, in this present Parliament assembled, and by the authority of the same, as follows:—

1. In section 1 of the principal Act (application of Part I), in subsection (2)(b) after the words "citizen of the United Kingdom and Colonies" there shall be inserted the words "and fulfils the condition specified in subsection (2A) of this section", and after subsection (2) there shall be inserted the following subsection:

"(2A) The condition referred to in subsection (2)(b) of this section, in relation to a person, is that he, or at least one of his parents or grandparents,—

* Reproduced from *Public General Acts, 1968* (London: Her Majesty's Stationery Office, 1969).
[In accordance with section 7, the Act, with the exception of sections 3 and 5, came into operation on March 2, 1968. Sections 3 and 5 came into operation on March 9, 1968.]
A text of the Act is also available in *International Legal Materials*, VII (1968), 395–401.

(*a*) was born in the United Kingdom, or

(*b*) is or was a person naturalised in the United Kingdom, or

(*c*) became a citizen of the United Kingdom and Colonies by virtue of being adopted in the United Kingdom, or

(*d*) became such a citizen by being registered under Part II of the British Nationality Act 1948 or under the British Nationality Act 1964, either in the United Kingdom or in a country which, on the date on which he was so registered, was one of the countries mentioned in section 1(3) of the said Act of 1948 as it had effect on that date".

2.—(1) The following subsections shall be substituted for subsections (1) and (2) of section 2 of the principal Act:

"(1) Subject to the following provisions of this section, on the examination under this Part of this Act of any Commonwealth citizen to whom section 1 of this Act applies who enters or seeks to enter the United Kingdom, an immigration officer may refuse him admission into the United Kingdom, or may admit him into the United Kingdom subject to conditions as mentioned in paragraph (*a*) or paragraph (*b*) of this subsection, or to conditions as mentioned in both those paragraphs, that is to say—

(*a*) a condition restricting the period for which he may remain in the United Kingdom, with or without conditions for restricting his employment or occupation there;

(*b*) a condition that, before such date and in such manner as may be specified in the condition, he shall report his arrival to such medical officer of health as may be so specified and shall thereafter attend at such place and time, and submit to such test or examination (if any), as that medical officer of health may require.

(1A) An immigration officer shall not impose such a condition as is mentioned in subsection (1)(*b*) of this section unless, on the advice of a medical inspector or, where no such inspector is available, on the advice of any other duly qualified medical practitioner, it appears to him to be necessary to do so in the interests of public health.

(2) The power to refuse admission shall not, except as provided by subsection (5) of this section, be exercised on any occasion in respect of a person who—

(*a*) satisfies an immigration officer that he is ordinarily resident in the United Kingdom or was so resident at any time within the past two years, or

(*b*) being a woman, satisfies an immigration officer that she is the wife of a Commonwealth citizen who is resident in the United Kingdom or of a Commonwealth citizen who enters or seeks to enter the United Kingdom with her.

(2A) Without prejudice to subsection (2) of this section, the power to refuse admission shall not be exercised on any occasion in respect of a person who satisfies an immigration officer—

(*a*) that he is under the age of sixteen;

(*b*) that he has at least one parent who is a Commonwealth citizen; and

(*c*) either that both of his parents are resident in the United Kingdom, or that both of them are entering or seeking to enter the United Kingdom with him, or that one of his parents is resident in the United Kingdom and the other is entering or seeking to enter the United Kingdom with him.

(2B) In paragraph (*b*) of subsection (2), and in paragraph (*c*) of subsection (2A), of this section any reference to a person entering or seeking to enter the United Kingdom shall be construed as not including a person who, on the occasion in question, is refused admission into the United Kingdom.

(2C) Where by virtue of subsection (2) or subsection (2A) of this section the power to refuse admission to a person on any occasion is not exercisable, or would not be exercisable apart from subsection (5) of this section, the power under this section to impose any such condition as is mentioned in paragraph (*a*) of subsection (1) of this section (in the following provisions of this section referred to as a 'restrictive condition') shall not be exercisable on that occasion in respect of that person except—

> (*a*) in a case falling within subsection (2)(*b*) of this section, where a restrictive condition is on that occasion imposed on the woman's husband or has previously been imposed on him and is then in force, or
>
> (*b*) in a case falling within subsection (2A) of this section, where a restrictive condition is on that occasion imposed on at least one parent of that person or has previously been imposed on at least one parent of his and is then in force".

(2) In subsection (3) of section 2 of the principal Act, for the words "subsection (2)" there shall be substituted the words "subsections (2) and (2A)", and for the words "admit subject to conditions" there shall be substituted the words "impose a restrictive condition".

(3) In subsection (6) of section 2 of the principal Act, for the words from " 'child' includes a step-child" to "illegitimate child" there shall be substituted the words " 'parent' includes a stepfather or stepmother and a parent by adoption and in relation to a person of illegitimate birth, includes a natural or putative parent of that person, and any reference to both parents, in relation to a person who has only one surviving parent, shall be construed as a reference to that parent".

3. In the principal Act the following section shall be inserted after section 4:

"4A.—(1) Subject to the following provisions of this section, if any person being a Commonwealth citizen to whom section 1 of this Act applies lands in the United Kingdom and does not fulfil either of the conditions specified in the next following subsection, he shall be guilty of an offence.

(2) The conditions referred to in subsection (1) of this section are—

(*a*) that, while on board the ship or aircraft from which he lands in the United Kingdom, he has been examined by an immigration officer;

(*b*) that he lands in accordance with arrangements approved by an immigration officer, and on landing, submits to examination in accordance with those arrangements.

(3) The Secretary of State may by order provide that subsection (1) of this section shall not apply to a person who lands from a ship or aircraft in such circumstances or combination of circumstances (whether relating wholly or partly to the nature of the voyage of the ship or aircraft, to his being a member of the crew of the ship or aircraft, to his intention to leave the United Kingdom in the same or another ship or aircraft, or to any other matters) as may be specified in the order.

(4) In any proceedings for an offence under this section, where it is proved that a person being a Commonwealth citizen to whom section 1 of this Act applies landed in the United Kingdom, and he does not prove that he landed there in circumstances which (by virtue of an order under subsection (3) of this section) exempt his landing from the operation of subsection (1) of this section, then unless he produces a passport which was duly stamped by an immigration officer—

(*a*) on or after the date on which he landed there, and
(*b*) before the end of the relevant period,

he shall, unless the contrary is proved, be presumed to have landed in contravention of subsection (1) of this section.

(5) For the purposes of subsection (4) of this section, a stamp purporting to have been imprinted in a passport by an immigration officer on a particular date shall, unless the contrary is proved, be presumed to have been imprinted by such an officer on that date; and in that subsection 'the relevant period', in relation to a person, means the period beginning with the date on which he landed in the United Kingdom and ending—

(*a*) twenty-eight days after that date, or

(*b*) at the end of the day on which his examination (including any further examination) in pursuance of paragraph 1 of Schedule 1 to this Act is concluded,

whichever is the later.

(6) The power to make orders under this section shall be exercisable by statutory instrument; and any statutory instrument containing any such order shall be subject to annulment in pursuance of a resolution of either House of Parliament.

(7) In this section 'land' means land from a ship or aircraft, 'ship' includes every description of vessel used in navigation, and 'crew', in relation to a ship or aircraft, means all persons actually employed in the working or service of the ship or aircraft, including the master of the ship or the commander of the aircraft, and 'member of the crew' shall be construed accordingly."

4. In sub-paragraph (2) of paragraph 1 of Schedule 1 to the principal Act (whereby a person cannot be required to submit to examination under that paragraph unless he is so required within twenty-four hours from the time of landing) for the words "twenty-four hours from the time when" there shall be substituted the words "twenty-eight days from the date on which".

5.—(1) Where a person lands from a ship or aircraft in contravention of section 4A of the principal Act, the master of the ship or the commander of the aircraft, as the case may be, if—

(*a*) he knows or has reasonable cause to suspect that that person intends to land from the ship or aircraft in contravention of that section, and

(*b*) he causes or permits him to do so, or does not take such steps as are reasonable in the circumstances to prevent him from doing so,

shall be guilty of an offence.

(2) A person guilty of an offence under this section shall be liable—

(*a*) on summary conviction, to a fine not exceeding £200 or to imprisonment for a term not exceeding six months or to both;

(*b*) on conviction on indictment, to a fine or to imprisonment for a term not exceeding two years or to both.

(3) The preceding provisions of this section shall have effect without prejudice to the operation—

(*a*) in England and Wales, of section 8 of the Accessories and Abettors Act 1861 and section 35 of the Magistrates' Courts Act 1952;

(*b*) in Scotland, of any rule of law relating to art and part guilt; or

(*c*) in Northern Ireland, of section 8 of the Accessories and Abettors Act 1861 and section 68 of the Magistrates' Courts Act (Northern Ireland) 1964.

(4) In this section "ship" has the same meaning as in section 4A of the principal Act.

6.—(1) In this Act "the principal Act" means the Commonwealth Immigrants Act 1962, and "enactment" includes an enactment of the Parliament of Northern Ireland.

(2) In section 14 of the principal Act (penalties, proceedings etc.), in subsection (2), after the words "offence under this Act" there shall be inserted the words "or under section 5 of the Commonwealth Immigrants Act 1968"; and in subsection (3), after the words "section four" there shall be inserted the words "section 4A", and at the end of subsection (3) there shall be inserted the words "or under section 5 of the Commonwealth Immigrants Act 1968".

(3) In section 18 of the principal Act (provisions relating to the Channel Islands and Isle of Man), in subsection (1), in paragraph (*a*), after "(2)" there shall be inserted "(2A)", and after that paragraph there shall be inserted the following paragraph:

"(*aa*) section 4A",

and in subsection (2), after the words "this Act" there shall be inserted the words "(either as originally enacted or as amended by the Commonwealth Immigrants Act 1968) or of section 5 of that Act".

(4) There shall be paid out of moneys provided by Parliament any increase attributable to this Act in the sums so payable under section 19 of the principal Act (which relates to expenses).

(5) Her Majesty may by Order in Council direct that section 4A of the principal Act shall have effect, subject to such exceptions and modifications as may be specified in the Order, in relation to persons entering the United Kingdom by land as it has effect in relation to persons landing in the United Kingdom from a ship or aircraft; and any such Order may be revoked or varied by a subsequent Order in Council under this subsection.

(6) No recommendation shall be made to Her Majesty to make an Order in Council under subsection (5) of this section unless a draft of the Order has been laid before Parliament and approved by a resolution of each House of Parliament.

(7) Except in so far as the context otherwise requires, any reference in this Act to an enactment shall be construed as a reference to that enactment as amended or extended by or under any other enactment, including this Act.

7.—(1) This Act may be cited as the Commonwealth Immigrants Act 1968; and the Commonwealth Immigrants Act 1962 and this Act may be cited together as the Commonwealth Immigrants Acts 1962 and 1968.

(2) This Act, except sections 3 and 5, shall come into operation on the day after the day on which it is passed; and sections 3 and 5 of this Act shall come into operation at the end of the period of eight days beginning with the day on which it is passed.

Bibliography

Acheson, Dean. "The Arrogance of International Lawyers." *International Lawyer*, II (1967–1968), 591–600.

Amerasinghe, C. F. "International Law and the Oil Expropriations in Ceylon." *Ceylon Journal of Historical and Social Studies*, VI (1963), 124–152.

American Bar Association, Special Committee on World Peace through World Law. *The Rule of Law among Nations: Background Information*. 1960.

Aziz, Ungku A. "Facts and Fallacies on the Malay Economy." *Straits Times*, February 28–March 5, 1967.

Bains, J. S. "Indo-Ceylonese Agreement: A Legal Analysis." *Indian Journal of International Law*, IV (1964), 522–526.

Barber, James. "The Impact of the Rhodesian Crisis on the Commonwealth." *Journal of Commonwealth Political Studies*, VII (1969), 83–95.

———. *Rhodesia: The Road to Rebellion*. London: Oxford University Press, 1967.

Barton, G. P. "Foreign Armed Forces: Immunity from Supervisory Jurisdiction." *British Year Book of International Law*, XXVI (1949), 380–413.

Bevans, Charles I. "Ghana and United States–United Kingdom Agreements." *American Journal of International Law*, LIX (1965), 53–57.

Blakeney, Valentine. "The Commonwealth in the United Nations." *Commonwealth Journal*, IX (1966), 11–12.

Borrie, W. D. *Population Trends and Politics: A Study in Australian and World Demography*. Sydney: Australasian Publishing, 1948.

Boston, R. "How the Immigrants Act Was Passed." *New Society*, no. 287 (1968), pp. 448–452.

Bowett, D. W. *Self-Defence in International Law*. New York: Praeger, 1958.

Brownlie, Ian. "The Relations of Nationality in Public International Law." *British Year Book of International Law*, XXXIX (1963), 284–364.

Buchan, Alastair. "Commonwealth Military Relations." In W. B. Hamilton, Kenneth Robinson, and C. D. W. Goodwin, eds., *A Decade of the Commonwealth, 1955–1964*. Durham, N.C.: Duke University Press, 1966.

Burns, Arthur Lee, and Nina Heathcote. *Peace-Keeping by U.N. Forces*. New York: Praeger, 1963.

Casey, R. G. *Friends and Neighbors: Australia and the World*. Melbourne: Cheshire, 1954.

Castel, J.-G. *International Law Chiefly as Interpreted and Applied in Canada*. Toronto: University of Toronto Press, 1965.

Clute, Robert E. "Nationality and Citizenship." In Robert R. Wilson, ed., *The International Law Standard and Commonwealth Developments*. Durham, N.C.: Duke University Press, 1966.

Cohen, Maxwell. "The Queen and the Constitution of Canada." *Commonwealth Journal*, VII (1964), 271–272.

Curtis, Lionel. *The Problem of the Commonwealth*. London: Macmillan, 1916.

Deener, David R. "Colonial Participation in International Legal Processes." In Robert R. Wilson, ed., *International and Comparative Law of the Commonwealth*. Durham, N.C.: Duke University Press, 1968.

Delson, Robert. "Comments on State Succession." *Proceedings of the American Society of International Law* (1966), pp. 111–117.

Donaldson, A. G. *Some Comparative Aspects of Irish Law*. Durham, N.C.: Duke University Press, 1957.

Dugard, C. J. R. Book review in *South African Law Journal*, LXXXIV (1967), 482–483.

Dunbar, N. C. H. "Australia and Collective Security." In D. P. O'Connell, ed., *International Law in Australia*. Sydney: Law Book, 1965.

Eayrs, James. "The Overhaul of the Commonwealth: Too Much Play in the Steering." *Round Table,* no. 225 (1967).

The Effect of Independence on Treaties. A handbook published under the auspices of the International Law Association. South Hackensack, N.J.: Fred B. Rothman, 1965.

Ehrlich, Thomas. "Cyprus, the 'Warlike Isle': Origins and Elements of the Current Crisis." *Stanford Law Review,* XVIII (1966), 1021–1098.

Fawcett, J. E. S. *The Application of the European Convention on Human Rights.* New York: Oxford University Press, 1969.

————. *The British Commonwealth in International Law.* London: Stevens, 1963.

————. *The Inter Se Doctrine of Commonwealth Relations.* London: Athlone, 1958.

————."Security Council Resolutions on Rhodesia." *British Year Book of International Law,* XLI (1965–1966), 103–121.

Feldman, Herbert. "The Communal Problems in the Indo-Pakistan Subcontinent: Some Current Implications." *Pacific Affairs,* XLIII (1969), 145–163.

Fenwick, Charles G. "When Is There a Threat to the Peace?—Rhodesia." *American Journal of International Law,* LXI (1967), 753–755.

Gibbs, N. H. *The Origins of Imperial Defence.* Oxford: Clarendon, 1955.

Glazebrook, George P. deT. *Canada at the Paris Peace Conference.* Toronto: Oxford University Press, 1942.

Goodhart, A. L. "The North Atlantic Treaty of 1949." *Recueil des cours,* LXXIX (1951), part 2, 187–236.

Goold-Adams, Richard. "The Problem of Malaya and Singapore." *Commonwealth Journal,* IX (1966), 63–68.

Green, L. C. "Malaya/Singapore/Malaysia." *Canadian Yearbook of International Law,* IV (1966), 3–42.

Groves, H. E. "The Constitution of Malaysia." *Malaya Law Review,* VI (1963), 245–275.

Guyana. London: Reference Division, British Information Service, 1966.

Hackworth, Green H. *Digest of International Law*. Washington: Government Printing Office, 1943.

Halderman, John W. "Legal Basis for United Nations Armed Forces." *American Journal of International Law*, LVI (1962), 971–996.

———. "Some Legal Aspects of Sanctions in the Rhodesian Case." *International and Comparative Law Quarterly*, XVII (1968), 672–705.

———. *The United Nations and the Rule of Law*. Dobbs Ferry, N.Y.: Oceana Publications, 1966.

Hamilton, W. B., Kenneth Robinson, and C. D. W. Goodwin, eds., *A Decade of the Commonwealth, 1955–1964*. Durham, N.C.: Duke University Press, 1966.

Harkness, Dennis. "There Is a Commonwealth Whether We Formalize It or Not." *Commonwealth Journal*, VIII (1965), 256–258.

Hartnetty, Peter. "Canada, South Africa and the Commonwealth, 1950–1961." *Journal of Commonwealth Political Studies*, II (1963–1964), 35–44.

Head, Ivan L., ed. *This Fire-Proof House*. Dobbs Ferry, N.Y.: Oceana Publications, 1967.

Hepple, B. A. "Commonwealth Immigrants Act, 1968." *Modern Law Review*, XXXI (1968), 424–428.

Higgins, Rosalyn. "International Law, Rhodesia, and the U.N." *World Today*, XXIII (1967), 94–106.

Holmes, John W. "The Political and Philosophical Aspects of U.N. Security Forces." In Bjorn Egge, Per Frydenberg, and John C. Sanness, eds., *Peace-Keeping Experience and Evaluation: The Oslo Papers*. Oslo: Norwegian Institute of International Affairs, 1964.

Howell, John M. "The Commonwealth and the Conception of Domestic Jurisdiction." *Canadian Yearbook of International Law*, V (1967), 14–44.

———. "Domestic Jurisdiction." In Robert R. Wilson, ed., *The International Law Standard and Commonwealth Developments*. Durham, N.C.: Duke University Press, 1966.

————. "Implications of the Rhodesian and Congo Crises for the Concept of Domestic Jurisdiction." *Australian Journal of Politics and History,* IV (1968), 358–372.

————. "A Matter of International Concern." *American Journal of International Law,* LXIII (1969), 771–782.

Huang-Thio, S. M. "Constitutional Discrimination under the Malaysian Constitution." *Malaya Law Review,* VI (1964), 1–16.

Jennings, Sir Ivor. *The Commonwealth of Asia.* Oxford: Clarendon Press, 1951.

Jennings, R. Y. *The Acquisition of Territory in International Law.* Manchester, England: Manchester University Press, 1963.

————. "The Commonwealth and State Succession." In Robert R. Wilson, ed., *International and Comparative Law of the Commonwealth.* Durham, N.C.: Duke University Press, 1968.

Jones, J. Mervyn. "State Succession in the Matter of Treaties." *British Year Book of International Law,* XXIV (1947), 360–375.

Kearney, Robert N. *Communalism and Language in the Politics of Ceylon.* Durham, N.C.: Duke University Press, 1967.

————."Sinhalese Nationalism and Social Conflict in Ceylon." *Pacific Affairs,* XXXVII (1964), 125–136.

Keatley, Patrick. "Jewel of the Indian Ocean." *Guardian,* May 27, 1969, p. 9.

Keith, K. J. "State Succession to Treaties in the Commonwealth: Two Replies." *International and Comparative Law Quarterly,* 4th ser., XIII (1964), 1441–1450.

Kelsen, Hans. *Principles of International Law.* 2nd ed., rev. and ed. Robert W. Tucker. New York: Holt, Rinehart and Winston, 1966.

King, Archibald. "Jurisdiction over Friendly Foreign Armed Forces." *American Journal of International Law,* XL (1946), 257–279.

Kizilbash, Hamid H. "United Nations Discussions on Asylum as an International Human Right." *Journal of Research (Humanities),* University of Punjab, II (1967), 123–154.

Kodikara, S. U. *Indo-Ceylon Relations since Independence*. Colombo: Ceylon Institute of World Affairs, 1965.

Kohn, Leo. *The Constitution of the Irish Free State*. London: Allen and Unwin, 1932.

Krishnan, V. Maya. "African State Practice Relating to Certain Issues of International Law." *Indian Year Book of International Affairs*, XIV (1965), 196–241.

Kunhi, M. K. Muhammad. "Indian Minorities in Ceylon, Burma and Malaysia." *Indian Year Book of International Affairs*, XIII (1964), 405–472.

LaForest, G. V. "Toward a Reformulation of the Law of State Succession." *Proceedings of the American Society of International Law* (1966), pp. 103–111.

Lauterpacht, Hersch. "Allegiance, Diplomatic Protection and Criminal Jurisdiction over Aliens." *Cambridge Law Journal*, IX (1945–1947), 330–348.

———. *Recognition in International Law*. Cambridge: Cambridge University Press, 1947.

Lawford, Hugh J. "The Practice Concerning Treaty Succession in the Commonwealth." *Canadian Yearbook of International Law*, V (1967), 3–13.

———. "Some Problems of Treaty Succession in the Commonwealth." Paper read before a regional meeting of the American Society of International Law at Greenville, N.C., April 25, 1967.

Legane, Colin. "New Hope for Nigeria: The Search for National Unity." *Round Table*, no. 230 (1968), pp. 127–136.

Legault, Albert. *Peace Research Reviews*, Vol. II (1968), no. 4.

Lester, A. P. "State Succession to Treaties in the Commonwealth." *International and Comparative Law Quarterly*, 4th ser., XIII (1963), 475–507.

Luard, Evan. *Peace and Opinion*. London: Oxford University Press, 1962.

Macdonald, R. St. J. "The United Nations High Commissioner for Human Rights." *Canadian Yearbook of International Law*, V (1967), 84–117.

McDougal, Myres S. "A Reply to Dean Acheson." *International Lawyer,* II (1967–1968), 729–743.

————, and W. Michael Reisman. "Rhodesia and the United Nations: The Lawfulness of International Concern." *American Journal of International Law,* LXII (1968), 1–19.

McNair, Lord. *The Law of Treaties.* Oxford: Clarendon Press, 1961.

Mallamud, Jonathan. "Optional Succession to Treaties by Newly Independent States." *American Journal of International Law,* LXIII (1969), 782–791.

Mansergh, P. N. S. "The Commonwealth and the Future." *International Studies,* IX (1967), 1–12.

————. *Documents and Speeches on British Commonwealth Affairs, 1931–1952.* London: Oxford University Press, 1953.

Menzies, Robert Gordon. *Afternoon Light.* 4th ed. London: Cassell, 1968.

Methrotra, R. "On the Use of the the Term 'Commonwealth.'" *Journal of Commonwealth Political Studies,* II (1963–1964), 1–16.

Miller, J. D. B. "British Interests and the Commonwealth." *Journal of Commonwealth Political Studies,* IV (1966), 180–190.

Nairn, N. B. "A Survey of the History of the White Australia Policy in the Nineteenth Century." *Australian Quarterly,* XXVIII (1956), 16–31.

Nehru, Jawaharlal. *Discovery of India.* 3rd ed. Calcutta: Signet, 1944.

Nkrumah, Kwame. "African Prospect." *Foreign Affairs,* XXXVII (1958), 45–53.

O'Brien, W. V. *The New Nations in International Law and Diplomacy,* Vol. III in the *Yearbook of World Polity.* New York: Praeger for the Institute of World Polity, 1965.

O'Connell, D. P. "Independence and Problems of State Succession." In W. B. O'Brien, *The New Nations in International Law and Diplomacy.* New York: Praeger, 1965.

————. *International Law.* Dobbs Ferry, N.Y.: Oceana Publications, 1965.

O'Connell, D. P., ed. *International Law in Australia*. Sydney: Law Book, 1965.
———. *The Law of State Succession*. Cambridge: Cambridge University Press, 1956.
———."Secured and Unsecured Debts in the Law of State Succession." *British Year Book of International Law*, XXVIII (1951), 204–219.
———. *State Succession in Municipal Law and International Law*. Cambridge: Cambridge University Press, 1967.
Palley, Claire. *The Constitutional History and Law of Southern Rhodesia, 1888–1965*. Oxford: Clarendon Press, 1966.
Palmer, Joseph. "Magnitude and Complexity of the Nigerian Problems." *Department of State Bulletin*, LIX (1968), 357–362.
Panter-Brick, S. K. "The Right to Self-Determination: Its Application to Nigeria." *International Affairs*, XLIV (1968), 254–263.
Parry, Clive. "International Law and the Conscription of Non-Nationals." *British Year Book of International Law*, XXXI (1954), 437–452.
———. *Nationality and Citizenship Laws of the Commonwealth*. London: Stevens, 1959.
Pearson, Lester. "A Bridge between Continents and Races." *Commonwealth Today*, no. 128 (1967), p. 1.
Peaselee, Amos J. *Constitutions of Nations*. Rev. 3rd ed. The Hague: Nyhoff, 1965.
Perham, Margery. "The Rhodesian Crisis: The Background." *International Affairs*, XLII (1966), 1–13.
Phadnis, Urmila. "The 1964 Indo-Ceylonese Pact and the 'Stateless' Persons in Ceylon." *India Quarterly*, XXXIII (1967), 362–407.
Phillips, Claude S. "International Law and Questions before the Congress of the United States, 1941–1945." Doctoral dissertation, Duke University, 1954.
Post, K. W. J. "Is There a Case for Biafra?" *International Affairs*, XLIV (1968), 26–39.
Preston, Richard A. *Canada and "Imperial Defense."* Durham, N.C.: Duke University Press, 1967.

Rabl, Kurt. "Involuntary Mass-Migrations as a Problem of International Law: Some Notes on the Indo-Ceylonese Issue." *Indian Year Book of International Affairs*, XIV (1965), 45–89.

Radakrishnan, N. "The Stateless in Ceylon." *Indian Year Book of International Affairs*, XII (1963), 487–563.

Ratnam, K. J. *Communalism and the Political Process in Malaya.* Kuala Lumpur: University of Malaya Press for the University of Singapore, 1965.

"Real Property Valuations for Foreign Wealth Deprivations." *Iowa Law Review*, LIV (1968), 89–114.

Reese, Trevor. "The Australian–New Zealand Arrangement, 1944, and the United States." *Journal of Commonwealth Political Studies*, IV (1966), 3–15.

Report of the Royal Commission on Bilingualism and Biculturalism. Ottawa: R. Duhamel, Queen's Printer, 1967.

Rhodesian Law Journal, V (1965), 2. Unsigned editorial.

Rusk, Dean. "Some Myths and Misconceptions about United States Policy." *Department of State Bulletin*, LIX (1968), 350–356.

Ryan, K. "Immigration, Aliens and Naturalization in Australian Law." In D. P. O'Connell, ed., *International Law in Australia.* Sydney: Law Book, 1965.

Scheinman, Lawrence, and David Wilkinson. *International Law and Political Crisis: An Analytical Casebook.* Boston: Little, Brown, 1968.

Schwelb, Egon. "Withdrawal from the United Nations: The Indonesian Intermezzo." *American Journal of International Law*, LXI (1967), 661–672.

Setelvad, M. C. *The Role of English Law in India.* London: Oxford University Press, 1966.

Sheridan, L. A. "The Changing Conception of the Commonwealth." *Year Book of World Affairs* (1957) pp. 236–256.

Singh, Harnam. "The Indo-Ceylonese Agreement of 1964: The Question of Separate Electoral Registers." *Indian Journal of International Law*, V (1965), 9–22.

Smith, Arnold. "The Commonwealth and Its Global Purpose." *Commonwealth Journal*, IX (1966), 53–58.

Snee, Joseph M., and A. Kenneth Pye. *Status of Forces Agreements and Criminal Jurisdiction.* New York: Oceana Publications, 1957.

Stanger, Roland J. "Criminal Jurisdiction over Visiting Armed Forces." United States Naval War College, *International Law Studies, 1957–1958,* LII (1965), 264–265.

Steed, R. H. C. "The Trouble about the Commonwealth." *Commonwealth Journal,* IX (1966), 167–171.

Stephens, Robert. *Cyprus—A Place of Arms: Power Politics and Ethnic Conflict in the Eastern Mediterranean.* New York: Praeger, 1966.

Stone, Julius. "Legal Bases for the Establishment of Forces Performing United Nations Security Functions." In Bjorn Egge, Per Frydenberg, and John C. Sanness, *Peace-Keeping Experience and Evaluation: The Oslo Papers.* Oslo: Norwegian Institute of International Affairs, 1964.

———. "Problems of Australian Foreign Policy, January–June, 1955." *Australian Journal of Politics and History,* I (1956), 1–26.

Thomson, Sir James, C.J. New Year's greeting in *Malayan Law Journal,* XXIV, (1958), ii.

Tinker, Hugh. "The Crisis in Commonwealth Asia." *Commonwealth Journal,* IX (1966), 87–92, 113.

Tregonning, K. G. *Malaysia.* Vancouver: Publications Centre, University of British Columbia, 1966.

Trindade, F. A., and S. Jayakumar. "The Supreme Head of the Malaysian Federation." *Malaya Law Review,* VI (1964), 280–302.

Tunstall, W. C. B. *The Commonwealth and Regional Defence.* London: Athlone, 1959.

Váli, F. A. *Servitudes in International Law.* 2nd ed. New York: Praeger, 1958.

Vallat, F. A. "Some Aspects of State Succession." *Transactions of the Grotius Society,* XLI (1955), 123–135.

Verbit, G. P. "State Succession in the New Nations." *Proceedings of the American Society of International Law* (1966), pp. 119–124.

Waldock, C. H. M. "The Regulation of the Use of Force by Individual States in International Law." *Recueil des cours,* II (1952), 455–517.

Wang Gungwu, ed. *Malaysia: A Survey.* New York: Praeger, 1964.

Weis, P. *Nationality and Statelessness in International Law.* London: Stevens, 1956.

——. "The United Nations Convention on the Reduction of Statelessness, 1961." *International and Comparative Law Quarterly,* 4th ser., XI (1962), 1073–1096.

Weston, Burns H. "The Taking of Property—Evaluation of Damages: A Comment." *Proceedings of the American Society of International Law* (1968), pp. 43–46.

Wheare, K. C. *The Constitutional Structure of the Commonwealth.* Oxford: Clarendon Press, 1960.

Whiteman, Marjorie. *Digest of International Law.* Vol. VIII. Washington: Government Printing Office, 1967.

Wilson, Robert R. "The Commonwealth and International Law." *American Journal of International Law,* LX (1966), 770–781.

——, and Robert E. Clute. "Commonwealth Citizenship and Common Status." *American Journal of International Law,* LVII (1963), 566–587.

——. "Commonwealth Prime Ministers' Conference of 1964." *American Journal of International Law,* LIX (1965), 570–573.

——. "A Decade of Legal Consultation: Asian-African Collaboration." *American Journal of International Law,* LXI (1967), 1011–1015.

——. "Gradations in Citizenship and International Reclamations." *American Journal of International Law,* XXXIII (1939), 146–148.

——. "International Law and Some Recent Developments in the Commonwealth." *American Journal of International Law,* LV (1961), 440–444.

——, *The International Law Standard and Commonwealth Developments.* Durham, N.C.: Duke University Press, 1966.

Wilson, Robert R. *United States Commercial Treaties and International Law*. New Orleans: Hauser Press, 1960.

Xydis, Stephen G. *Cyprus*. Columbus: Ohio State University Press, 1967.

Yearbook of the Commonwealth. 1969.

Index

Abdul Rahman, 19n, 67, 68n, 69
Addison, Viscount, 63n
Admiralty Islands, 169n
Al Shehadeh and Another v. *Commissioner of Prisons. . . . ,* 24n
Algeria, 120n
Alport, Lord, 105
American Bar Association and sources of international law, 13n, 14n
Angola, 120n
Anguilla, 92, 130, 199
ANZUS Pact, 19, 179, 180, 180n, 181, 187, 201
Argentina, agreement of as to treaty succession, 29, 30
ASEAN, 39
Asian-African Legal Consultative Committee: authorization to, 37n; custom as influenced by, 194; work of on law of treaties, 14n, 36
Australia, 94, 134, 169, 170; constitution, 113n; control of migration and immigration, 134–135, 135n, 147, 150; defense arrangements, 168n, 176n, 177, 178, 179, 187, 188; formation of Commonwealth of, 43–44; naturalization in, 49–50; policy as to Vietnam, 5; position of, as to Rhodesia, 112, 112n; attempted secession from, 113; and separation of Singapore from Malaysia, 69; treaty with New Zealand, 23; transfer of islands to, 54

Bagdad Pact, 178
Barbados, 28, 122, 150
Basutoland and succession to treaties, 35n
Bauer v. *Acheson,* 158
Belgium, succession to rights of, 25
Biafra, 92, 124, 127, 198
Blackstone, doctrine of, 11, 148
Borneo, 70
Botswana, 113n; succession to treaties, 35; agreement with United States, 31
Boudin v. *Dulles, Secretary of State,* 160
British Caribbean Federation, 113
Bunche, Ralph, 88n
Burma, 44

Canada, 113n, 188; defense, 168, 168n, 169, 188; Department of External Affairs on Newfoundland treaty, 37n; ethnic relations in, 59, 60n; freedom of travel, 160n; human rights, 204; immigration laws, 144n, 147n, 150; immigration practice, 153n; international status of, 110n; policy of, as to Vietnam war, 5; status of visiting forces, 202; Supreme Court of, 188
Carl Zeiss Stiftung v. *Rayner & Keeler, Ltd.,* 111
Castlereagh, Viscount, 167
CENTO, 82
Ceylon, 83; agreement with India, 73–74, 75n, 76, 76n, 78, 79, 82, 196; bases in, 46, 56, 170, 171; citizenship, 150; human rights, 80–81, 196; introduction into, of Roman-Dutch law, 71; linguistic and religious divisions in, 72–73, 74, 196; membership of, in United Nations, 29; population elements in, 71; self determination in, 85; Soulbury Report on, 71, 72; succession of, to treaties, 29; withdrawal of troops from, 170
Charles O. Porter v. *Christian A. Herter,* 159
China, 135, 159, 185
Churchill, Winston, use of Commonwealth by, 6
Cocos Islands and Christmas Island, 54
Colombo Plan, 69
Commonwealth of Australia v. *New South Wales,* 113n
Cook v. *Spring,* 42n
Co-operative Committee on Japanese Canadians v. *Attorney General for Canada,* 57n
Court of Human Rights, 203n
Cuban missile crisis, 185
Cyprus: bases in, 46, 56, 173; citizenship, 150; communalism in, 17, 62, 82, 84, 90, 196, 201, 202; EOKA in, 84; and European Convention on Human Rights, 203n; as republic, 47, 197; succession of, to obligations and responsibilities, 29n; and United